Praise for *Whole Leaders, Wild Trust*

Throughout my career as a CEO, corporate board director, and CEO coach, I have witnessed leadership at its most challenging and transformative moments. And rarely have I encountered a book as honest, empowering, and simply humane as Whole Leaders, Wild Trust. Rob McKenna's insights reach far beyond conventional wisdom; he illuminates the courageous interplay between trust, vulnerability, and wholeness that defines truly exceptional leadership. In *Whole Leaders, Wild Trust*, Rob McKenna doesn't just write about the importance of trust—he provides the tools that leaders can use to develop and earn it. In my experience in leading, overseeing, and advising on complex global transformations, I've learned that true leadership isn't measured only by strategy or even results, but also by the courage, emotional maturity, and trust that undergird it. This book bridges the gap between intention and practice. The WiLD Toolkit's assessments and the WiLD Trust Index deliver insightful and measurable ways to understand leadership under pressure. Rob's work is a call for leaders to be both driven and compassionate, data-informed and deeply human. He reminds us that we're not just shaping organizations—we're shaping people's lives, we are shaping the future. *Whole Leaders, Wild Trust* is a real must-read for every leader.

—**Ana Dutra,**
Former CEO, Korn Ferry Consulting;
Global Corporate Board Director

Rob McKenna has built a career helping leaders cultivate organizations based on wild trust—and he's got the research and the results to show it works. In this approachable and clear book, he lays out why this is important and how to build it in your own teams.

—**Alexis A. Fink, Ph.D.,**
Senior Research Scientist, Former VP,
People Analytics & Workforce Strategy, Meta

As a leader, I've learned that trust is both fragile and essential, and never easy to build or sustain. *Whole Leaders, Wild Trust* is a timely guide for those committed to the hard but vital work of leading with authenticity and impact.

—Dr. Deana L. Porterfield,
President, Seattle Pacific University

In a time when trust feels scarce, *Whole Leaders, Wild Trust* is a breath of fresh air. Dr. Rob McKenna offers a practical and deeply insightful framework for developing leaders who lead with courage, humility, and authenticity. This book is more than theory—it's a guide for anyone who wants to build trust that lasts.

—Dr. Kent Ingle,
D.Min., President, Southeastern University

Dr. Rob McKenna's *Whole Leaders, Wild Trust* is a must-read for leaders who understand that high performance and deep trust go hand in hand. Based on my own experience this framework can revolutionize how organizations operate. Rob makes it clear: trust is measurable, investable, and essential for lasting results.

—Alex Shootman,
CEO, Alkami Technology

In a world hungry for leaders we can believe in, Rob McKenna delivers both hope and a blueprint. *Whole Leaders, Wild Trust* shows us that trust isn't abstract. It can be built, rebuilt, and multiplied when leaders choose to grow whole. Rob McKenna writes with rare honesty and wisdom about what leaders need most: the courage to be whole and the grit to build trust that lasts. This book is a companion for every leader who longs to make their work matter without losing themselves—or their people—along the way.

—Ron Carucci,
Managing Partner, Navalent, bestselling and award-winning author of Rising to Power and To Be Honest.

Dr. Rob McKenna's new book, *Whole Leaders, Wild Trust*, offers a fresh and practical perspective on leadership by drawing a bold connection between who leaders are, how they build trust, and the results their organizations achieve. With decades of research and real-world experience, Rob delivers more than just concepts—he equips leaders to deliberately strengthen themselves, those around them, and the entire culture they shape, especially in times of uncertainty and high stakes. It is a must-read for leaders who want to build cultures where people and performance thrive together.

—**Scott C. Furman,**
Chief Information Officer, Chesterfield County

In a time when leadership is often defined by performance alone, *Whole Leaders, Wild Trust* is a step towards what really matters. Dr. Rob McKenna offers more than a leadership model; he delivers an impactful framework that blends personal growth with organizational trust. With insight and heart, this book equips leaders at every level to lead with both purpose and vulnerability, and to become the kind of leader that the world needs—one that is whole, grounded, and trustworthy.

—**Tim Neville,**
President and CEO, Echoing Hills Village Inc.

Reading *Whole Leaders, Wild Trust* is like finding that missing sock in the dryer—suddenly everything makes sense. Dr. Rob McKenna's WiLD Trust Platform has multiplied trust in my own business, and I have recommended his work to leaders in multiple arenas because it consistently transforms both people and organizations. Every leader should "Go WiLD"!!

—**Ethan Brizzi,**
Owner/Broker, Brizzi Financial

A few years ago, I met Dr. Rob McKenna, and his call to intentional leadership, know your specific purpose and live it out on purpose, changed my life and leadership. In *Whole Leaders, Wild Trust*, drawing on his WiLD Trust work, he shows that the systems and structures we build are only as strong as the trust and people who sustain them. Trust isn't just relational; it's systemic. When leaders invest in their people with honesty, vision, and care, cultures grow stronger, and performance endures. Simple idea, critical practice. Read this book and you will be blessed, and if you put its teaching into action, those you lead will be blessed as well.

—**Josh Wiley,**
President, Villara Building Systems

As a leader, I've seen firsthand how trust can make or break a business. Rob McKenna brings this truth to life with wisdom, real-world examples, and practical guidance. This book isn't just about leadership—it's about building relationships that inspire loyalty, collaboration, and lasting success.

—**Jeff Smiley,**
Senior Sales Executive

"Leading is an incredible experience, and likely one of the hardest of your life." But Dr. Rob McKenna just made it a little bit easier by helping us to better understand the heart of leadership—genuine relational trust—and how to build it within our teams, organizations, and companies. This book serves as a roadmap for anyone wanting not just to lead but to lead well!

—**Patrick Bertsche,**
Owner and CEO of Matrix Design LLC

In a complex world that focuses on what seems like many of the right things like systems and processes, it is refreshing to have Dr. Rob McKenna focus on what REALLY matters, empowering leaders to build trust so that leaders can build a foundation that enables true human thriving.

—**Tami Heim,**
President and CEO, Christian Leadership Alliance

The most effective leaders understand that culture is their greatest competitive advantage. In *Whole Leaders, Wild Trust*, Dr. Rob McKenna shows how building trust from the inside out creates high-performing teams and enduring relationships. Having led in global organizations like Google, Microsoft, and now Protiviti, I can confidently say this book is a must-read for leaders who want measurable results that last.

—**Greg Hunter,**
Global Marketing Leader, Protiviti

Trust is the hinge on which every creative endeavor turns. Without it, projects collapse; with it, visions take shape. In *Whole Leaders, Wild Trust*, Dr. Rob McKenna lays out a framework leaders and creatives cannot afford to ignore. I've known Rob for 15 years, and I can attest these insights are not abstract theories but hard-won truths from a life lived with integrity. This book is as necessary as the trust it demands we build.

—**Jason Pamer,**
Producer of *After Death*, the highest-grossing faith documentary of all time; Partner, Dream Hospitality

Having worked across the globe in high-pressure environments, I know that trust is both critical and hard-earned. *Whole Leaders, Wild Trust* by Dr. Rob McKenna provides leaders with a roadmap for developing trust as a measurable, actionable function—essential for influencing stakeholders, driving change, and building resilient organizations. This book is a must-read for anyone leading in complex, multicultural, or high-risk settings.

—**Wendy Bashnan,**
Senior Director, Security and Fire Protection, Scout Motors Inc.

You can't build a house with just one hand tool. Neither can you build a company or a life with just one leadership tool; you need the whole leadership toolkit. WiLD leaders is about all of you, not just part of you. Dr. Rob McKenna knows we are integrated human beings who bring our whole person to our leadership life. In *Whole Leaders, Wild Trust*, Dr. McKenna shows you how trust is the foundation upon which your leadership is built. When you build your life and organization using the whole leadership toolkit, you'll create a company that survives and thrives in today's unpredictable business climate.

—**Greg Leith,**
CEO, Convene Corporation

As a Member of Harvard Business Review Advisory Council, and a CEO who has worked with leaders across 56 nations and multiple industries, I have seen both the promise and the pitfalls of leadership in complex environments. In *Whole Leaders, Wild Trust*, Dr. Rob McKenna captures what few can—how trust, resilience, and intentional development form leaders who both get results and give care to people. Having known Rob and the WiLD Leaders community for years, I can attest this is not theory but a lived practice that transforms individuals and organizations alike. Every leader who seeks to thrive amid global complexity should embrace and apply the knowledge and wisdom in these pages.

—**James McPherson, JD, MBA,**
Founder & CEO, Purpose and Legacy Center; Member, Harvard Business Review Advisory Council

In higher education, I've seen that the most effective leaders are those who invest deeply in people, not just outcomes. In *Whole Leaders, Wild Trust*, Dr. Rob McKenna equips leaders to bring together courage, humility, and accountability in ways that inspire growth in both individuals and communities. This book is a timely resource for faculty, students, and anyone preparing to lead with integrity and purpose.

—**Suzanne Davis,**
President, Greenville University

I've seen many ideas take shape over a long career in real estate, strategy, and leadership—but few capture both clarity of purpose and depth of human insight like *Whole Leaders, Wild Trust*. From the first chapter, Dr. McKenna bridges big vision with actionable wisdom, equipping leaders to build trust and to lead with strength and compassion. Having worked with Rob and WiLD Leaders for many years, I know this isn't abstract theory but a lived practice that transforms individuals, teams, and communities. If you're searching for something to sharpen your leadership, inspire authentic connection, and reimagine what's possible in work and in life—this is it.

—**Ann Klein,**
License Partner & Area President, Engel & Völkers

In a world full of leadership hacks and shortcuts, Rob McKenna offers something far more valuable: depth, trust, and transformation. *Whole Leaders, Wild Trust* isn't just a book—it's a blueprint for growing leaders from the inside out. Rob's insights are as timely as they are timeless, rooted in research and refined through real-world experience. Every page challenges you to lead with greater courage, wisdom, and wholeness.

—**Les Parrott,**
Ph.D., #1 New York Times Bestselling Author of *Love Like That*

In *Whole Leaders, Wild Trust*, Dr. Rob McKenna delivers both a wake-up call and a roadmap. He makes the powerful case that trust isn't a soft ideal—it's a measurable, buildable asset that fuels performance, connection, and culture. Drawing on decades of research and real-world leadership experience, Rob invites us to lead as whole people—courageous enough to be seen, intentional enough to keep learning, and committed enough to build trust that lasts. This is not another leadership theory book; it's a practical, deeply human guide for anyone serious about creating organizations where people and purpose thrive together.

—**Garry Ridge,**
USA Today Bestselling Author of *Any Dumb-Ass Can Do It*;
Chairman Emeritus, WD-40 Company; and The Culture Coach

FOREWORD BY **STEPHEN M. R. COVEY**

Whole LEADERS Wild TRUST

The Courageous Path to Personal, Relational, and Organizational Change

ROB McKENNA, PhD

WILEY

Copyright © 2026 by WiLD Leaders Inc. All rights reserved.

Published by John Wiley & Sons, Inc., Hoboken, New Jersey.

No part of this publication may be reproduced, stored in a retrieval system, or transmitted in any form or by any means, electronic, mechanical, photocopying, recording, scanning, or otherwise, except as permitted under Section 107 or 108 of the 1976 United States Copyright Act, without either the prior written permission of the Publisher, or authorization through payment of the appropriate per-copy fee to the Copyright Clearance Center, Inc., 222 Rosewood Drive, Danvers, MA 01923, (978) 750-8400, fax (978) 750-4470, or on the web at www.copyright.com. Requests to the Publisher for permission should be addressed to the Permissions Department, John Wiley & Sons, Inc., 111 River Street, Hoboken, NJ 07030, (201) 748-6011, fax (201) 748-6008, or online at http://www.wiley.com/go/permission.

The manufacturer's authorized representative according to the EU General Product Safety Regulation is Wiley-VCH GmbH, Boschstr. 12, 69469 Weinheim, Germany, e-mail: Product_Safety@wiley.com.

Trademarks: Wiley and the Wiley logo are trademarks or registered trademarks of John Wiley & Sons, Inc. and/or its affiliates in the United States and other countries and may not be used without written permission. All other trademarks are the property of their respective owners. John Wiley & Sons, Inc. is not associated with any product or vendor mentioned in this book.

Limit of Liability/Disclaimer of Warranty: While the publisher and author have used their best efforts in preparing this book, they make no representations or warranties with respect to the accuracy or completeness of the contents of this book and specifically disclaim any implied warranties of merchantability or fitness for a particular purpose. No warranty may be created or extended by sales representatives or written sales materials. The advice and strategies contained herein may not be suitable for your situation. You should consult with a professional where appropriate. Further, readers should be aware that websites listed in this work may have changed or disappeared between when this work was written and when it is read. Neither the publisher nor authors shall be liable for any loss of profit or any other commercial damages, including but not limited to special, incidental, consequential, or other damages.

For general information on our other products and services or for technical support, please contact our Customer Care Department within the United States at (800) 762-2974, outside the United States at (317) 572-3993 or fax (317) 572-4002.

Wiley also publishes its books in a variety of electronic formats. Some content that appears in print may not be available in electronic formats. For more information about Wiley products, visit our web site at www.wiley.com.

Library of Congress Cataloging-in-Publication Data is Available:

ISBN: 9781394379279 (Cloth)
ISBN: 9781394379286 (ePub)
ISBN: 9781394379293 (ePDF)

COVER DESIGN: PAUL McCARTHY
COVER ART: © SHUTTERSTOCK | SE_VECTOR

SKY10133718_120825

*To my Dad and Mom, David and Janet McKenna,
who led with joy and grace and
always encouraged me to keep asking the hard questions.*

Contents

Foreword	xvii
Preface	xxi

Part I	**Whole and Trusted**	**1**
Chapter 1	A Vision of Trust: From Blueprints to Belief	3
Chapter 2	Our Greatest Need: From Deep Desperation to Wild Aspiration	9
Chapter 3	The Systems and the Souls: Bridging the Visible to the Invisible	17
Chapter 4	Whole Leaders, Wild Trust: The Courage to Be Seen. The Risk to Trust Again	33
Chapter 5	Mindset, Methods, and Measures: Moving from Gut Intuition to Intentional Change	47
Chapter 6	The Chemistry of Trust: The Formula Behind the Feeling	57
Part II	**Becoming a Whole and Trusted Leader**	**73**
Chapter 7	Ready: Prepare for Whatever Comes Next	77

Chapter 8	Purposeful: Start with a Why That Won't Let Go	95
Chapter 9	Productive: Crush the Important Things	107
Chapter 10	Composed: Stay Anchored in the Storm	115
Chapter 11	Learning: Enter the Leadership Laboratory	129
Chapter 12	Competent: Build Trust Through Excellence	135
Chapter 13	Motivated: Inspire the Deeper Forces Behind Your Effort	145
Chapter 14	Invested: See Others Clearly	157
Chapter 15	Supported: Move from Solo to Surrounded	165
Chapter 16	Intentional: Lead a Whole and Intentional Life	181
Part III	Creating a Whole and Trusted Team	187
Chapter 17	Truthfulness and Transparency: The Courage to be Candid	189
Chapter 18	Productivity, Consistency, and Conflict: Forward Progress, Faithful Practice, and Fighting Well	195
Chapter 19	Clarity and Planning: Plans Don't Kill Trust, Confusion Does	201

| Part IV | Building a Whole and Trusted Organization | 205 |

Chapter 20 Leadership Maturity: Convicted and Caring 207

Chapter 21 People and Culture: Where People Belong, They Build 213

Chapter 22 Engagement and Performance: Visible Progress Builds Invisible Trust 219

Chapter 23 Whole Leaders Building Wild Trust: The Fight for What Matters Most 225

Bibliography 231

Acknowledgments 235

About the Author 237

Index 238

Foreword

There are times when a book does more than add to the conversation on leadership. It issues a call. A call to return to something essential and timeless, and at the same time to reimagine how we lead in a world of accelerating change and complexity. *Whole Leaders—Wild Trust* is that kind of book.

When I first connected with Dr. Rob McKenna, I was struck by both the depth of his thinking and the clarity of his conviction. We had a deep and meaningful conversation on his podcast about trust, and it became clear to me that we share more than a professional interest in the subject.

We share a belief that trust is not simply a soft, social virtue, but rather a hard-edged, economic driver—a strategic imperative. We share a conviction that leadership is not about position or power, but about responsibility and stewardship. And we share a hope that the transformation our world so urgently needs will come not from better strategies and systems alone, but from better leaders. Leaders who are whole, trustworthy, trusting, humble, and courageous.

For years I have written and spoken about my conviction that "trust is the one thing that changes everything." Rob has taken that timeless principle and built a framework that shows leaders how to put it into practice. His vision of "whole leaders" and "wild trust" is not just compelling language; it is a roadmap for living and leading with greater intentionality, purpose, and impact. He reminds us that trust doesn't grow only at the organizational level; it starts within us, expands through our teams, and then extends into our cultures.

What Rob has done here is bold. He names the fractures and the fears that often accompany leadership today—leaders under pressure, teams under strain, cultures that feel fragmented. But he doesn't stop there. He shows us how to move toward integration, wholeness, and trust that is not fragile but resilient. Trust that is not abstract but measurable. Trust that can be built and rebuilt in real relationships, in real time, in the real challenges leaders face.

This is not mere theory. Rob has walked alongside leaders in the trenches. He has done the empirical work. He has built practical tools—like the WiLD Trust Index—that help leaders and organizations see where trust is strong, where it is weak, and how to strengthen it. His work reflects decades of science and experience, yet it is written with a human touch and connection that invites leaders to bring their whole selves into the process.

Reading this book, I was reminded of my own work in *Trust & Inspire*. At the heart of both is a conviction that people are not just assets to be managed, but human beings (whole people) to be trusted and inspired. That organizations are not merely entities delivering products and services, but communities of purpose, meaning, contribution, and potential. And that the highest calling of a leader is to unleash that potential by modeling the behavior we would like to see, by extending trust intentionally and generously, and by inspiring others through connecting with people and connecting to purpose.

If you are a leader—or becoming one—this book will stretch you, challenge you, and strengthen you. It will not flatter you with easy answers. Instead, it will invite you to take the harder, better path: to become a whole leader, and to build the kind of trust that endures. And that transforms and inspires.

I admire Rob's courage in writing this book. He is calling for nothing less than a transformation in how we think about leadership. He is reminding us that culture follows the leader, and trust follows culture. He is showing us that while distrust has become the default in too many places, whole and sustaining trust remains our greatest hope. And that a high-trust culture remains our greatest multiplier.

I am humbled and grateful to add my voice to Rob's. I consider him a friend. We are fellow travelers in a movement that is bigger than either of us, a movement that is profoundly needed in our world today. A movement toward leaders who are real, human, whole, and trusted. Leaders who see and understand the responsibilities and stewardships implicit in their roles as leaders. Leaders who model the way by demonstrating humility and courage simultaneously. Leaders who are both trustworthy and trusting. And leaders who inspire others through connection, caring, and purpose.

So I invite you to read this book with openness and excitement. Wrestle with its ideas. Test its tools. Apply its frameworks. Be influenced by its research. And most of all, seek to live its core message in becoming a whole leader yourself and in building the kind of trust that lasts. Because leadership is not a game to win, but a life to live. And, as Rob says, trust isn't optional; rather, trust truly is *the one thing that changes everything*.

Stephen M. R. Covey
The New York Times and #1 *Wall Street Journal*
bestselling author of *The Speed of Trust*
and *Trust & Inspire*

Preface

While I'm not a superfan of too many things, I am a massive fan of *The Speed of Trust* by Stephen M. R. Covey. Published in 2006, its truth is just as piercing and relevant today. He says, "There is one thing that is common to every individual, relationship, team, family, organization, nation, economy, and civilization throughout the world…That one thing is trust."

That line has haunted me in the best way. It's true—and yet, too often, trust is treated like vapor: vital but intangible, something we hope to feel rather than something we know how to build. But what if it's more than that? What if trust is measurable? What if it's something you can intentionally and systematically build within yourself, with those around you, and across every sphere you touch? And what if that effort to build trust can't be separated from the effort to become whole—because those two things are, in fact, the same? This is the heart of the book you're about to read.

You already know that without great leaders, your teams suffer. Without growth in your people, your mission lags. You've seen the damage one unprepared, unaware, or immovable leader can cause. You've seen how dysfunction and silence can take down momentum and morale. But you've also seen the opposite—a leader with clarity, courage, conviction, and compassion—and how one person like that can shift everything. You already know that without a deep, ongoing investment in people, nothing else really matters.

And if you're reading this, I suspect you've tried. You've made an effort. You've taken courses, held offsites, maybe even brought in coaches or read your share of leadership books. You may have tried tools around personality, strengths, or styles, and you've probably seen some things help. But you may also still feel like something's missing—like you're building, but not sustaining. Like you're growing, but unsure how to scale that growth across your organization or your life. If you've solved all that, if trust is high and alignment is seamless, I applaud you. But if you're like most leaders I know—including me—then you're still learning. You still feel the pressure to get it right for your people. You still see the cracks and wonder how to build something stronger. This book is for you.

It's for emerging leaders stepping into their leadership potential. It's for seasoned executives navigating complexity. It's for managers, parents, entrepreneurs, educators, and anyone who wants to build something lasting and good. Because here's the thing: we have systems for everything—sales, marketing, operations, workouts, meal prep. But when it comes to developing people, we often default to hope and instinct. And when we do try to systematize development, it can go stale fast—feeling robotic, overly generic, or disconnected from the real stories people carry. That's why what we need is different. We need a system that breathes. One that's whole and intentional. One that honors complexity and humanity. One that doesn't reduce people to parts but helps them become more whole. That's what this book is about.

And now, I want to pause and share something directly from the heart of a leader—something I hope every person reading this will imagine as a letter written from your own leader, or even from yourself to the people you lead. It's a letter I believe so many would want to receive:

Team,

First off, I am so grateful for each and every one of you. When I started this and landed in the role I'm in now, I knew I would build with an incredible group of people. And you are more than I ever could have imagined. And as we go forward, I have so much in my heart that has been stirring for a long time. Things that I hope you will feel inspired by. Here is what has been calling me.

I don't want this to simply be a place where we just get things done. I don't want this to be a place where we achieve our goals but lose each other in the process. I want this to be a place where we become something—together. I want to know you. Not just what you do here. I want to know what drives you, what you carry, what matters most to you when no one's looking. And I want you to know me. Not just the title or the voice in a meeting—but the human being who cares deeply about what we're building, and even more deeply about how we build it. And, I want everyone here to know each other in the same way. Their strengths, their purpose, their deepest aspirations for our work together.

Here's what I'm hoping for: I want to build a different kind of trust with you. A wild trust. The kind that doesn't ignore the fact that we'll let each other down and miss the mark—but believes we can still tell the truth, still grow, and still rise. A trust that includes faith in each other, belief in each other, even when it would be easier to pull away.

I want this to be a place where your growth and our investment in each other is not optional—it's essential. Where who you and I are becoming is just as important as what you and I produce. I want to invest in you—not just as an employee, but as a whole person. I want you to look back and know that being part of this team shaped you in the best possible ways.

We are building something here. But we can't build anything great if we aren't also building each other. That's the commitment I'm making, and I hope you'll make it too.

Let's do this. Together.
—Your Leader

This letter, in some form of your own words, is what I want for you and every person who serves with you. What would you say if I told you there is a way to build that kind of place—a trust that lasts? That there's a way to increase performance and well-being at the same time? To reduce destructive conflict and build alignment without losing authenticity? And that the system is not only research-based and wildly effective, but also simple, repeatable, and customizable—because it was built for human beings? The only requirement is your courage. Your courage to ask better questions. To invite people to edit. To stay in the process, even when it's messy. And to believe that something better is possible.

This book introduces the system I've spent most of my life building—based on decades of research and deep trenches of experience with leaders and organizations around the world. I believe in it because I've seen it work, time and time again. And by the time you finish reading, I believe you'll not only understand what I mean by a system that breathes—but how to build one in your own world. Here's what to expect: This book is about you and it's about others. It's about the long game and the right-now. It will challenge how you think, how you lead, and how you invest in those around you. It will help you see the layers upon which trust is built—personally, relationally, and organizationally. And it will show you what becomes possible when leaders commit to becoming whole and trusted.

At the end of each chapter, you'll find a section called "For a Conversation." These are sets of questions designed to help you pause, reflect, and process what you've just read. Whether you're reading this on your own, discussing it with a team, using it in a classroom, or leading a group through the book, these prompts are there to create space for deeper insight and honest dialogue. Because trust doesn't grow in silence—it grows in conversation.

To every leader reading this—whether emerging or experienced—I have deep respect for you. It takes guts to admit you're still learning, even when others expect you to have it all figured out. It takes humility to acknowledge where things could be better. And it takes hope to believe we can still build what we've always needed most. But I believe we can.

My promise to you is this: I won't shrink back from the hard stuff. I'll give you frameworks, language, tools—and also truth. I'll invite you to see trust as more than a concept. I'll ask you to take action, to get honest, and to go first. Because if we do this together, we won't just change our leadership. We'll change our organizations. We'll change our culture. We'll change our world.

So let's go. Let's develop whole leaders and build wild trust—together.

PART I

Whole and Trusted

We are living in a world starving for leaders we can trust—and longing to become those leaders ourselves. Not perfect leaders. Not always-right leaders. But whole leaders—willing to be seen, willing to keep growing, and willing to lead in ways that require both courage and sacrifice. These are the leaders who know that trust is not a trait; it's a practiced and powerful choice. They are not defined by the masks they wear, but by the risk they take to be honest about who they are. We don't just need better leadership models. We need leaders who are becoming better humans.

Part I lays the foundation for that kind of leadership. It explores why trust is both our greatest need and our most neglected strategy—and why becoming whole is not a luxury but a necessity for anyone leading in this moment. These chapters will walk you through the internal and external systems that shape us, the mindsets and methods that drive our behavior, and the chemistry of trust itself—what it's made of, how it breaks down, and how it can be rebuilt. This section is meant to reframe your assumptions, connect the dots between your personal and professional life, and set the stage for what's to come.

The path toward trust is both strategic and deeply personal. It is both, and every leader carries a blueprint—some conscious, some buried—shaped by experience, pain, belief, and hope. But blueprints aren't buildings. What transforms the structure of a life or an organization is both the plan and the builder's belief in what could be. The call in front of us is not to fabricate something shiny or flawless, but to construct something real, something intentional and something that can withstand pressure because it's grounded in truth. Trust isn't the absence of conflict. It's the presence of integrity, consistency, humility, and clarity—even when the winds pick up.

This is a reformation, not a trend. It is a return to something elemental: the capacity to lead ourselves and others from a place of wholeness. And it's not for the faint of heart. Because once you've seen what trust can do—once you've led a team that tells the truth or worked with a leader who owns their humanity—you can't unsee it. You'll want more of it. And you'll want to become the kind of person who builds it.

CHAPTER 1

A Vision of Trust

From Blueprints to Belief

> *We are completely dependent on others for most everything. When we face that truth, trust becomes non-negotiable.*

The Parable of the Builder

From the time he was child, he loved to build things. Log cabins out of blocks of wood, driftwood forts on the beach, fortresses full of battalions of plastic army men—you name it. He loved to build them. Imaginary worlds where people could live, work, and even fight make-believe wars against armies of bad guys. He loved to build imaginary places where imaginary people could do their thing and do it together. In fact, his mother and father would often watch in wonder from the kitchen window as he would construct complex tunnels in the dirt where his pretend people could live, work and move freely while also feeling protected. He was fascinated by the need for shelter and protection for his pretend friends—not only from the elements, but from bad actors who would threaten their communities. There was something in him that knew that the things he built had to serve the people, and that excited him.

As he got into his 20s, he started to work, and without much surprise, he continued to hone his passion for building into his early adult life. His make-believe buildings and people had become real-life structures where he learned the specifics of his craft—of working with wood and metal and the necessity for understanding architecture and the need for structures to serve those who would walk the halls of the things he built. At the age of 30 though, something struck him. He realized he didn't just want to build, he also wanted to make a difference in the world. He wanted to grow and expand and use the knowledge and skills he had gained to do something profound—something that would change the world around him for the better. And so, he set off on a journey. As he traveled, he continued to build real structures that people could thrive in, and as he did, others got excited to build with him. He had never imagined that others would follow the vision he had been driven to follow, but they did. They traveled together, building larger and larger structures with even more interesting aesthetics that solved more problems for people. This team of people weren't in it for the money, but they were being paid well and able to sustain themselves and their own families so that they could continue to build. His team was inspired, creative, conscientious, on time, and they trusted each other. He felt the cohesion in his team like a rhythmic pulse within his chest that told him that things were so good.

As more time passed, his vision and the vision that he now shared with his team inspired many people to join them and to build with them. The work was so good. He was doing what he was designed to do—what he was called to do, but as the number of people serving with him grew, new challenges emerged. While the work was still incredible and inspired him every day, he noticed something changing. While the building part of the work seemed easy, as the number of people on mission with him grew, so did the number of interpersonal challenges they faced. While everyone knew each other in the beginning and the excitement for the building was enough to cover any pressures that came up, now it was different. People had become so focused on the work that they no longer talked as often or as easily as they used to. While in the past they would have solved a problem together right on the journey, now they were working in their own spaces and not talking as much. Or, when they did talk, it was apparent that some people weren't getting along like they had in the past. There were so many people on-mission together that it had become much more difficult to know anyone as well. While the group who had joined him had all the building skills in the world, there was a sense that something else was beginning to break down. There were rumors that some who had joined weren't as skilled or as reliable as they had been in the past. At the most fundamental level, people seemed to have lost trust in what he had built, in each other, and even in themselves. And that trust seemed to be particularly tough when they were under pressure or tried to do things differently.

What was once a team of people he worked closely with every day had become multiple teams, and while they were dependent on other teams, they didn't talk with them as much and it just felt like things weren't as inspiring as they used to be.

Something had also begun to change in him, and around him. He was responsible for resourcing it all and for the well-being and performance of his builders. The pressure for resourcing would sometimes be so high that he thought he might break. Building had become more expensive as it took far more than plastic army men and a hill of dirt and mud to build. But things were also changing inside of him.

The journey had been long. He had gone from unrestrained excitement about the mission and the journey, to watching dozens and then hundreds of people begin to build with him. And now, he was no longer building at all. His time in the backyard of his childhood home seemed like a long-lost dream. His job was no longer to just build, but now to inspire other builders. And he wasn't always sure he knew how to do that.

The number of people building with him had grown so much that he realized that he just wasn't sure what to do. He wanted to keep building and loved the growth he had experienced, but he had lost sight of that original purpose within him, lost connections with others with whom he was building and was wondering if they felt the same. His deepest desire was still there, but as he journeyed for many years and the number of those traveling and building with him grew, he could feel something breaking down.

He knew how to build and where to find materials for his people, but something else was happening. He felt alone, off course, and was daily questioning his purpose and his abilities. He even questioned whether he ever knew how to build anything at all. He felt rudderless and lacked the motivation he once had. And, worst of all, he wondered if others felt the same. He wondered because he could see evidence that things had changed. People were talking behind the backs of others, and the politics and jockeying people were doing for power felt like a disease. Many of the best builders who had joined him were starting to leave, and it was even getting to the point that the things they were building were just not as good. The integrity of the structures had always been really important to him, and the expert builder in him knew that it just wasn't the same.

He wasn't done with the journey, but he knew something had to change. He was at an important breaking point—a moment where he would either break out or break down. "The building or the people?" And then, something changed in him. A new inspiration. An idea that was so wild, it felt both impossible to achieve, but clearly in reach. He felt inspired, with a fresh vision for a future ahead. "I must do both." He knew how to build things, but realized his most important question at that moment was, "How do I build people?" A deep and renewed desire to not only build structures for others, but for those who had joined him on the journey—other leaders and team members. He knew he must be as intentional about building his people as he had been about building things for people. He needed a way to see them, to increase their own capacity, and to develop deep and sustaining trust between them.

He felt like it was a skillset he had never fully grown, but he was hungry to develop it. He started building structures for people, but never imagined that he would have to build people and increase their capacity to build together if they were not only going to continue to trust one another, but also to fulfill their mission. Like the necessity for measuring the length of a board or the number of nails to build a wall, his deepest desire was to be able to apply that same level of specificity to the opportunity and challenge of building his people. And so, he began again.

We Are Builders

Within every one of us is a builder. Whether we will join the team of another master builder or start building on our own, we all want to

A Vision of Trust

be a part of something. You may be trained as a plumber, an engineer, a doctor or nurse, an accountant, a psychologist, or in some other craft or specialty, but you are also a builder—or at the very least, someone who will build with others. Whether you are just starting off on the journey as an emerging leader, watching your own child play in the backyard, or have had many join you on the journey and you too are struggling to understand how to connect your people-building efforts to whatever it is that you do in the world, you are not alone. Within each one of us is a builder, but early on we often don't fully realize what it will take to build together over the long haul.

When others join us on a mission, we call that a team. And as even more join us, we call that an organization. Building together is the process of organizing, which allows us to build larger and larger things for more and more people. As we build, what we often don't realize until it is too late is that building together requires us to know each other, to see each other, and to trust each other. We realize that as we grow, if we fail to tend to the garden of relationships that either thrives or dies at the base of whatever it is we are building together, our organizations will not thrive, and neither will we.

Every one of us has dreams and aspirations that we will be a part of something bigger than us. No matter what industry you work in or where you are from, deep within each of us is a desire for a greater purpose and to be a part of something that is making a difference in the lives of others. Sure, we need resourcing for ourselves and we need wins and rewards that keep us moving forward, but we also want to be a part of something that is making a difference for others. In too many organizations, we've lost sight of that reality. And we've lost sight of why we got started in the first place.

My hope is that you are inspired to something more, and you will see a pathway to understanding what it means to create long and sustaining value as you build. To increase the returns of your building efforts by creating an irreconcilable connection between your efforts to build things and to build people. And, at the core of that effort will be your ability to build trust that spreads across your entire organization, between every team member, within yourself, and even in your family—a wild and extraordinary trust that connects that childhood builder in every person on the journey with you to the childhood builder in you. That kind of trust is whole, it is sustaining, it is life-changing, and it is wild. It is a wild trust that allows you to see what is invisible, measure what is too often left as an intangible feeling, and build an unbreakable and life-changing level of trust for everyone who builds with you.

For a Conversation

1. What are you building? A business, a family, a product, a service, a life?
2. What does trust have to do with the performance and well-being of the people you are building with? What does it have to do with you?
3. What would change if you were not only a builder of things, but a builder of people?

CHAPTER 2

Our Greatest Need
From Deep Desperation to Wild Aspiration

We are wired for trust but too often drowning in doubt—and the distance between those two is where our lives, our teams, and our organizations begin to break down.

Who can we trust? It's one of the most challenging questions of our generation. Employees are asking this question. So are team members, sons and daughters, leaders—each of us. At a time when information is readily accessible and polarization is often the default, it's hard to know what or who to believe. We're built with an innate need to trust. But we're living in what may be the widest gap in history between that need and our actual capacity to trust others.

When a need that deep goes unmet, hope is often the first casualty.

The information revolution has only made it harder. We have more data at our fingertips than ever before, but data fed to us by intelligent systems is often tailored to our biases—offering a curated view of the world that feels complete but isn't. Too little data, and we don't have what we need to decide. Too much, and we lose confidence that anything we hear is true. If you're skeptical, just pick up the phone of a friend or family member and compare your news feeds. The contrast might lead to a lively dinner conversation—or maybe a critical insight about what (and who) we can actually trust.

In the past, we trusted what we were told—what we read in the newspaper, heard on the radio, saw on the news. But that's not trust. That's information. That's belief without relationship. Real trust isn't one-way. It's worked out. It's a conversation. It's tested in conflict and proven in vulnerability. And here's the problem: the information we get today isn't just one-way—it's personalized. Tailored to our preferences, shaped by our clicks. It doesn't challenge our biases; it confirms them. That's not evil. But it's not trust either.

Here are two litmus tests. First, if someone can't articulate the other side or even argue the possibility that they may be wrong, they're not earning trust—they're reinforcing their narrative. And second, one of the greatest litmus tests of our ability to be trusted is our interest in our own trustworthiness. It is really hard for you to trust me if I'm only interested in whether or not you are trustworthy. That's a one-way ticket into oblivion.

So why is this interesting now? Because it used to be that trust was hardest in our closest relationships—at home, at work, in the tension between us. But now? It might be easier to build trust in a team than in the data we're fed every day. Why? Because in relationships, we get to work it out. We get to name the truth, test it, measure it. We can build trust—within us, between us, and around us.

And that's why we're here. Because the future doesn't need more noise. It needs more trust. Real trust. The kind that grows when we choose to work it out—together. Today, the trust script has flipped. We have an opportunity to build trust between us at work in ways that have now become increasingly difficult in other areas of our lives. We have the opportunity to measure and build trust between us in a world where we have begun to assume that the information we are fed is true—but between us—we get to work it out.

Our Need for Trust

Some call it a crisis of distrust. I think of it as a misplacement of trust. We all trust something—but often, it's the wrong thing. We trust our phones, data-hungry corporations, distant governments, and strangers we follow online who happen to share our worldview. Meanwhile, we struggle to trust those closest to us.

And far too often, we're unwilling to do the work to rebuild what's been broken, or we simply don't know where to start.

"Widespread distrust in a society... imposes a kind of tax on all forms of economic and social transactions. Distrust poisons the channels of communication and discourages cooperative behavior." (Fukuyama 1995)

This misplaced trust is costing us. The disengagement, distraction, and disconnection across a generation are taxing our organizations—and our people. Some estimates suggest it's costing us trillions. But more than that, it's eroding our well-being and plunging us into a global mental health crisis. We're investing most of our time and energy in symptom management—momentary relief.

What we need is a radical shift in how we think about leadership development, how we build teams, and how we structure organizations where people don't just perform—they thrive. That shift begins with a whole new conversation. A conversation about whole leaders and whole trust.

Think about your own need for trust. You need it to have an honest conversation with your spouse. To drive down the road believing others will stay in their lanes. To buy something and trust the money you're using holds value. To send a critical message to a colleague. Your customers need trust to buy what you're offering. And you need trust to take a risk—trust that someone will have your back.

Trust means believing people will be honest and care for you at the same time. Trust is what gives us the confidence to follow our leaders—and what others must feel to follow us. Our collective breakdown in trust has infected every layer of our lives: schools, governments, teams, organizations, leaders, and our personal well-being. If we don't know who to trust, we are lost. Trust builds the foundation of friendship, helps us seek support, and gives our work purpose. It deepens families and marriages. It makes peace possible. And it gives us the strength to build together, to tend to the garden of relationships that keep us whole as we grow.

And at the heart of that trust isn't just competence—it's character. It's consistency. It's clarity. The same traits that make us trustworthy as individuals make our systems, our leadership, and our cultures worth investing in.

The Business Imperative

"Above all, success in business requires two things: a winning competitive strategy, and superb organizational execution. Distrust is the enemy of both." (Covey 2006)

Trust is the bedrock of effective relationships, strong teams, and thriving organizations. Yet we're facing a significant trust challenge. According to Gallup, only 21% of US employees strongly agree they trust their organization's leadership.[1] And this isn't just a leadership issue.

It's a systemic breakdown in how we relate to each other. The data is clear: trust is essential to performance. Here's why:

- **Improved Employee Engagement:** When employees trust their leaders, they're more engaged. Gallup reports that high-trust workplaces see 13% higher productivity and greater job satisfaction.[2]
- **Enhanced Collaboration:** Teams with high trust communicate and problem-solve better. According to *Harvard Business Review*, they avoid unnecessary conflict, innovate more, and create progress.[3]
- **Increased Innovation:** Trust empowers risk-taking. Research in the *Journal of Applied Psychology* shows that employees in high-trust environments share more bold and unconventional ideas—leading to growth.[4]
- **Reduced Turnover:** PwC reports that 55% of trusted employees are less likely to leave their jobs.[5] Retaining the right people protects performance and preserves your culture.

---

[1] Gallup. *State of the Global Workplace 2023 Report.*
[2] Ibid.
[3] Paul J. Zak. "The Neuroscience of Trust." *Harvard Business Review*, Jan–Feb 2017.
[4] Carmeli, A., Brueller, D., & Dutton, J. "Learning Behaviours in the Workplace: The Role of High-Quality Interpersonal Relationships and Psychological Safety." *Journal of Applied Psychology*, 2009.
[5] PwC. *2021 Trust in the Workplace Survey.*

- **Improved Customer Loyalty:** Edelman Trust Barometer reveals that 81% of consumers remain loyal to brands they trust.[6] When trust is high inside your organization, your customers feel it too.
- **Stronger Crisis Response:** Deloitte found that organizations with high trust levels recover 30% faster during a crisis.[7] Trust creates confidence, coordination, and calm.

Trust isn't just nice to have. It's a performance multiplier. But here's the catch: people don't trust us just because we talk about trust. Trust is what follows the equal sign. It's the outcome of our actions. If we do the right things, trust grows. If we don't, it fractures—and it breaks fast. Broken people are hard to trust. Broken leaders are hard to follow. But whole leaders—people becoming more integrated, aware, and intentional—can rebuild trust. And organizations filled with those kinds of people? That's what we need to build. In a conversation on our podcast, Garry Ridge—Chairman Emeritus of WD-40—captured this idea with striking clarity:

> "Success in the business is the will of the people times the strategy." (Ridge 2025)

Strategy alone isn't enough. Execution alone isn't enough. Without the will of the people—the trust, belief, and commitment of your team—strategy collapses. That will is built in the quiet, daily decisions of leaders who choose to be trustworthy.

Not long ago, I asked a friend of mine, a senior leader, how she was doing. Her response stopped me: "I'm beaten and broken. I feel like an icebreaker, cutting through resistance that feels frozen. And I feel so little trust." She's a phenomenal leader. And her story is not rare. Like so many of us, she's desperate for trust.

LEADERSHIP = TRUST

Leadership is not ultimately about charisma, strategy, or even performance—it's about trust. Because without trust, none of the other

---

[6]Edelman. *2023 Edelman Trust Barometer.*
[7]Deloitte. *Trust as a Catalyst for Performance and Recovery*, 2021.

things matter for very long. Teams fracture. Systems break. Influence fades. Trust is the glue, the fuel, the hidden architecture beneath every healthy leader, team, and organization. And it's not just about being liked. It's about being counted on. Believed in. Known.

Trust is the thread that runs straight through culture. And that's where Edgar Schein said it best:

> "Neither culture nor leadership, when one examines each closely, can really be understood by itself. In fact, one could argue that the only thing of real importance that leaders do is to create and manage culture and that the unique talent of leaders is their ability to understand and work with culture." (Schein 2010)

Leadership and trust, just like leadership and culture, are inextricably linked. And, culture is the echo of trust—or the absence of it.

A leader doesn't just set direction—they set tone. They don't just cast vision—they create conditions. And those conditions either cultivate trust or corrode it. What's fascinating is how often we talk about leadership development as if it's a set of competencies, when in reality, it's the process of becoming the kind of person others can trust with their future. And that's not theoretical—it's observable. It shows up in how a leader responds under pressure, whether they invest in others, whether they invite truth, and whether they align their behavior with their values.

Leadership is not a solo act. It's not a title. It's a relationship. And trust is the foundation of that relationship. The deeper truth is this: culture follows the leader—and trust forges culture. So if we want to build the kind of cultures where people thrive and missions endure, it begins with whole leaders who understand the sacred weight of trust.

Our Wildest Aspiration

While distrust has become the default, whole and sustaining trust is our most powerful hope. I want to invite you to imagine a different future—for yourself, your team, and your organization. Not a fantasy. Something real. Something wild—not because it's chaotic, but because it's extraordinary. Because it's what we long for but haven't fully seen.

Imagine walking into work with absolute clarity about your role. Imagine solving problems quickly. Imagine alignment between your work and your life. Imagine working with people who are becoming better for your sake and theirs. Imagine leaders who aren't perfect but are working at it. Imagine a culture where stress and anxiety happen, but they're not the norm. That future is within reach. With intentionality, structure, and care—we can build it.

Why does this matter?

It matters because when we trust each other, we feel secure. Trust transforms hesitation into action. It turns emotional labor into energy. It helps us build identity, not just performance. When trust is low, we question everything. When it's high, we still ask questions—but to move forward, not to protect ourselves. If we want to build trust, we can't hide. We have to know and be known. At its core, trust is about relationships. It's about seeing and being seen.

Trust isn't simply a concept we analyze—it's the foundation we stand on. It's the very structure that supports our hardest conversations and our most courageous risks. It's the force that allows us to move from fear into focus. And that's why it's our wildest aspiration. Not just because it's what we want, but because it changes everything when we get it right. Because if we're going to build what matters most, we can't just build things—we must also build people. Just like the builder you met in Chapter 1, the deeper challenge isn't only about the materials in our hands, but the trust being built within us and between us. And the good news? We can begin again.

For a Conversation

1. Where are you currently experiencing a deeper need for trust?
2. Who are the people you trust most—and why?
3. If you imagined a future where everyone around you trusted each other more fully, what would be different?

CHAPTER 3

The Systems and the Souls

Bridging the Visible to the Invisible

> *We were never meant to choose between building the mission and tending the soul. Trust begins where the blueprint meets the heart.*

If you had to pick between getting results or caring for people, which would you choose and why? If you had to choose and you couldn't game the question into doing both, which would matter more? It's a frustrating question because most of us want both.

What do we know about leadership and organizations after decades of research on their effectiveness and growth? A healthy and high-performing organization is one that has a strong focus on both the visible and the invisible—the process and the people. The visible things include the operational systems, the budgets, the mission statements, the products, the machines, the resourcing, and the job descriptions. And the most visible thing of all, results. If we are to run effective and high-trust organizations, we must see results. But results aren't enough. We must also focus on the things that are more difficult to see. The invisible things include the thinking, the feelings, the wellness and fulfillment of the people, and everything that occurs within and between us as human beings. If we are to run effective and high-trust organizations, we must also focus on the things that are more difficult to see.

While the invisible parts of our efforts are often considered the soft side, it is more accurately described as the harder side. It is harder because it isn't as immediately apparent the way the visible sides of our lives are to us. And the invisible and visible pieces of our lives and work—our systems and the thoughts and feelings of the people who use them—are in constant tension with one another in spite of the reality that in our best world they are aligned. This is why when I've asked my friends who are CEOs if they could go back and study two things, the most common answer I hear is—accounting and psychology. Most of them will say that leading is about resourcing and it is about people—and you have to master both. The most fundamental paradox of leading that is at the core of our need for trust is the tension between human being and human doing.

The Leadership Timewarp

Before we dive into what's next, let's take a brief walk through where leadership theory has come from. What follows is a creative dramatization of key ideas that have shaped the last century of thinking about leadership effectiveness.

If each of us could understand the wealth of research and thinking over the last 100 years on leadership and organizational effectiveness, what would we see? I want to invite you into a timewarp, and more specifically, to a house party in the 1940s that will last for decades. Somehow we got on the guest list, and all they told us was that we should be prepared to meet some interesting characters. Like any good partygoer who doesn't know many people at the party, we walk in and find a seat on the couch near some strangers talking about work and leadership.

And then, in walks Gordon Allport—an early pioneer of thinking about leadership. Gordon enters the party and says, "Traits! Leaders are born and not made. They are born with what it takes to lead. They just have it, and if we can find what they have, we can make organizations effective by looking for those same things in others. It's a huge idea I know, but it's possible! Let's figure out the traits we need and go find those leaders! The trait approach—I claim it! This is my theory. It's all about personality and traits."

The Systems and the Souls

As Gordon grabs a beer and takes a seat in the kitchen ruminating on his thoughts about traits, in walks a cast of researchers from Ohio State University. They walk in somewhere between 1940 and 1970 and they say "Gordon, sure traits matter, but there's more. It's not just traits, but behaviors—things leaders are doing. Some of them are more about showing consideration for people and others are more about initiating and building structure. We call it the "Styles Approach"—the idea that certain behaviors are more or less effective for a leader. Some of us are good at structure and some of us are good at consideration for others."

During their rant about "styles" from the living room—another group of researchers (wolverines, if you will) from the University of Michigan, two fisting beers and chanting hail to the victors—barge in from another room. With blood in their eyes as they are going for the jugular of their Ohio State enemies—"Sorry to interrupt, but there's more! It's not just leadership styles that matter. We discovered that leaders have preferences between those styles. Some are focused on the people and some are focused on the task."

As these Ohio State and University of Michigan experts argue, in a dark corner of the room, a research assistant from Ohio State whispers to her peer from Michigan, "I know we aren't supposed to like or learn from each other, but have you all figured out how leaders do both at the same time? We have this two-by-two that looks like yours that tells us that both people and operations matter, but it takes work to have strong operational systems and people systems at the same time. Are you seeing the same things?" To which the supposed enemy research assistant from Michigan whispers back in fear his colleagues might see him talking to the Buckeye, "Yes, we are working on that same problem."

Suddenly, as if on cue in this conversation that has literally been occurring in this room for decades, in walks a man named Robert Katz from about 1955 declaring—"Stop! We know more! Skills are quite different from traits or qualities of leaders. Skills are what leaders can accomplish, whereas traits are who leaders are. It's not enough to talk about preferences or a simple 2×2 between tasks and people. We must talk about what a leader has to get done. To which the Ohio State research assistant says to her new friend from Michigan, "I'm looking at his list of skills and abilities, and it looks like half of them are people-oriented and half of them are task-oriented. Are you noticing that too?" After which she realizes she's whispering to no one because her surprising Michigan friend actually had left to relieve himself in the bathroom.

After a heated discussion over lunch regarding artificial intelligence, the future of energy production, and Taylor Swift's latest album, those still at lunch hear a ruckus coming from the living room as two men declare, "I am Ken Blanchard and I am Paul Hersey and we are the fathers (we like to call ourselves that) of what from henceforth shall be called "Situational Leadership theory!" We will blow your minds because it's not only about traits, or styles, or preferences, or skills and abilities of leaders. We introduce to you a new actor in the play of life that changes everything. It is the context and even more importantly, the follower!" We proclaim that a leader's behavior along two dimensions of being directive or supportive (the way the leader should respond) is dependent upon the motivation and the ability of the follower. If the leader knows those things, they will know how to respond! Isn't that amazing?"

The crowd gathered in the living room mutters in disbelief. Our two surprising friends in the corner whisper to each other, "Makes good sense. I think he's onto something. It's really an extension of our 2 × 2 of operations and people, but it hadn't occurred to us to think about the follower, and that the leader's response of focusing on being task directive or people centric might depend on the motivation and ability of the follower. To which the Michigan man says to the Ohio State friend, "You need another drink? Ya, me too. This has gotten good."

As evening approaches and the martinis, bottled water, and cheap beer roll on, the air in the room is lighter and more inviting… almost as if the partygoers had begun to learn something together. At just the moment where it seemed like it was time to call it a night, the number of people at the party had increased as more theorists, leaders, practitioners, and experts had shown up. Even Fred Fiedler was in one corner talking about contingency theories of leadership and that the relationship between followers and leaders matters. It was based on his research that task-motivated styles were different than relationship-motivated styles, and that there is a dynamic exchange between leaders and members of the organization. His theory made sense to the others on the chairs and couches around him, but there was some speculation about whether his theory could be proven.

So much learning had been shared in so little time. As the party-goers began grabbing their coats and sharing contact information and LinkedIn profiles, someone showed up late and barged through the front door, "I'm Peter, Peter Drucker, and let's pull it all together."

WHAT WOULD YOU HAVE LEARNED?

If you had been at this party, what would you have learned? What we have learned over the last century about leading, leadership, and the connection between people and organizations has taught us something. If we are to lead and organize well, we must focus on two things—processes and people. Whether we call it smart organizations and healthy organizations, initiating structure and consideration, compassion and accountability, operations and human resources, we will always be responsible for providing clarity and providing care.

At the heart of this story is this. If we are going to create better organizations—wildly trusted organizations, we are going to have to constantly attend to the fundamental tension between people and process. It is a universal truth in leadership. From a personal level that means that the connection between what we do and who we are will always be at the center of our learning. Learning is so much more powerful when we connect our deepest thinking, ideas and calling to what it is we are trying to get done. The lesson is this. Your strategy must never be separated from your people. You must align them in a way that every person understands where your organization is going and the systems that support you getting there together. At the same time, you must never lose sight of your people and their fundamental need to be driven by a purpose that includes them, but is also bigger than them. That level of integration requires you to always align your people development efforts with your strategic mission as an organization—connecting the visible to the invisible.

> The party metaphor is a creative retelling of landmark contributions in leadership theory and should be read as a narrative synthesis, not a formal historical timeline. The scholars and theories referenced include foundational work from the following:
>
> Gordon Allport: Trait theory
> Ohio State and University of Michigan studies: Behavioral theories
> Robert Katz: Skills theory
> Hersey & Blanchard: Situational leadership
> Fred Fiedler: Contingency theory
> Peter Drucker: Management by objectives and organizational effectiveness

The Paradox of the Visible and Invisible

A whole leader building wild trust embraces tension between the visible systems that are necessary to make progress and the often invisible story of the people who will use those systems.

You are designed to get things done, to achieve goals, and to build systems and operational structures for your life and work and for the life and work of others. You were put here for a purpose, and that purpose will continue to reveal in layer upon layer. As that purpose becomes clear, it will become a north star that will likely guide you for the rest of your life. But, that is not all you are. As we build throughout our lives, we realize that life is more than simply building. What we discover is that as we build and build on purpose, we will also be responsible for the well-being and building of others—for those who build with us. As we build, we realize that the structures can be strong and can work for everyone, but that they will only work to the extent that people are thriving as they build. We realize that if we spend all of our time building and ignore the garden of fragile and powerful relationships that sits at the base of our building, things will get difficult and politicized, and require a level of emotional labor that we never planned for. We realize that to lead well we will need to be both builders and gardeners at the same time. And, those two parts of our job and our identity will often be in tension with one another—a necessary tension between building with courage, conviction, and purpose while tending to the incredible people who will build with us for the rest of our lives.

> "People want to feel valued and respected. But they also want to know what is expected of them, how they fit in, and how their work contributes to a greater mission." (Ulrich 2006, 219)

Think about your day today. If you are like me you have things that you want to achieve, people for whom you are responsible, and you have things that you have to do and get done. For most of us, the things that we need to get accomplished are tangible and pretty easy to identify. You may need to mow the lawn, to make a few phone calls to the electric company or to a customer, or you may need to check your inbox to see if that person you reached out to for a job responded to you yet. If you are a student, you may need to check and see when your assignment is due. If you are a business owner, you may need to check your sales projections, and if you are an operational manager, you may need to check on your team's productivity and creativity today.

No matter what your day holds, looking back and saying that this was a good day likely has some measurable and visible results that would tell you things are moving forward. But, that's not all your day likely included. Every one of the things you are trying to accomplish includes relationships with others and things that are much more difficult to see immediately. Doing any of those things requires us to understand what is going on inside of others, whether it's their motivations, their mental health on any given day, or their commitment to helping us get those things done. In the end, the progress we are making includes both the actual things we are trying to accomplish as well as the people who we will work with to get them accomplished. Our days include the visible and the invisible—the human being part of life, and the human doing part of life.

The builder part of us is powerful because it is visible and easier to identify. It has visible results and it is necessary. It's easier to pay attention to the builder in us because we can see the results of our efforts most readily and others can see those results too. And, the results of our building are what also provides the physical resources to keep going. Without financial resources, measurable results, and increasing profit and margins, nothing else happens. Being a builder doesn't just give us a definable and measurable purpose, it all creates the necessary flow of resources to sustain our work into the future. The challenge is that we are not only builders, we are gardeners. We are not only designed to scale and grow the value that has been placed in our hands, but in the end, we know that we are stewards of something more. We are stewards of a gift—the gift of giving back, of investing in the lives and purpose of others, and of seeing something more than measurable financial growth or a known brand.

We are here to care for those we build with. We are here to give people an opportunity to thrive, to sacrifice, to grow, and to learn. We are here for something more. We are here to cultivate the garden of fragile and miraculous relationships for all who build with us and will be served by what we build. Some of us struggle with the operational sides of life and organizing, and others of us struggle more with managing the relationships in our lives, but we must become masters of both. We must be both builders and gardeners—focused on both what we can see, and what we can't.

If we must focus on the visible and the invisible, then what's the problem? Our focus on building systems and structures often conflicts with the people challenges we face. We have ways we talk about that challenge when we say things like, "I'm tired of being treated like a number." The reason people feel like a number and not a person in our organizations is because as organizations grow and scale, they sometimes lose sight of the individuals who serve and work within them. It's a reality. As we grow, we must have systems that scale and grow with us, but in that growth, we will always face the pressure to lose sight of the individuals. Both are necessary. Our systems must scale. We must have them. And, we must not lose touch with the thoughts, needs, and feelings of individuals. We must do both, and if we are to do both well, we must realize and move toward the paradox they offer us.

The Bridge of Trust

So, if the invisible and the visible are the two principles—what is it that ties the two together? We already know that both are necessary. Picture an iceberg. Above the surface are your systems—visible, structured, measurable. Below the surface are the emotions, motivations, and hidden drivers of your team. What connects them? Trust. Trust is the bridge that links the seen to the unseen and connects our operational reality to our human experience. See Figure 3.1.

Whether we are running our home, trying to get organized for our first class in college, or running an organization or a team, we are each fully aware that we must be masters of the system while dealing with our feelings about how it's going. There is an irreconcilable connection between the systems and the resources it takes to do anything, and our feelings and thinking about how it's going. And, what gets even more interesting is when the feelings of one person bump into the feelings of another person. At that moment, even the best systems in the world will likely break down if there isn't something that is connecting the systems and the people. What is it that ties them together and connects the visible and invisible pieces of our lives and work and leadership? What ties them together is trust. And we are desperate for it right now. Trust is the bridge between our being and our doing that causes every relationship to flow as opposed to fight, and every system to function as opposed to falter.

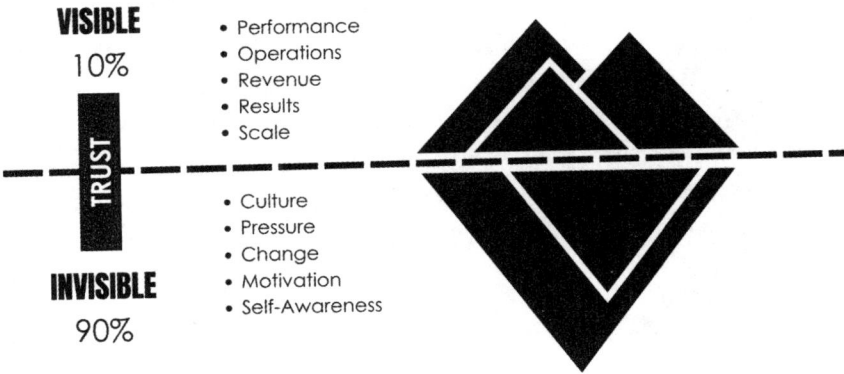

Figure 3.1 Seeing the Unseen

The greatest systems in the world are only as effective as the trust between the people who will use them. If I don't trust you, it will cause me to spend most of my energy managing the dynamics of our relationship over making progress. And, it isn't enough to simply trust people. We must put operational systems for our lives and work in place that are aligned and connected to the needs of the people. This is precisely why most learning and development approaches inside organizations fall short. Most training and development efforts fail because they become boxes to check without a real connection to the motivations and nuance of the people in them, or they are too disconnected from the actual work to be meaningful. We must connect them together and trust provides that bridge. And we don't become whole and trusted leaders, create whole and trusted teams, or become whole and trusted organizations by simply talking about trust. Whole and sustaining trust is built through both our systems and our people, and by paying ongoing attention to measuring it, building it, and maintaining it over time.

What Does It Mean to Trust

Trust is the bridge between the visible and invisible pieces of our lives, the builder and the gardener in us, because trust increases our capacity to be both. If I trust you with my finances or with leading my organization, it means that we know each other. We know each other for who we really are, and when that occurs, trust deepens. If we are to begin to build trust and question our trust in others less often, we must understand what trust is all about. Trust is more than a feeling or a gut reaction. Trust is a choice, an intention, and a faith in someone else. It says to us and to others, "I trust you even though I cannot know for sure that you won't let me down." Trust is what causes us to take a calculated risk. Trust gives us the courage to say "I do" at the altar. It gives us the courage to take the job and move our family for it, and it's what causes us to make a financial investment in a product or service that will help our business. Trust is powerful and it is multifaceted.

Trust is your *belief* in my *integrity*, my *ability*, my *reliability*, my *strength* and that I am telling you the *truth*—and my belief in the same in you. If you trust me, you believe that I will do what you're asking me to do (integrity), that I can do it (ability), that I will do it consistently (reliability), and that I will do it well or improve where I need to (strength). Most importantly, trust means that I will be honest (truth) when any of those things are missing, and that I will have your best interest at heart as I do.

Trust is a belief, and a belief in all of those things. It is a promise to each other to either deliver on our commitments or to improve, and it never stops. Trust is the linkage between our being and our doing, and when it is being built and maintained (yes it will always require maintenance), it will make the visible, operational systems of our lives work like magic and the human and more invisible sides of our lives less laborious and more glorious. When trust is there, everything works better.

Emerging from the Dark

If trust is so important and bridges the paradoxical tensions of our human being and doing, the builder and the gardener in us, how then do we build it and why is it so challenging? Trust is challenging because it puts the most fundamental dilemma of our human experience right in the middle of the spotlight—the tension between being known and hiding—of functioning in the dark versus in the light. You've likely seen this repeatedly in your own life. In situations where your trust in others is low, there is almost always something being hidden or kept from us. We have all hidden something from others and others have hidden things from us. In some cases, it's not some deep dark secret, but simply a feeling of insecurity to do our jobs, or it is based on a hurt within us that causes us not to trust others, which often escalates into us not being trustworthy.

> "We all live with the fear that our inner light will be extinguished or our inner darkness exposed. We fear the loss of trust—our own and other people's—in what we see within. But when we refuse to face our shadows, they take up residence in the leadership we offer." (Palmer 2000, 92)

It's not that trust is always about an evil kind of hiding where we are intentionally and nefariously keeping the truth from each other. Because we are talking about human relationships, it's more complicated than that. In some cases, we hold back the whole truth because we don't feel safe to talk about what we are experiencing, or in many cases we can't even find the words to effectively describe what it feels like to be us, or that we haven't had great experiences with being honest and lacked the support necessary to try again. Regardless of that reality, our ability to be truthful with each and to come out of the darkness matters.

That moment in each of us is our fundamental problem and solution when it comes to trust. To walk vulnerably toward the tension of our temptation to hide and our deepest need to be known. I trust you says to another, I see you—the whole of you—and because of that and in spite of your brokenness, I trust you. But too often, we walk in the dark. We don't know ourselves, or we hide what we do know. What we hide comes out eventually. The arrogant leader who is insecure beneath the surface but attempts to project strength. The disconnected leader who doesn't see their impact on others. Or even the leader or team member who believes they are self-aware, when everyone around them knows they aren't. Or the team member who is afraid to admit their weaknesses or lack of confidence to do their job. We see this all the time.

> "To love at all is to be vulnerable. Love anything and your heart will be wrung and possibly broken... The only place outside Heaven where you can be perfectly safe from all the dangers of love is Hell." (Lewis 1960, 121)

What is the impact on the visible side of our organizations? People leave, talk about each other behind the backs of others, or they simply can't perform their jobs. We must trust each other in spite of our temptation to hide, and that will require vulnerability and a willingness to make the invisible things occurring within our hearts and minds as visible as the things that surround us every day. And that level of trust will require intentionality, courage, and a level of vulnerability we may not have experienced before.

Your Moment and Your People

What is the strategic moment you are attempting to seize right now? What purposeful thing are you working on right now and what role are others playing in that? What is it that you or your organization must do to achieve the goal and to make the difference you set out to make? That question eludes far more people than you realize, but when that mission is clear and the moment is identified, all your efforts to invest in your people will not only make sense to you, but to every person who serves with you.

For emerging leaders and young adults, that moment is often their preparation for a career, or their search for that first full-time job. For many organizations, their moment is defined by a transition in leadership, a new product or organization you are launching, or the hiring of new leadership that is changing things. Sometimes it is exponential growth or an unprecedented decline in the business, or the launching of a new product or service that is predicted to disrupt an entire market or industry. For others, it is rising interest rates that have put your carrying costs of inventory through the roof, or your realization that your organization has outgrown its capacity to develop leaders fast enough. And for others, the most deeply rooted call on their lives is to solve poverty in the world, the need for water, or for education, and hope and resources for the poorest of the poor. Whatever your strategic moment, it is necessary to identify it before you can begin your efforts to connect your people to the mission of your organization.

Why is this so important? We know a lot about learning and leadership development in organizations. We know that most learning occurs on the job as people are trying to fulfill the expectations of their roles and as they are simply trying to get things done. While training and books are important for learning specific tasks, most of our learning is occurring through trial-by-fire and even crucible experiences that occur in high-pressure moments on the job. People learn the deepest lessons as they are attempting to get things done, and learn even deeper lessons if the stakes are high and they have to draw on other people like never before. And, when that moment is intentionally connected to their learning and humanity, unprecedented things begin to happen.

What is the relevance of nearly 100 years of research and great thinking about leadership and organizational effectiveness today? Other than the reality that we must focus on people and processes, we must also bring alignment between the two. They will always be in tension with one another, but we could do a better job of aligning them. The problem is that we are too often drawn to oversimplified solutions over solutions that capture our reality as leaders of organizations. Developing the people side of your organization apart from your strategic reality is not only a miss, it is likely the reason that most of your efforts in the past to develop your leaders and teams have left them wanting more.

Where do you begin? You begin with a set of questions to excavate your mission and the strategic moment you're seizing as you seek to fulfill that mission. As soon as you are clear about this moment you and your organization are experiencing, your leader and team development efforts will not only begin to come into alignment with that mission, you will then begin to understand the urgency you feel better and the plan you will need to get everything on track.

Ask yourself two questions:

- What is the moment you are experiencing right now in the life of your organization that is a moment that matters?
- What does the performance and well-being of those around you have to do with your ability to seize that moment effectively?

Building wild and extraordinary trust across your life and organization begins with understanding your moment and the moment impacting every person who serves with you. For most of us, making progress and work are such important parts of our identity. While some suggest that we are not defined by what we do, that is simply not the whole truth. Our ability to make progress and get things done leaves imprints on our psyche and our character that tell us something about ourselves. It tells us what motivates us and what we are capable of accomplishing, and it moves us forward. It reminds us that we are here for a purpose—to build and make progress. We were put on this earth to work it, to establish systems and plans for production, and to make a difference. And, in so many cases, our place to build is what we call an organization (or a business) and an organization is about people. And, whenever it's about people, it is about being known and knowing others versus our pull to hide and protect. Whenever we have to get something done together, we must face this reality head-on. To trust each other, we must know each other and we must know ourselves. We must unveil and stop hiding. There is no way around it—and trust is what creates health and progress because it is the bridge between the visible and the invisible.

As closing time approached at our party that has been going on for decades, Peter Drucker walked in at the end in about 1966. While the party would surely continue in the future, Peter had one last thing to say that would be repeated in one way or another at every party for decades to come. He said this.

> "Only executive effectiveness can enable this society to harmonize its two needs: the needs of organization to obtain from the individual the contribution it needs and the contribution of the individual to have the organization as his tool for the accomplishment of his purposes. Effectiveness must be learned." (Drucker 1966, 52)

Dr. Drucker's point? Change for our organizations, our families, and even society must begin with us, and we must be ready to learn. We must connect the visible and the invisible.

For a Conversation

1. What is the strategic moment you are experiencing right now?
2. Who are the people who play an important role in your progress?
3. In what ways does trust connect the people and the systems in your life that make everything work better for you?

CHAPTER 4

Whole Leaders, Wild Trust

The Courage to Be Seen. The Risk to Trust Again

You don't have to be perfect to be trusted, but you do have to be honest about who you are becoming.

Leading would be easy if we were robots. I'm not sure we'd be any better at it, but it sure would be easier. If we were robots, our programming would just tell us what to do and we would do it. We wouldn't have to fuss with all the feelings of other people, what they think about themselves and what they think of us. We wouldn't have to be concerned with whether people are motivated or inspired. We would simply be responsible for getting the results we were built to get, and when we didn't get them, we would just be replaced by a better robot.

Until leaders are robots, it's not going to be like that. Leaders aren't machines and neither are the people we lead. And as long as human beings are the leading stewards of the resources and functioning of our world, trust will not be optional. Human beings require trust to function, and more importantly, to thrive. And the universal truth is that to trust each other, we must know each other better.

"A person is a person through other persons... My humanity is caught up, is inextricably bound up, in yours." (Tutu 1999, 31)

It's hard to trust someone whose brokenness has taken over their leadership. Like a cracked bucket can't carry water, a leader unaware of their own fractures can't carry the trust of others. This isn't about perfection—it's about progress. About the journey toward becoming a more whole and trustworthy version of ourselves. That journey often starts with telling just one small part of your wild story.

The common theme when we label something as wild is that it's oftentimes beyond surprising, defying reason, unexpected, obviously important, possibly undeserved, and even somewhat scandalous. Something that's the opposite of wild is something that's tame and cultivated, civilized, cultured, relevant, disciplined, calm, indifferent and sensible. Many of us don't live in that world, or at least our unspoken sides don't. Our unspoken world is wild, and we often feel like misfits in the sensible world. The world says that what is relevant makes sense, and we know that the real story of our lives—our jobs, finances, marriages, personality, faith, successes, failures, losses, suffering, happiness, and redemption—is anything but sensible. We are wild things in a world that will always be too sensible to handle us.

It's the wild and whole stories others have shared with us that have opened a door to hope, possibility, and trust. Not a trust that says it all happened for good, but a trust that says you're not alone, and there is the possibility of light right in the midst of the darkness. It's our wild, surprising, shocking, uncivilized, unordered, undisciplined, and sometimes scandalous stories that open a door to insight. Those stories have shaped us, and they continue to shape the wild ride ahead. While it would be irresponsible to go "all in" and share everything all at once (that would be weird by the way—so don't do that), beginning to tell even part of the story is where it starts. It all begins with an invitation, and far too often we fail to be invited or to invite others. This is an invitation to not only see yourself more accurately as a leader or potential leader, but to get intentional on the journey ahead.

Is it possible for two broken people to trust each other? Yes it is possible, because on some level we are all fragmented. But trust is only built between us and among us if we are making intentional progress out of our brokenness toward wholeness. You do not have to be perfect to be trustworthy as a leader, but you do need to be making strides toward becoming more whole. Why is it important to understand that we all have a wild story? If we are to trust each other, we must know each other. And how in the world can we know each other if we aren't willing to share who we really are? To build trust, we are going to have to know one another. And, knowing one another will require courage, intentional vulnerability, and a plan for how to build it over time.

Each of us, whether we are leading or following, brings a wonderfully complex and nuanced combination of capacity to get results, feelings about our world, good and bad experiences, and a deeper drive for purpose that makes us all so incredibly interesting and capable of unbelievable things. But that same complexity that makes us so wonderful is also what makes us difficult. We aren't robots, and I'm thankful for that. Sure, we bring some wiring in our DNA regarding our personalities and our strengths and limitations, but we also bring an experiential story that has shaped our capacity to lead and who we are. The problem is that too often we understand so little about who we are and the person or leader we've become. Sometimes it feels like too much work to become just a bit more self-aware, let alone more effective. But, for some of us, we simply haven't been invited to understand our whole story and its impact on the leader or person we could become.

Vulnerability, Transparency, and Trust

Vulnerability, while important, is challenging because its literal definition is the openness to being hurt. If I share something with you that matters there is a very real chance that you could either hurt me with it or that you could completely misunderstand what I shared. It's a risk. And yet, vulnerability is required for trust. In the same way that vulnerability is the openness to being hurt, transparency is the openness to being seen. And like vulnerability, it is required if we are to become trusted and to trust others. We must be seen (be transparent) and in order to be seen, we must share something important and potentially dangerous to share (something vulnerable). Vulnerability is necessary for change and inspiration and trust building, but it takes courage because there is a reality that others may hurt you or misunderstand you, and yet, it is still required to build trust. Transparency is like a clean window. When unobstructed, it allows us to be seen and see others—a key ingredient for trust.

Both vulnerability and transparency are required for trust. This doesn't mean that we will share everything, but that we will need to practice a bit of appropriate vulnerability and share more than we have in the past if we are to become more trusted and trusting of others.

Your Wild Story

What's the story of how you came to this moment you are in right now, and what impact has it had on who you are and the influence you have on others? Whether you are a parent, a president, a manager, or someone who doesn't aspire to lead but may in the future, your whole story is important. Our whole leader story is the uniqueness behind our personalities, our competence, our lessons learned, our relationships, our purpose for being here, and how others will experience us and experience themselves. Seeing and telling our whole story is one of the most important developmental steps we can take toward becoming more whole as leaders and human beings, and for deepening trust with others. Some of us might feel like it's all just too strange or broken to share, while others of us feel that it isn't weird or different enough to deserve much attention at all. What we do share as humans with responsibility for others is that when we think about our whole story, in most cases there is something wild about it. We have a story we tell when we're asked what we do for a living, when someone asks us about our family, or when we're asked what we are doing after college. We have a story we tell when we're asked how things are going, or when someone asks us in an interview, "Tell me about your strengths and weaknesses." Like you, I have an answer in response to most of those questions. But it gets complicated when I realize someone is interested in more than the easy answer—when they are interested in hearing more of the whole and real story behind my more surface responses to the different pieces of my life. Those parts of my story include so many interconnected parts, a lot of uncertainty, some surprises, unexpected successes, some pain, mistakes, and wrong turns. Our whole and wild stories of our development as leaders or as people are always there, but not always easy to share. The problem is that, as leaders, we navigate some of the most important decisions of our lives without connecting the different parts of our whole story to the choices we're making today. In hopes that you'll share some of your story with someone else, here's part of mine.

My first date with my wife Jackie, I got her to skip finance class in college. I'm so glad she did because now we've been married longer than we were single. I am a father of two young men who have taught me so much about leading and life. I was a university professor for over 20 years, and during that time I also had my own business. I am an outdoorsman, a gamer, a truck enthusiast, and I'm pretty handy with tools. I am an unlikely Ph.D. because I was a B student through most of college. I applied to twelve Ph.D. programs and got into one. I feel socially awkward in many situations, but I believe that most other people feel that way too. I feel much more qualified to do the work I do today than I did when I was younger. I am invested in leaders who bring courage and sacrifice to their world, and you might be surprised by that underqualified feeling I sometimes have. I'm fully aware that I come from what others might see as privilege and plenty, but I also know that I don't have the privilege of being without brokenness, shame, doubt, fear, or a feeling of not fitting in. I got a late start at being comfortable in my own skin, and I'm still getting there. I care a little too much about what you think of me. I believe deeply that there is a God who has plans for my life, but I struggle sometimes when it feels like God is silent. While I've always been a driver, innovator, and creator of new things, I feel like I hit my deepest stride later in life. I'm generally a grateful and hopeful person. My biggest excitement for when I die is to be able to ask God a ton of wild questions, and then play Call of Duty together. I aspire to be slightly endearing to others, but also sometimes know I'm not. I have only first and sixth gear. The first gear is "goofy and playful" Rob and the sixth gear is "let's get it done or get to the hard questions" Rob. I'm more introverted than most people think. I'm comfortable speaking in front of large groups of people, but am sometimes more uncomfortable in small groups.

Finally, I am the youngest brother by 8, 13, and 17 years to two sisters and a brother. My parents had leadership responsibilities all my life because my dad was the president of two different universities and a seminary. I watched my parents navigate leadership together and in many ways our dinner table conversations were more like an advisory board session than a normal family dinner conversation. My parents are amazing people and leaders, and still, their journey as leaders was challenging. If my dad was in the middle of a campaign to raise money for a science building on campus there were always many who were pushing in different directions. There was likely a neighbor in the community who might sue the university because they didn't want another building built, a parent who was frustrated that the building wouldn't be completed soon enough for their son or daughter to study in that new science building, and even faculty in the humanities who might push back against a science building being built at a liberal arts college. And those competing desires landed squarely on my mom and dad's shoulders. In the midst of all that, my parents were navigating all the normal things of life, marriage, and raising kids. As public figures and leaders, their lives were on display. And, in many ways, that dinner table was the "McKenna" safe place to ponder, to ask questions, and to be whole as people. Witnessing that as a kid gave me such an appreciation for leaders and leading, and for the need for spaces to be whole. As a leader said to me recently, "So Rob, what you've spent your career doing is attempting to rebuild that dinner table for other leaders." I think he was right. Like my parents and so many others around me, I have found myself in the position of leader and of being responsible for the experience, work, and development of a lot of people.

What's your wild story? What is important for others to understand if they are to trust you and you are to trust them? If my story seems better or worse than yours, trust me when I say that if I let you in deeper there are places where our brokenness and our redemption would cause us to realize we share far more than we don't. The only reason I don't share more is either because those parts of me aren't quite baked enough to pull out of the oven, or because I hold some of those stories in solidarity with others. What I do know is this. Every one of us has a whole story, and that story is impacting the leaders we are today, the leaders we will become tomorrow, and the trust we must continue to assess and build that will serve as the lifeblood of our lives and leadership.

Whole Leaders

When I launched my organization many years ago, I named it WiLD Leaders for two reasons. First, every person has a wild story that is necessary to understand if we are to develop the next generation of world-changing leaders. But second, the acronym stands for "whole and intentional leader development," and those four words play such a critical role in all of our efforts to measure and build trust together. Your trust-building efforts will begin with embracing and understanding your own capacity to become a whole leader, and to live a life full of both intention and learning.

When we were kids, we knew who the leaders were. We played a game called "Follow the Leader," and no one ever had to tell us the rules. The only unspoken rule was that the leader goes first. For whatever reason, when someone started doing something, if we were willing to play, we started to follow. Whether the leader climbed over rocks, started running, or crawled under furniture, we followed if we wanted to play the game.

Has our way of seeing leaders really changed all that much in our adulthood? We follow leaders every day who have taken the initiative to do something first, and oftentimes, we're drawn to follow leaders who bring the greatest amount of conviction that somehow aligns with our current way of thinking about our world. While we so often define a leader by the extent to which they embody what's important to us, the greatest leaders will both align with us and challenge us. Leaders are going first all over the world and doing things that we may find unimaginable or deeply disturbing. However, they are leaders nonetheless. When we think about an individual going first, we quickly realize that their position is quantitatively and qualitatively different from not going first. We are not all leaders all the time. We hear that statement said often and it absolutely minimizes just how challenging it is to actually be the leader. Furthermore, the common statement that leaders are followers is attractive because it highlights a servant characteristic that we desire in our leaders, but it minimizes the experience of what it means to step out in front in the face of very real resistance and powerful voices that may sabotage our ability to remain in that position, and stay there well.

The first time you are promoted from team member to leader of that same team is important. The people who were once your peers are now your direct reports, and in many cases, you know things about each of them that you cannot share with others. To be honest and constantly truthful and open would not only be illegal in some cases, but could be downright reckless. Trust is no longer built by telling the whole truth, but by being honest that there are things you can talk about and things you can't. And most leaders cannot even do that. That level of honesty is oftentimes something the rest of us couldn't handle, or might even use against them when we are at our worst. Leading is isolating because it is difficult to know who you can trust, what they can handle, and what you can share. At the same time, a strategic and intentional community of support is absolutely necessary if we are to prepare and encourage whole leaders. It's not only work-related challenges that isolate leaders, but also our life challenges. Challenges in marriage, parenting, caring for parents, and life stress are impacting leaders every day, and so often they feel little hope that they can get help.

Everything changes for a person in the role of leader.

As a leader, you are no longer only responsible for your truth. You are also responsible for understanding and communicating the truth of others, and for what it means to move forward together as opposed to moving forward alone. Simply living or speaking our truth and leaving it at that would be easy if we lived our lives in a cloister—in a vacuum outside of relationships to others.

Leading is inherently about us in the role of leader with others. As leaders, we are not only responsible for understanding and living into ourselves, but also for understanding the truth of others and how those truths interact. Transparency looks different for leaders because you now are responsible for holding solidarity with individuals and will likely know things about each of your followers or team members that you can't share with others. And, while it's easy to blame leaders when we are not one, we now become responsible and accountable in ways we weren't before because so much of the experience and progress of others rests on our shoulders. You will get too little credit when things go right, and receive the blame when they don't. You will have to draw on other people like never before. You will succeed and fail, and all of it will happen in a more public way. You will have the opportunity to inspire people and deal with moments or seasons where the people around you feel disengaged or unmotivated.

Leading is an incredible experience, and likely one of the hardest of your life. Going first is especially difficult for leaders who have even an ounce of compassion or connection into the needs of others. To develop a whole and intentional leader is to pay close attention to the actual experience of going first—of stepping out into a position of isolation, of courage, and of unprecedented complexity. To prepare a generation of thoughtful and courageous leaders for that moment will mean radically reforming the paradigms that define what it means to develop a whole person as a leader.

So what does a whole leader actually look like? What are they made of, and what are they moving toward?

Whole leaders are not content to stay fragmented. They know they are a work in progress—but they don't use that as an excuse. Instead, they live in the tension between strength and humility, continually becoming a more complete version of themselves. They are aware of their gifts and their gaps. They lead with conviction, but they're not afraid to change their minds. They are willing to be edited—even in places that feel core to who they are. They can take the hits, admit when they're wrong, and stay in the room when things get hard. That's not weakness—it's fortitude. As Brené Brown reminds us in *Daring Greatly*, "You can't get to courage without walking through vulnerability. Period." (Brown 2012, 33) Her words ring especially true for whole leaders. Vulnerability isn't a detour around leadership—it's the path through. Staying in the room when things get hard isn't just about resilience; it's about the raw courage to lead with our full selves. Because the kind of leader who owns their mistakes and asks better questions is the kind of leader people want to follow.

Whole leaders carry both heart and mind into the work. They care deeply about the people they lead, and they never lose sight of performance and progress. They don't reduce people to tasks, and they don't reduce strategy to spreadsheets. They know that sustainable impact comes when people and mission align. That means they keep their roots in purpose, but they're open to pruning. They are listeners and learners. They ask questions more often than they fill the room with answers. They play the long game—and they are fully present in the now. They see the individuals on their team, and they see the system those individuals live in. And they are building both.

We need more of them. Whole leaders are out there—sometimes quiet, sometimes overlooked, sometimes waiting for someone to believe in them. I cannot emphasize this enough: if we are to build trust between us, our efforts must begin with an intentional investment in developing whole leaders—leaders who will go first, who will go deep, and who will carry both courage and sacrifice into their roles. They are the leaders we hope to follow. And they are also the leaders we must become.

Intentional Development

Would you rather be around someone who intended to be something better and fell short, or around someone who never had the intention in the first place? Why do we beat up on people for having good intentions? Even if they fell short, at least they intended to do something good. While we have good intentions, a lot of things happen by mistake. Our problem is that we assume that intentions and mistakes are in a contradictory relationship to one another. To the contrary, at our best, our intent serves as the foundation and guide, keeping us somewhat centered for the multiple attempts that will be necessary to become more whole versions of ourselves. Think of a director on a movie set. Whether it's 1 or 50 takes to get a scene right, the process and learning necessary in getting there plays a key role in finishing the scene. While things certainly happen by mistake (multiple fails until we get what we were intending in the first place), our mistakes or mis-takes are the ways we move from intention to destination.

Intention requires that each of us see that we have the ability to choose. Psychologists call that ability agency, or the fundamental belief that not only can I make a choice, but that my choice will matter. With regard to our learning and growth, whether we're leaders in the world or not, intention is the ingredient in our change recipe that makes the difference between us being told to change, and feeling a sense of having the capacity to become something different. Every attractive cultural concept of change, whether it's a growth mindset, adaptive performance, learning agility, self-development, vulnerability, emotional maturity, leadership development, engagement, or meaning is not only built on the assumption of agency, but on the assumption that if we changed how we thought, we could change—and even more powerful, could become more whole. If we want to get intentional about developing ourselves and others as whole leaders, we must face the realities of change.

Development is change, and change is a chaotic and disruptive process. It just is. When we ask a person to develop, we are asking them to change—to intentionally become a different version of themselves, for their sake and for the sake of others. We are asking them to make a choice to enter into a moment that will produce pressure, resistance, and a temptation to move back to the equilibrium that makes us more comfortable—even if that equilibrium isn't the best thing for us. "Leader" is neutral. Leaders cannot be. While leader is a neutral term, I have very little interest in preparing, developing, or launching neutral leaders. Like you, I want leaders who have a sense of themselves and enough efficacy, fortitude, and conviction to step out into the position of being first, and a willingness to edit for the sake of others.

What is the most important place to start?

If there was one thing that I would look for in leaders beyond competence, results, personality, or behavior styles, it would be editability—a willingness to have the backspace key hit on things that may require deep change, even changes that feel like they are a part of their character. Developing whole leaders is about creating pathways into the real experience of leaders that connect their purpose, personality, character, competence, and networks of support in a way that opens up agency and belief for them—pathways that give them permission to ask the harder questions out loud. For every one of us, agency isn't given or demanded, it's invited.

Wild Trust

Few of us would deny that our world is in the midst of a reformation—a radical change in values and dividing polarities that are attacking our trust in each other like endless volleys of artillery. Those polarities have put us in the middle of the most profound crisis of trust the world has ever seen. Whether it's the tension between relativism and fundamentalism, liberty and security, justice and mercy, love and truth, or diversity and unity—these are the paradoxes of our time. These tensions are not only political and ideological, they are also practical, structural, and even theological.

While global and organizational shifts in cultural assumptions are important, just as important is the impact of these shifts on individuals and leaders. Oversimplified solutions to our less than simple problems will always leave us wanting more.

> "We have a crisis of trust in our world today. It's pervasive. It's in our institutions, in our companies, in our cultures, in our relationships. The reality is that while we may be aware of the problem, most people don't know what to do about it." (Covey 2022, 3)

If we focus on oversimplified leadership principles or the five steps to effective living and ignore the polarizing context within which each of us will exist or lead, we risk prescribing overused clichés or airport book solutions that will leave all of us underprepared and undersupported. It's not enough to talk about leadership or to talk about principles. It's time to talk about leaders and about us—and more specifically—improving our efforts to develop whole leaders and whole people for the whole world. Whether it's an individual emerging from poverty, a business leader desiring a deeper connection of faith in their work, a tradesperson who begins to manage others for the first time, someone called to serve but challenged to lead an organization, or a young adult on a university campus, it's time to change the paradigm.

While a revolution is a movement against existing realities, a reformation is a movement of change based on a reality that's right in front of us. To that end, a whole-leader reformation that will change the trajectory of our crisis of trust is a strategic and intentional focus on the needs of leaders, and away from leadership as an abstraction from the real and gritty experience of leading. The whole reality of leaders is that they are human. They ask themselves hard questions, they make mistakes, they fail, and they have fears and even moments of hopelessness that can either define them or inform them. The difference for leaders is that their mistakes happen in public and their fears are easily labeled as weaknesses. We are surrounded by those leaders who need us to do a better job of meeting them where they are and offering them another way. A leader, whether by choice or by necessity, is responsible for the experience of so many others and for our progress forward. With that burden comes a whole different level of responsibility and they need trust within themselves and trust for everyone who serves with them.

And, there is hope. A wild aspiration.

- **Wild trust is a miracle hiding in plain sight.** Given how flawed we are—how prone we are to self-interest, misunderstanding, and fear—it's actually quite surprising that any of us can trust each other at all. We are unreliable narrators of our own stories, often unsure of what we even want, let alone how to be honest about it with others. We misread each other, we let one another down, and we carry histories of hurt. And yet, trust shows up. Sometimes slowly. Sometimes in a rush. But always as something more than we had a right to expect. That kind of trust—the kind that grows not because we're perfect, but because we keep showing up anyway—is *wild trust*.
- **Wild trust is faith and belief exchanged in both directions—even when we know how often we fall short.** It's not naïve, and it's not blind. It doesn't ignore past wounds or pretend failure hasn't happened. Instead, it chooses to hope in the face of that reality. Wild trust is your faith in me and mine in you, even though we both know we've disappointed each other before. It's the decision to believe that what we're building together—whether a team, a mission, or a relationship—is worth the risk. It's the courage to say, "I'll go with you anyway." That kind of trust doesn't emerge from sanitized relationships. It is born in the mess—in the truth-telling, in the apologies, in the rebuilding, in the slow and sacred work of believing again.
- **Wild trust is an aspiration—an audacious hope—for something better.** It imagines a different kind of world. A different kind of organization. One where people tell each other the truth, even when it's hard. One where we don't pretend that brokenness doesn't exist—but we refuse to let it define us. Wild trust moves us from fragmentation to wholeness, from silence to courage, from suspicion to clarity. And

when it works—when we look back and realize what we built together—we say something deeply humbling and profoundly true: *We did that in spite of ourselves.* That's wild trust. Not because it was easy. But because we chose to stay, to speak, and to build anyway.

So I ask you this.

What can we do to better prepare a generation of whole and trusted leaders with hearts to serve, a willingness to learn, a capacity to lead at the next level, and a wisdom to discern and provide clarity in these complex times? Answering this question is critical, but it will take a reformation—a radical shift in how we intentionally prepare them for the journey ahead. A shift in our mindset, our methods, and the way we see our measures of progress.

For a Conversation

1. What's the wild story that others need to understand in order for them to see you more effectively, and to trust you? It doesn't need to be long, but consider sharing something important for others around you to know.
2. Who are the leaders you would describe as whole leaders and why?
3. If you were to change just one thing in your life that would be an intentional shift for you that would not only benefit you, but others, what would that be?

CHAPTER 5

Mindset, Methods, and Measures

Moving from Gut Intuition to Intentional Change

> *You can't build trust on instinct alone. True leadership begins when your mindset shifts, your methods deepen, and your measures start telling the whole story.*

Trust is one of the most important currencies in our world today, but too often it feels like the air we breathe. We know we must have it to survive, but when we reach out to grab it, it floats between our fingers like a vapor and disappears. What if I told you that you could not only measure trust and take decisive action to build it, but also that your efforts to develop the people and leaders around you are one in the same? I spent most of my career developing a system of whole leader assessments, all contained in the WiLD Trust Platform, that were designed to build whole leader capacity. What we discovered over the years changed everything. Developing whole leaders and building sustaining trust involves more than measures of our progress. It also includes a shift in our mindset and the way we actually do the hard and important work of developing ourselves and others—a methodology that changes everything.

Before we can invest in developing ourselves and others as whole leaders—or begin measuring and building the trust we long for—we must first clarify our mindset, our methods, and the measures that will drive real change.

Mindset: The Way We See Everything

We've all heard the phrase "mindset matters." It sounds like a motivational poster, but what we believe about ourselves, others, and the nature of growth actually determines what we're willing to try, risk, or change. What we don't often say out loud is that development is hard. It takes guts to look in the mirror, let alone help someone else do the same. Mindset is about how we interpret not just our potential, but our limitations. It's a belief system that informs whether we see development as a process that we endure or as an opportunity we engage.

A whole leader mindset includes a few core truths:

- Development is both a *process and an outcome.* It is not linear, and that's okay.
- You must get a *handle on where you are*, even as you accept that where you are will change.
- We learn *individually and together.* Transformation is personal, but never private.
- Different people require different things. *One size doesn't fit all.*
- Thinking and doing are both essential. *Reflection without action leads to stagnation.* Action without reflection leads to recklessness.
- Change your *mind*, and your *behavior* will follow. Change your *behavior*, and your *mindset* will shift. It's not either/or.
- You matter. Others matter. *And this isn't all about you.* The organization matters too.

This mindset challenges one of the most ingrained myths of leadership—that you must either be selfless or self-focused. In reality, whole leaders hold the paradox. They recognize that they are stewards of more than their own story. That's the sacrificial part. It's not that your needs don't matter; it's that leadership invites you to consider something bigger than yourself.

Abraham Heschel once said, "To see what we know is not enough. We must know what we see." (Heschel 1965, 76). Developing a whole leader mindset means being willing to see differently, and then act accordingly.

Method: The Way We Practice Change

The most significant shift in how we approach development today isn't just in *what* we develop, but *how*. Traditional development approaches often focus on competencies or behaviors detached from context. But a whole and intentional approach to developing whole leaders and building wild trust is different. It's rooted in real-time awareness, shared vulnerability, and a line of sight that extends from the individual all the way to the mission of the organization.

The WiLD Line of Sight: Individual → Team → Organization → Mission.

Every tool, question, and practice in the WiLD Trust Platform is designed to create clarity across this line. The goal is not just increased performance, but increased awareness—of yourself, of your team, and of the organization you're building.

At the core of the method are seven practices.

PRACTICE 1: ASK QUESTIONS BEFORE GIVING ANSWERS

The research on leaders has made it clear that failure is as powerful a teacher as any success, but that doesn't make it any easier when it happens. Development is change, and change is hard. Learning to be a leader requires change. These transformational moments are rarely framed by clear answers. Whole leader development is about creating a pathway into the questions that each of us are already asking ourselves, but are often forbidden to speak out loud—the questions we ask over a cup of coffee or a beer with a trusted friend in a moment of vulnerability:

- Why am I here?
- Why do I feel lost?
- Why do I struggle in relationships?
- Why do I keep making the same mistakes?
- Why would someone hire me?
- Why do I sometimes feel uninspired?
- Why do I feel isolated and alone?
- Why am I making it all about me?

Who among us hasn't asked these questions at some point? For some of us at different seasons of our lives, even approaching these questions or giving them voice feels a little dangerous. It's almost as if asking them gives them the power to overwhelm us. The reality is that these are just some of the questions that open up a lens on our actual experience. The problem begins when we or others attempt to resolve these questions with answers that wrap our lives up with tidy little bows. Remaining in these questions long enough creates the necessary awareness to begin to imagine versions of them that maintain their urgency while opening a pathway forward. Questions that provide a pathway invite us to see a different potential future while keeping us in the tension between where we are and where we could be. The first set of questions become invitational questions like…

- What would change if you knew why you are here and what you should do next?
- What would change if there was purpose driving your next step forward?
- What would change if you were more composed under pressure?
- What would change if you were applying lessons from your past experiences?
- What would change if you knew your unique skills and competencies, and your blind spots?
- What would change if you knew what motivates you?
- What would change if you were surrounded by cheerleaders, mentors, and people who give it to you straight?
- What would change if you were intentionally investing in the learning and growth of those around you?

The most important developmental questions occur in repeating cycles over our lifetime. The problem is that we often desire quick answers that promise massive impact, but at the very same moment, we want deep and sustaining change. Deep change requires reflection and asking questions we know are important. There is hope though. Like any change at the personal level, it takes a sustained emphasis on making learning the goal, and questions the key prescription. A focus on questions doesn't assume that answers aren't important, but that getting to the deeper resolution to our developmental challenge must involve as many courageous questions as answers.

When we move from giving answers to asking questions—especially questions we don't know the answer to—we invite others into a process of mutual growth, and we invite them to see the possibilities that have been living in them all along.

PRACTICE 2: TAKE RISKS IN REAL TIME
The best development doesn't happen in a classroom. It happens in the moment where you make a decision, have a difficult conversation, or try something new. The WiLD method involves *real-time development*, where leaders are encouraged to engage courageously in the present moment, not just reflect on it later. This requires vulnerability, but with discretion. Vulnerability doesn't mean oversharing. It means being honest enough to admit you don't have it all figured out, and wise enough to know when and how to share that truth.

PRACTICE 3: INTEGRATE MEANING, MISSION, MECHANICS, MINDSET, AND MEASURES
One of the most common breakdowns in leadership and organizational trust is the misalignment between what we believe, what we say matters, and what we actually do. We often focus on the mechanics—what to do and how to do it—without aligning them with deeper meaning or mission. But whole and trusted leadership doesn't start with mechanics. It starts with mindset—the way we see people, purpose, and pressure. That mindset should inform our methods—how we structure our systems, teams, and goals. And both must ultimately connect to how we measure what matters.

That's why meaning, mission, and mechanics aren't new categories—they're expressions of mindset, methods, and measures in action. *Meaning* asks the mindset question: Why does this matter? *Mission* is the method: How does our purpose translate into strategic priorities? *Mechanics* are where our systems and measurements show up. And the best leaders, the most trusted teams, are the ones who align all of them with intention.

Because at the end of the day, the real question isn't whether we can build systems that function. It's whether we're building something worth sustaining—and doing it in a way that reflects what we say we value. Without that alignment, trust erodes. But when mindset, methods, and measures all point in the same direction, trust becomes not just possible, but operational.

PRACTICE 4: SEE DEVELOPMENT AS A LONG PLAY

Whole and intentional leader development isn't a sprint. It's not a quick fix, a coaching hack, or a training day—it's the long play. And that changes everything. When we see development as a long game, we're no longer obsessed with immediate returns or next-quarter wins. We're building with the awareness that the people we're investing in today may be the ones who carry the mission forward tomorrow—even if we're not in the room to see it happen.

That long view reframes the way we define success. It shifts our expectations from output to legacy. It invites us to develop people not only for what they can do now, but for who they're becoming, and who they'll help others become. It acknowledges that some of the most important outcomes of our leadership may never show up on our watch—but that doesn't make them any less vital.

Long play development means we speak to future impact, not just present performance. We encourage people with the kind of vision that transcends deadlines. We plant seeds we may never see grow, because we trust that someone else will water them. That kind of perspective demands humility—and it demands faith. Because if we truly believe that leadership is about transformation and not just transaction, then we have to be willing to invest in people who may never return the favor, but who will absolutely multiply the impact.

If we adopted this mindset fully, how would it change our efforts to develop those around us? How would it affect the metrics we track, the stories we tell, the patience we practice? The impact could be massive. Because long play development doesn't just produce more leaders—it produces more trusted leaders. And that changes the culture not only of our organizations, but of the generations that follow us.

PRACTICE 5: DEVELOP LEADERS TOGETHER

Whose we are shapes who we are. Leadership doesn't develop in isolation—it's forged in the friction, feedback, and faith of relationships. We are wired for connection, which is why we feel disoriented—less whole—when we try to lead or grow alone. We were created to work together, to build together, and to become together. Yes, solitude matters. There are moments when silence is essential and being alone clarifies everything. But those moments are preparation, not the destination. In the end, we always come back to each other.

A whole perspective on leadership demands that we take relational development seriously—not just as a nice-to-have, but as a fundamental pathway to growth. That means intentionally surrounding ourselves with people we invest in and who invest in us—truth-tellers, supporters, challengers, and fellow builders. It means recognizing that leadership is not just about who we are, but about who we're becoming together.

If you're married, do you get to be whoever you feel you're supposed to be? If you're leading a team, is it enough to just "be yourself?" The truth is, growth often means editing ourselves in response to the people who count on us most. That doesn't mean abandoning our core—it means refining it. It means asking, "What part of me needs to stretch for the sake of those I love, lead, and serve?" That question is uncomfortable, but it's also the birthplace of trust.

Unless we've chosen a life in a cloister, disconnected from the purpose and presence of others, we are constantly navigating the tension between who we are and who we're becoming—for the sake of others. Whole leadership is never just about self-actualization. It's about interdependence. And the leaders we become in community are almost always braver, wiser, and more trustworthy than the ones we try to become alone.

PRACTICE 6: FOCUS ON THE ONE WITH AN EYE TO THE MANY

All of us will face the temptation to either focus on individuals or on organizations. When our sphere of influence is smaller, it's easier to pay attention to the needs of every person, but as organizations grow, we are forced to think about the many. That process is called scale. As we scale and grow, it becomes necessary to put systems in place that can serve the needs of the many for whom we are responsible. The problem is that as we grow the number of people for whom we are responsible, we can often lose sight of the one. A whole and intentional approach to leaders and trust requires us to do both, and to put methods in place that will allow us to see the needs of every individual while also creating systems for the many. It is a necessity that has been around as long as humans have been organizing. A whole approach requires us to continually focus on the one while maintaining an intentional eye on the many.

This is also necessary for us personally. Every leadership challenge begins with the one—*you*. But it cannot end there. Our work to develop whole leaders and build wild trust must start with individual awareness and extend to the team and organizational level. If we want to shape culture, we must start with the person. Sometimes, that person is the most reluctant leader in the room. And sometimes, the best thing we can do is look with them rather than at them. When we do that, we create environments where leaders are seen, heard, and invited to become more whole—not just more effective.

PRACTICE 7: MAKE PEOPLE DEVELOPMENT A STRATEGIC RHYTHM, NOT A ONE-OFF MOMENT

One of the most limiting mindsets in leadership today is the belief that developing people is an event. A book. A workshop. A personality test. A moment on the calendar. But whole and trusted leadership development isn't a pit stop—it's a rhythm. And unless we reframe it as such, we will continue to treat leader development as a checkbox rather than a core strategic and operational function of our organizations.

What's required is a mindset shift that must be reflected in your methods. Leader and people development isn't ancillary to your strategy—it *is* your strategy. It's the engine that fuels performance, drives retention, builds belonging, and accelerates trust. When conversations about personal growth, relational dynamics, and team-level trust become part of the normal operating system—not just the off-site agenda—something changes. Trust becomes measurable. Culture becomes shapeable. Strategy becomes more human.

This is more than theory. When development becomes a consistent rhythm—woven into check-ins, team meetings, one-on-ones, performance reviews, and decision-making processes—you stop seeing your people as fixed entities with static styles. You begin to see them as whole human beings with potential, pressure, and purpose. That shift doesn't just impact engagement; it impacts execution. Because people who are seen, known, and intentionally developed tend to stick around—and they tend to perform.

So don't treat leadership development as an extracurricular. Bake it into your culture. Make it part of how your teams think, act, and build. If you want to create a culture of trust and performance, start by turning development into a rhythm your organization can feel. Because when you lead with that kind of intention, you're not just checking a box—you're changing what's possible.

Measurement: The Way We Understand the Story

Measurement of anything in our organizations serves three purposes. First, it tells us where we are. Measurement is not about judgment—it's about *orientation*. While you may know where you want to go, knowing where you are is just as important for mapping the journey ahead. Second, measurement gives us a way to track our progress. We can then either course correct or accelerate. Third, measurement inspires the goal. When we can see small and measurable wins, it inspires us to win more, to move the mission forward, and tap into specific actions we can take to meet our goal. Finally and maybe most importantly, measurement starts the important conversations that move us toward transformational impact.

Imagine trying to get somewhere without a map. You may eventually stumble on the destination, but you'll likely waste time, energy, and resources along the way. A whole and intentional leader measures what matters. And what matters is *who you are becoming*, not just what you are doing. Personal, team, and organizational assessments work, but are most transformational when they are not only focused on providing you with a profile, a score, or a category within which to see yourself, but also the story behind that score. The *WiLD Trust Platform* includes assessments rooted in decades of psychological research, not to create boxes, but to tell a fuller story. Every metric is designed to offer clarity and insight, not just scores. As we always say, the score matters, but just as important is the story behind your score.

The purpose of measurement in whole and intentional leader development is fourfold:

- **Self-Awareness:** Where am I now? What's my current state? Knowing where I am is the first step in mapping where I want to go.
- **Shared Language:** How do we talk about what we're experiencing together? A shared language and common framing allows us to start powerful and personal conversations.

- **Progress Mapping:** How do we track growth over time? Progress builds confidence and efficacy for the new challenges that will emerge.
- **Strategic Alignment:** How does my development connect to the organization's direction? Known as line-of-sight, one of the most important things that measurement does is in its power to invite a person to see the impact of their work on the larger mission occurring around them.

In the following chapters, I am going to connect some incredible science regarding whole leader development and what it means to build wild trust within yourself, in your relationships and teams, and across your organization and sphere of influence, but remember this: building whole leaders and deepening trust is dependent upon your mindset, your method, and the way you approach using assessments and measures to get there. Once you embrace that reality, you are ready for what's next.

For a Conversation

1. As you reflected on what it means to adopt a WiLD mindset, what was affirmed in you and what do you feel compelled to change?
2. When you consider your current paradigms for change and your methods for investing in others, what is different about the methods described in this chapter?
3. What role have assessments played in your past and how will you use them in the future in your own development and the development of others?

CHAPTER 6

The Chemistry of Trust
The Formula Behind the Feeling

Trust isn't a leap in the dark—it's a step in the light. And when we have the courage to name it, measure it, and build it together, we stop hoping for change and start leading it.

During a conversation in 1987 between President Ronald Reagan of the United States and Mikhail Gorbachev of the Soviet Union, President Reagan said,

> "The Soviet Union and the United States have a long history of arms control agreements, and we have learned that it is important to trust each other—and we do—but also to verify. You always say that, Mr. President. You say, 'Trust, but verify.'" Gorbachev, smiling, responded: "You repeat that at every meeting." And Reagan replied: "I like it." (Reagan 1987)

Presidents Reagan and Gorbachev saw something important. They knew that their relationship must be built on a mutual knowing of one another—a kindredness and even a brotherhood of shared understanding. But trust required more. Each of them understood that trust requires evidence, discernment, and wisdom, and not simply blind belief in each other. We should never measure trust in each other for the sake of proving us to be untrustworthy, but it would be unwise to fail to verify our progress forward.

I'll never forget the CEO sitting in the front row at a recent speaking engagement. As I was describing our unending need for trust and introducing the audience to our work measuring and building it at the personal, team, and organizational levels, he was glaring at me with a very serious look in his eyes that communicated disdain at its worst, and a lot of questions at best. Even though the audience was large, I had been told that this particular CEO was running a several billion dollar business and would be my toughest audience. The day with these leaders was great, but I have to admit that my front row friend was in the back of my mind as I was hoping to inspire him along with all the rest. As I was walking to catch my ride at the end of the engagement, he caught my attention in the parking lot. He said, "Rob, great job today. Very inspiring. Most importantly, it never occurred to me until today that I could measure trust."

In my car ride to my hotel I was full of the greatest joy any speaker can feel. Even my toughest audience caught hold of the vision I was casting. Trust is the most important currency in your life and business, and you can measure it. You can not only measure trust, but you can measure the drivers that build it as well.

As I've already described, too often trust feels like vapor. Something we can see floating in front of us, but when we reach out to grab hold of it, it disappears or slips through our hands. It feels like that because so much of trust is invisible and occurring within and between the hearts and minds of individuals and the people they live and work with every day. Our ability to trust each other, as well as the organizations, institutions, and governments that shape our future, is not only the key to our effectiveness—it is also the largest contributor to our well-being and the hope we feel for what lies ahead. Trust is our biggest problem and our most important solution, but it is more than a feeling or a vapor. Trust has a chemistry. And because it has a chemistry, that means we can measure it. And if we can measure it, we can begin to understand it and build it.

My organization did not set out to build trust. We set out years ago to develop whole leaders and teams. What we didn't understand in the early years was that while we were helping organizations develop leader and team capacity, something else was occurring.

Trust was being built. By focusing on the foundational drivers of leader and team performance, well-being, and wholeness, the deepest transformation was in their capacity to trust each other. We had discovered the drivers at the personal, team, and organizational levels that were building a whole and sustaining trust.

The WiLD Trust Index™

While our need to trust has always been at the center of our functioning as human beings, it has now become one of the most critical issues of our time. To that end, we created the WiLD Trust Index ™ (the WTI), a 33-question assessment of trust at the personal, team and organizational levels. While the WTI provides leaders with insights and tools to begin this vital work, it also allows us to study trust at an unprecedented level. The findings are disturbing as well as inspiring.

According to our research, nearly 50% of people report they are working in a "jungle of trust"—environments where their trust in team members, leaders, and organizations is alarmingly low. Yet, while we all bear responsibility for addressing this crisis, there are clear, actionable steps we can take to change this reality for ourselves and others. What we also learned is that organizations that prioritize the measurement and building of trust through an investment in their leaders and investing in trust at all levels see transformative results—not just in culture, but in measurable business outcomes. And, those transformative results require an understanding of some of the challenges organizations face in getting there.

Here are just a few of our key findings:

- **Distrust is being experienced by too many.** Within organizations, 48% of employees experience a daily reality of distrust, with low trust in both their team members and in their organization and leaders. Even in high-trust organizations, 43% of employees experience a lack of trust.
- **Conflict isn't the problem.** One of the biggest challenges teams face is managing conflict while staying composed. Self-composure in high-pressure moments is key to building trust. Conflict, when handled well, can strengthen trust within teams.

- **There are widespread trust challenges.** Trust-related challenges were reported by 73% of employees—whether in their teams, their organizations, or both.
- **Trust looks different across four different generations in the workplace.** Trust starts strong for people in their 20s, dips to unprecedented lows in their 30s, and then begins to climb back up from there.
- **Performance and truth are key drivers at the team level.** Getting the job done with excellence and being truthful with each other are key drivers of trust. Most people trust their managers more than their team members, and trust is more fragile at the team level than at the organizational level.
- **Emotional maturity matters.** Individuals and leaders who are able to be both clear and honest while also being caring and compassionate help to drive and build trust.
- **Personal trust and organizational trust are related.** In the Jungle of Trust—where team and organizational trust are low—76% of employees have significant developmental challenges at the personal level. Conversely, 79% of employees in the Stronghold of Trust—where both team and organizational trust are high—those people are feeling competent, supported, purposeful, and on track. The implication—personal trust is not just an individual issue—it has a direct and profound impact on workplace culture.

The Chemistry of Trust

In the pursuit of excellence, every leader and every organization must master two things—what is seen, and what is unseen. A whole approach to trust requires a focus on both the visible pieces of the organization (i.e., systems, resourcing, strategic plans, capital assets, etc.) as well as the invisible dynamics occurring within the heart and mind of every individual in the group (i.e. competence, motivation, personality, readiness, support, learning, etc.) Trust not only occurs between people as they put their confidence in each other, it also is impacted by the systems and processes and resources that provide the necessary conditions for trust to grow. Trust connects the person and the team to the organizational structures that make it all possible.

When we trust someone with something as significant as our finances, we trust a team member to have our back, or when we trust someone with the leadership of our organization, it reflects a profound connection. Trust deepens when we know each other—when we truly see each other for who we are.

To build trust, sustain trust, and make meaningful progress, we must understand its makeup, because trust has a chemistry. It is more than a feeling, and includes a combination of elements, that when they are engaged, build trust. At its core, trust is the belief in someone's integrity, ability, reliability, strength, and truthfulness. Trust is relational in nature—something that occurs between people and spreads throughout entire groups. It's a confidence in each other—a belief. It's the belief that someone *will do* what you need and want them to do and have your best interests at heart (integrity), that they *can do* it (ability), that they will do it *consistently* (reliability), and that they will perform competently and *well* (strength). It is also the belief that they will be *honest* with you if any of these things are lacking (truth).

Trust is both a belief and a promise—a promise to deliver on commitments or to improve when necessary. It is the crucial link between the person and their work. When trust is built and maintained, it transforms the operational systems of our lives into seamless mechanisms and makes the invisible aspects of our humanity—our emotions and relationships—less burdensome and more fulfilling. Simply put, when trust is present, everything works better. Fulfilling the promise of trust requires us to not only define trust, but to understand the layers that contain the more specific drivers of trust at every level—the Circles of Trust.

Circles of Trust™

Trust operates on three interconnected layers: personal, team, and organizational, shown in Figure 6.1. They build upon one another, with the personal layer serving as the most fundamental layer where trust must first be developed in order to build trust at the team and organizational levels. The team level is where the learning, development, and actions of the individuals join together to test and refine their belief in each other. Finally, at the organizational layer is where

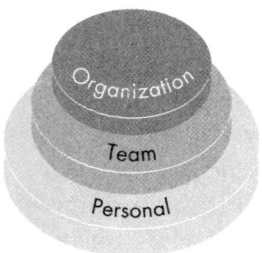

Figure 6.1 Circles of Trust

necessary systemic conditions are established that allow trust to flourish from an individual to their team and throughout the mission of an organization.

PERSONAL TRUST: BUILDING THE FOUNDATION

It is impossible to trust someone who doesn't trust themself, and that very same person will also have difficulty trusting others. Insecurity within us breeds insecurity between us. At its foundation, trust begins within each of us. To be trusted and to trust others begins with an increasing understanding of who we are, where we are going, where we are most effective, what motivates each of us, and what we must develop to move ourselves and our teams to the next level. This is why every leader or people development initiative is also a trust-building initiative. We already know that in order to develop leadership capacity in our organizations, we must make an intentional investment in building up readiness, purpose, progress, composure, learning, motivation, investment in others, support, and intention for every person who serves with us. What we now know is that those efforts to develop individual capacity also build trust, especially as that learning is shared with others.

Personal trust is about awareness within us. As leaders and team members begin to learn and grow and develop across the most important lanes of their development, they build the personal foundation to build trust with others. Without this foundation, it becomes nearly impossible to extend genuine trust to others or to be seen as trustworthy. The fundamentals of leadership and personal development have remained the same. Personal trust is about growth, not perfection. It requires self-awareness to identify our strengths and weaknesses, a commitment to continuous improvement, and the ability to act authentically in alignment with our values. This foundation lays the groundwork for the confidence, vulnerability, and consistency needed to foster trust at the team and organizational levels. When we prioritize building trust in ourselves and being trustworthy people, we create a ripple effect that positively influences our interactions with others. We show up with confidence and authenticity, ready to navigate the complexities of trust in teams and organizations.

TEAM TRUST: THE GLUE OF COLLABORATION, INNOVATION, AND EFFECTIVENESS

If personal trust forms the foundation, team trust represents the structure that rises from it. Trust within teams is what enables collaboration to flourish, creativity to emerge, and challenges to be overcome. Without trust, teams often become fragmented, with hidden agendas, unspoken tensions, and a lack of accountability eroding their potential. The WiLD Trust Index measures overall team trust by assessing 11 key drivers of trust at that level including variables such as the ability, reliability, strength, integrity of team members, and the extent to which they are open and honest with one another.

Team trust is the extent to which team members within an organization are developing the necessary patterns between them for trust to be built. "Relationship trust is all about behavior…consistent behavior" (Covey 2006, 124). At the level of a team, trust becomes a relational reality. It reflects the extent to which team members establish the necessary conditions for trust to thrive—a process that is often more complex than trust at the personal level. While personal trust is about an individual's self-awareness, team trust emerges from the behaviors, interactions, and shared experiences between us. Because team trust is built on the interplay between individuals, it is naturally more dynamic and complex than personal trust. As relationships and workplace conditions change, team trust fluctuates more than individual perceptions of trust in oneself.

Team trust is about more than just getting along; it's about creating an environment where team members feel safe to take risks, voice their ideas, and admit mistakes. This requires openness, mutual respect, and shared goals that unite the group. It requires a great deal of personal awareness about ourselves to be shared with others. Strong team trust doesn't just happen—it's built intentionally over time. It requires consistent effort, clear communication, and a willingness to address conflict constructively. Teams that prioritize trust unlock their potential, achieving results that go beyond the sum of individual contributions.

ORGANIZATIONAL TRUST: THE CONDITIONS FOR SUCCESS

At the organizational level, trust is the connective tissue that binds systems, culture, and strategy together. It is about creating the environment within which trust can grow and be sustained over time. Organizational trust determines whether employees feel empowered and engaged, whether clients remain loyal, and whether the organization can adapt to change and achieve its vision.

Organizational trust starts with leadership, and is about establishing the conditions around us that allow trust to thrive. Leaders set the tone by modeling transparency, accountability, and necessary levels of vulnerability. But trust also extends to the systems, processes, and culture of the organization. Are the right people staying in the organization? Are people clear about the measures of their progress? Are leaders trusted and honest, as well as caring? Does the organization invest in its people and consistently deliver on its promises? Organizations that prioritize trust don't just benefit from happier employees and stronger relationships with customers—they also achieve measurable business results of positive progress. While the specifics of how to build trust at this level vary, the principle is universal: when trust is embedded in the culture, it creates the conditions for sustainable success.

The WiLD Trust Quadrant™

While understanding the Circles of Trust gives us insight into the foundational layers of trust, imagine now if you could understand and map trust in your organization.

The WiLD Trust Quadrant maps an organization's trust levels along two critical dimensions: team trust and organizational trust (see Figure 6.2). This creates four distinct quadrants, each reflecting a unique organizational trust profile:

The Chemistry of Trust 65

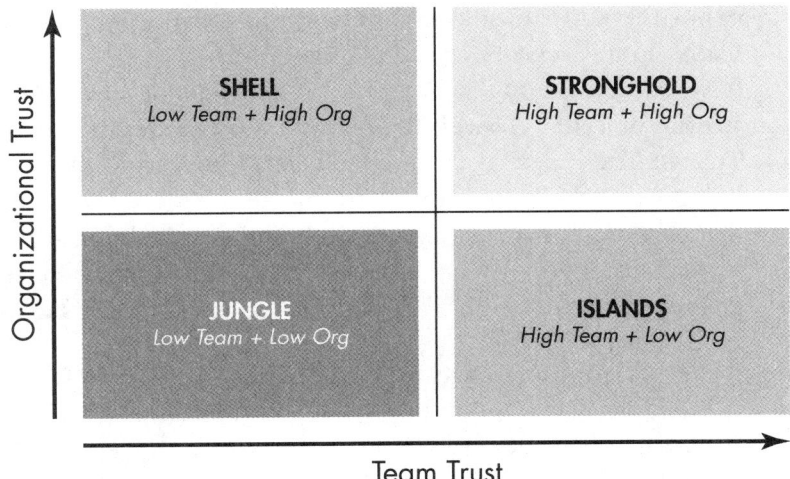

Figure 6.2   WiLD Trust Quadrant

- **Stronghold of Trust (Higher Team Trust, Higher Organizational Trust):** A stronghold is a place of safety, providing both strong walls and security within. These organizations enjoy high levels of trust at both the team and organizational levels. Employees trust their teammates and their leaders, and they believe in the organization's systems and mission. These are the high-performing, resilient organizations where trust grows, employees thrive, and innovation expands.
- **Islands of Trust (Higher Team Trust, Lower Organizational Trust):** Islands are secure—once you're on land. But surrounded by deep waters, the island itself is only a half measure toward true security. In these organizations, trust is strong within teams but lacking at the organizational level. Employees trust their immediate teammates but may not have confidence in leadership, other teams, organizational systems, or the overall direction of the company.
- **Shell of Trust (Lower Team Trust, Higher Organizational Trust):** A shell can protect from the outside, but what about the trials within? While a strong shell of organizational trust

exists, these organizations experience low levels of trust within teams. Employees may not trust their colleagues, but they may have confidence in the organization's leadership and systems.

- **Jungle of Trust (Lower Team Trust, Lower Organizational Trust):** The jungle is dark, chaotic, and incredibly difficult to navigate. These organizations are plagued by low trust at both the team and organizational levels. Employees lack trust in their teammates, their leaders, and the organization as a whole. This environment is often unproductive, and at times toxic and unsafe.

THE WiLD TRUST QUADRANT STORY

In our study of trust, we wanted to not only understand where most organizations fall in the WiLD Trust Quadrant, but also some of the story within each quadrant and their relationship to personal trust (see Figure 6.3).

Demonstrating high levels of trust at both the team and organizational levels, 30.6% of organizations achieved the Stronghold of Trust. Another 24.5% landed in the Shell of Trust, where organizational trust was high, but trust within teams was lacking.

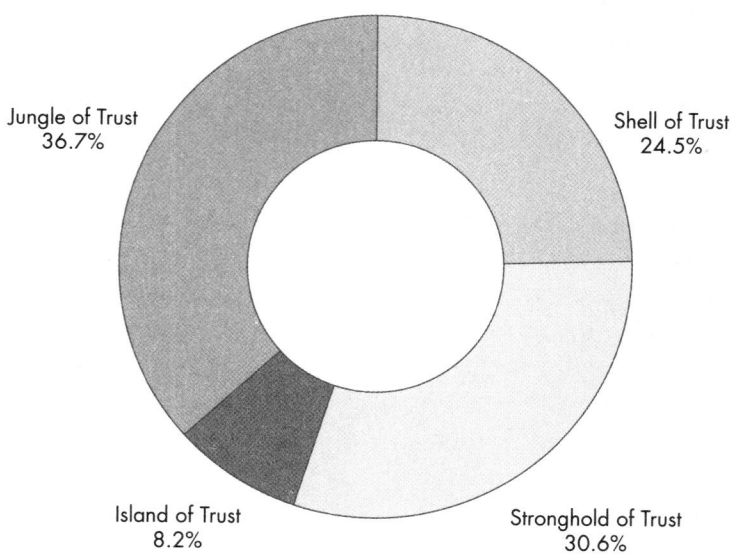

Figure 6.3 WiLD Trust by Organization

Only 8.2% of organizations scored in the Islands of Trust, signifying strong team trust but weaker trust at the organizational level. A total of 36.7% fell into the Jungle of Trust, where both team and organizational trust are low.

This stark reality highlights the critical challenge many organizations face in building and sustaining trust. A staggering 69.4% of organizations—over two-thirds—live outside the Stronghold, with 36.7% languishing in the Jungle. Organizations in the Jungle often experience low morale, high turnover, and diminished productivity as a result of the pervasive lack of trust in colleagues, leaders, and the organization itself. These environments demand urgent and focused efforts to cultivate trust, not only to improve employee well-being but also to achieve business objectives.

Our study also revealed that organizations struggle more with team trust than organizational trust: 61.2% of organizations scored low in team trust, compared to 44.9% scoring low in organizational trust. While addressing organizational trust is so important, this finding underscores the critical need for organizations to prioritize building trust within teams. Trust within teams fosters open communication, effective collaboration, and psychological safety, which enable teams to navigate challenges and achieve collective goals. In environments where team trust is low, employees often feel disconnected, unvalued, and unable to contribute their best work. Building team trust, therefore, is not merely a tactical concern—it is foundational to organizational success.

UNDERSTANDING YOUR STORY OF TRUST

No story of trust is the same. In fact, in our research there was a wide variability in how organizations scored across the two dimensions of trust. It demonstrates that trust challenges aren't universal but instead reflect the unique dynamics within each organization. Drivers such as leadership style, communication practices, organizational structure, and past experiences all contribute to where an organization falls on the WiLD Trust Quadrant. There is no one-size-fits-all solution to building trust. Each organization must understand its distinct trust dynamics to design and implement effective interventions. Tailored approaches are essential for addressing the specific trust challenges at both the team and organizational levels.

As I was describing the different possibilities in the WiLD Trust Quadrant, I would guess that you were already beginning to imagine where your organization would fall. Maybe you see high levels of trust within teams, but not at the organizational or senior leadership levels and you feel like you are functioning with Islands of Trust. Or maybe you resonate with the Shell of Trust where things may be shaky within teams, but there is strength and alignment at the level of your organization. Or you may feel like a stronghold is where you are and you want to reinforce and keep it that way. Or, for many, the jungle is the reality, and you must begin a deep process of change. Wherever you find yourself, I want you to know that you can begin to measure trust, and turn that feeling you have into an intentional reality.

Many leaders assume that trust issues are similar across organizations, but it's just not true. Every organization has its own trust story shaped by its culture, history, and leadership. Telling this story accurately requires a nuanced understanding of your trust dynamics at both the team and organizational levels. By addressing the trust strengths and issues specific to your story, you begin to take the first steps toward moving your organization into a Stronghold of Trust, or reinforcing the stronghold you already have.

THE WiLD TRUST QUADRANT BY INDIVIDUALS

While the organizational and team perspective on trust provided so much, we also wanted to understand the experience of individuals in the Quadrant. At that level, we discovered an important challenge related to the personal realities of employees and their day-to-day experiences. In Figure 6.4, each circle represents one or more employees, with the size of the circle indicating the number of employees scoring at that level.

One of the most sobering insights from the data is that nearly half of all employees (48.1%) report that their daily work experience is in the Jungle of Trust. This is both tragic and urgent, as it underscores the prevalence of low-trust environments in the workplace. Employees navigating the Jungle often experience feelings of isolation, stress, and disengagement, which hinder their ability to contribute effectively and thrive in their roles.

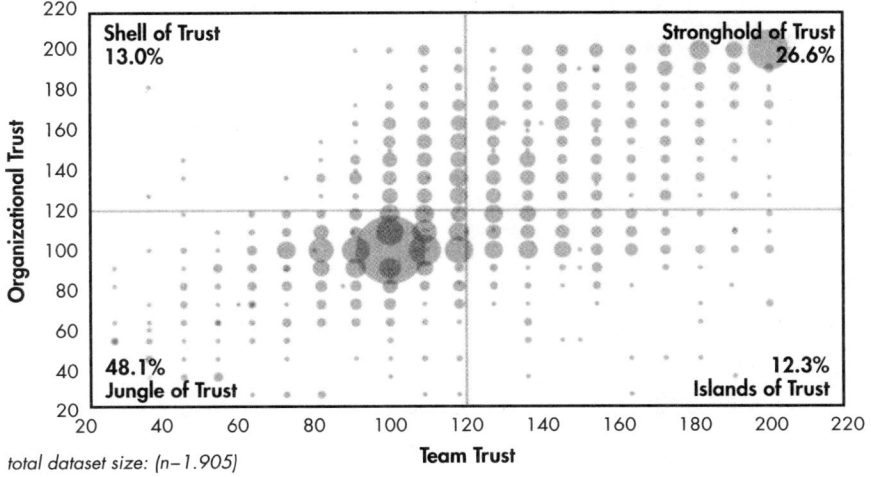

Figure 6.4   WiLD Trust Quadrant by Individuals

RETHINKING TRUST ACROSS THE AGES

We often hear that young people don't trust leaders or organizations anymore—but the data tells a different story.

When we looked at trust levels using the WiLD Trust Quadrant (see Figure 6.5), we saw something surprising: people in their 20s actually report the highest levels of trust in their teams and organizations. Far from being skeptical, early-career professionals tend to show strong confidence in those around them—likely driven by optimism and the excitement of starting out.

But things shift for people in their 30s. Trust takes a noticeable dip, with many people reporting their lowest levels of trust during this decade. Why? By this point, expectations have met reality. People face more responsibility, see how things *really* work behind the scenes, and may feel let down by leadership or systems that once seemed solid. It's a time of learning hard truths—what we call the "Jungle of Trust." The good news? Trust starts to rebuild when people reach their 40s, 50s, and beyond. With more experience, people often gain a clearer view of how to navigate challenges, build strong relationships, and see the bigger picture. Trust at this stage is more grounded—less idealistic, more resilient.

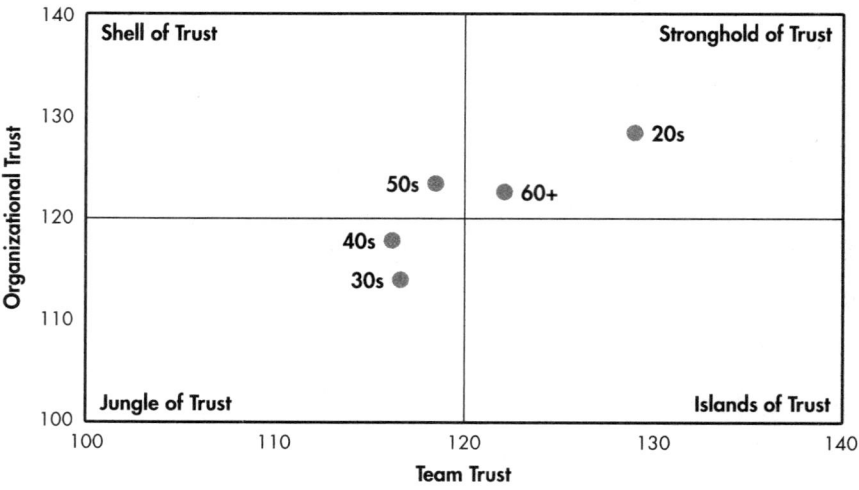

Figure 6.5 WiLD Trust Quadrant by Age Group

What does this mean for leaders? First, don't assume low trust is a generational thing—it's more about life stage. Support younger employees by nurturing the trust they already bring. Pay close attention to those in their 30s, when trust is most vulnerable. And lean into the wisdom of mid-career and seasoned employees who can help steady the ship. Trust isn't static. It grows, breaks, and rebuilds throughout our careers. The more we understand that journey, the better we can lead through it.

THE JUNGLE WITHIN THE STRONGHOLD

Too often leaders assume that trust is ubiquitous—that if trust is somewhere, it's everywhere. That is simply not true. Even in organizations that scored in the Stronghold of Trust, **an average of 41.3% of their employees still find themselves in the Jungle.** This disparity highlights the complexity of fostering trust. An organization's overall trust score does not necessarily reflect the lived experiences of all its employees. Individual experiences of trust are shaped by drivers such as team dynamics, relationships with managers, and perceptions of fairness and transparency within the organization.

There is hope though. A closer look at the data shows that the majority of employees in the Jungle are situated near the border of the Stronghold. This proximity suggests that with targeted and intentional efforts—such as improving team dynamics, strengthening relationships with peers, and fostering a sense of belonging—organizations can help employees navigate out of the Jungle and into higher-trust environments. However, those efforts would need to include both building trust within the individual's team, and their organization.

QUESTIONING TRUST

During a debrief with a CEO regarding his placement in the WiLD Trust Quadrant, he was grappling with the fact that nearly 30% of his employees were still reporting a daily experience in the Jungle, despite the organization's overall high trust score. His experience did not make him strange, it actually made him normal. Too often we assume that trust is something we either have or don't have, and that it is everywhere. As I tell leaders all the time, trust is less often broken for good, and more often questioned now and then. While we would all love to function within the stronghold and our hope is that everyone in our organization, or even our family for that matter, is experiencing high trust all the time, trust is more dynamic than that. There will always be work to be done, and that is why trust is not built and left, it is intentionally maintained.

While breakdowns in trust are never fun moments to navigate, breakages are necessary if we are to build strength and become strongholds of trust. Our trust in each other and across our organization is in a constant dance between strength and breakage, and ironically, the breaking points can become strengths if they are seen as moments to ask questions, to get honest with each other, and see the potential on the other side.

Leaders aim to create environments where people can thrive, perform, and feel valued. And yet, even in high-trust organizations, many employees face low trust in their immediate work environments. Too many individuals experience dysfunction, even in organizations promoting trust at higher levels. It's a reality. But imagine if you could build trust systematically within teams and across your organization. Your aspiration can become a reality as you begin to focus your attention on the Circles of Trust, and the key developmental drivers of trust at all three levels—developing awareness within your people and leaders at the individual level, developing their relational and team capacity by focusing on the patterns between them, and setting the conditions around everyone so both individuals and teams thrive and trust is built for the long haul.

For a Conversation

1. Which Circle of Trust is strongest for you right now? At a personal level, a relational level, or at an organizational level? At which level does it need to be reinforced or built?
2. Where is your lived experience right now in the WiLD Trust Quadrant? Are you experiencing Islands of Trust, a Shell of Trust, a Stronghold of Trust, or a Jungle of Trust?
3. What would change for you if you embraced the reality that trust is questioned in moments more than it is broken forever?

PART II

Becoming a Whole and Trusted Leader

Building trust in our relationships and across our organizations and society, our journey will begin with an intentional investment in ourselves.

We are desperate for great leaders. At a moment in history where we wish we had a full bench of incredible leaders ready to step up and bring the deepest wisdom, competence, experience, and discernment, we are too often left wanting. We see too many leaders who are fundamentally driven by ambition, an invisible agenda over a compelling and visible strategy, or a facade of confidence without much experience to back it up. We see too few leaders we can trust on every side of the aisle.

If we are to change the game and ensure we have a crowded bench of great leaders we can trust for the generations to come, the beginning is within us. Developing and preparing a generation of whole and trusted leaders who will satisfy our desperation will start with us. It does not begin with blame on the systems or the people who are in control, but a healthy conversation within and between us regarding who we are, why we are, and what we must consider if we are to be a part of the movement of developing a generation of whole and trusted leaders.

If we are to create trust between us in our teams, our families, and in our communities, and if we are to create the conditions where trust can thrive everywhere in our organizations and our lives, we must begin with ourselves. We must begin by making an intentional investment in becoming the leaders we are so desperate to find, deepening our understanding of ourselves and our awareness of our own worth and the worth of others.

In Part II, Chapters 7 through 16 walk through 10 dimensions of whole and trusted leadership—from readiness and purpose, to motivation, competence, and the courageous choice to invest in others and live with intention. While you may be used to developmental tools and assessments that label you and leave you there asking, "What's next?" the following chapters will help you answer that question at different turning points in different seasons of your life. You'll likely feel more nudged toward intention than you've ever experienced before. Development and learning are like that. The incredible challenge of creating structure around our whole and wild story is that it requires some guardrails to help us from slipping off the edge to developmental oblivion. That's why these guardrails are there. Intentionally chunking the important developmental pieces of our experience and growth is necessary at the start, and the open space in your own emerging story provides the skeletal structure that connects the living and breathing parts of your experience. We have no business asking ourselves or others to be vulnerable without those guardrails. I created a system of whole leader assessments known as the WiLD Toolkit that provides that developmental scaffolding I've described. But the following chapters will speak to you regardless of whether you have access to the WiLD Toolkit or not. The transformational elements of your whole and intentional developmental journey and the assessment associated with each element include:

1. Getting Ready—*The WiLD Profile*
2. Purposeful & Called—*The Purpose & Calling Inventory*
3. Productive—*The Meaningful Goals Assessment*
4. Composed—*The Leading Under Pressure Inventory*
5. Learning—*The Transformational Experiences Audit*
6. Competent—*The Skills & Knowledge Inventory*
7. Motivated—*The Motivational Drivers Inventory*

8. Invested—*The People Investment Plan*
9. Surrounded—*The Strategic Support Assessment*
10. Intentional—*The WiLD Plan*

If you are using the WiLD Toolkit as an intentional process for your development, the following chapters will take you deeper into the structure and ideas behind each of the assessments step by step. My hope is that providing structure for your intention won't box you in but will liberate you into a level of learning and growth you may have never imagined. Most important, as you begin to invest deeply in your own learning and development, it will serve as the foundation for your trust and trustworthiness. It will begin with you becoming more deeply aware of the many things about you that need to be affirmed or need to change, and will continue as you share that learning and awareness with others.

CHAPTER 7

Ready

Prepare for Whatever Comes Next

> *The whole and trusted leader is always getting ready for what's next.*

The Whole and Trusted Leader

Who are the leaders you would trust with your life and work, and why? Who are they and what are their names? What is it about them that makes them trustworthy? How do they see their world? Who are the people in your family that you trust? Who are the people on your team at work that you trust, and what is it about them that causes you to put your trust in them? The leaders we should trust and will trust over the long haul are incredible human beings. They are both clear and compassionate. They know themselves well—their convictions, values, competencies, weaknesses, and they stand on a firm and supported foundation. They are people of integrity—like an integer—a number that cannot be divided within itself. The whole and trusted leader is defined, purposeful, and full of clarity. In the same moment they are not only people of integrity like a castle, but permeable, willing to change and to see our side. They are willing to open their gates and lower the drawbridge to let us in. They may not change their mind, but they will honestly work hard to hear and continue to learn. The whole and trusted leader is a truth speaker and a peace keeper, a communicator and a listener. The challenge and reality that many of us face is that we function in organizational cultures and environments that don't support health and performance and trust, but instead pound on the greatest leaders until they either tap out, or tap in somewhere else. Nevertheless, we can do something about it and it is our job to start with us.

Whole and trusted leaders are rare, but they are out there waiting to be seen for who they are and who they could become. Our small and large businesses, our universities, our churches, and our communities are full of them. Even our families are full of them. They are there to be developed if we could only see the potential that is there. Some of them are reluctant to lead because they know how much is at stake. Some may not feel that they are qualified, but we cannot let that scare them away from the very possibility that they are the ones who should hold our future.

Whole and trusted leaders are willing to edit, to learn, to change and to do those things not only for their own sake, but for the sake of others. The rub here is that we often don't prop up leaders who are willing to change. We prop up leaders whose convictions we agree with, or those who made the big sale and got the biggest trophy. We often don't want someone who is still learning—and that is where we miss the point. To be whole and trusted, we must be thinking at an entirely different level—willing to learn and change while deepening our convictions at the same time. And to truly know ourselves and to participate in our own development is to also know what is hard for us to sacrifice. Editability is the key. If I won't hear you and consider what you need from me or for me to be, will you ever trust me? It is unlikely, especially for the long haul.

Where Do We Begin?

To become a whole and trusted leader is to realize that the developmental challenge of every person is nuanced. Every leader's story is different, and at the same time they do share some things. This is one of the reasons that so many other attempts at building trust and healthy and whole organizations have failed. They have failed to face that reality and respond accordingly. It does not matter who you are. You may be sitting in a classroom in a high school or in a college campus, standing at the window of your executive office, sitting behind the desk you come to every day to run your small business or not-for-profit, or you may be considering the possibility of becoming a leader. No matter who you are, it will begin with your willingness to change, to deepen, and to grow. Are you willing to edit for the sake of others and at the same time deepen your convictions? This question is key because it is our willingness to change, to learn and to grow in the face of a deepening within us that is going to be the fundamental litmus test of our capacity to become the whole and trusted leaders we could be. The whole and trusted leader is a leader who will learn and change until their last breath, and will do it for the sake of others and not just because of the rewards along the way.

SCAFFOLDING OUR LEARNING AND DEVELOPMENT
Think about the last time you saw scaffolding on a building. Scaffolding exists to help us access parts of the building that we otherwise couldn't reach. It also allows us to climb up and down as necessary and solve problems that may come up as we become aware of them while we're climbing. We might be able to see that the windows are dirty from the ground, but without scaffolding we couldn't safely get up to clean those windows, or replace the leaky siding causing mold to grow inside our house. While we so often want answers to our growth and development that look more like clean and easy trips between point A and B, the reality of our learning, growth, and experience over our lifetime is more like a climb from point A to point B, back to point A, up to E, and then a meandering journey between D and C. If the first part of this book was dealing with our desperation for trust and for whole leaders, then the next part of the book is designed to provide structure for your journey. To that end, I'm going to prescribe a path that I've seen work for so many people, while encouraging you to maintain a complete openness that the following chapters, as prescribed parts of your story, could be read or could serve you in whatever order your experience as most helpful.

GETTING INTENTIONAL
While inspiration and understanding are important, without an intentional connection between our progress and story, we risk feeling like kids at summer camp whose inspiration quickly left them two

weeks after coming home. What would change if you believed that both inspiration and intent were possible? What would change if inspiration and intent were interwoven in a way that what inspires you produced intentional direction, and the progress you're making produced repeating and increasing inspiration?

One thing I've tried to instill in my sons is the power of intent in getting them to the outcomes they desire. Each summer in their teenage years, my wife and I had an expectation that they would each have a job that may or may not carry forward into their next school year. Later in life, we understand this, but the longer you wait to search for a job, the higher the likelihood that returning college students and other high school students will take up most of the best available options. If it stopped there, our entire focus would be on the goal of getting the best job—or in the case of applying late, the job that's available. How different would a high schooler's job search look if they started reflecting and taking action two months prior to school ending?

I had an aha moment when one of my sons submitted his first job application online and he said, "that was a little bit stressful." It wasn't the stress of applying that impacted him, but the stress of submitting an application which would then be evaluated. He had never experienced that before. Would any of us question whether that moment of awareness will establish a foundation for how he will approach job searches for the rest of his life? Probably not. And those job searches will matter because they will be inseparable from his seeing pathways to apply his unique design and capacities in the places he will be called to serve. Our challenge isn't admitting that learning and performance are important, but in intentionally integrating them in a way that they no longer contradict each other, but serve each other.

As opposed to a one-off solution that says just get to know your strengths and that will be enough, or know your personality type and you will be good, or discover your purpose and you will feel fulfilled, I want to invite you to see something you already know. Your development as a whole and trusted leader includes those things and so much more. The following chapters are designed to provide structure and scaffolding for your personal developmental story, while leaving open space for your emerging narrative. These are developmental topics that you will revisit multiple times over your lifetime.

I'll never forget the moment after our first son was born and my wife and I headed for our car in the hospital parking garage to head home. I have never felt more obviously not ready to do something or to be trusted with anything, let alone a baby. The day before it was just my wife and me, and now we were fully responsible for this small human. I'll never forget clipping his seatbelt over his car seat and thinking, "Good Lord, I hope I did that right!"

When we were children, we played a game called hide-and-seek where the person who was "it" would count to 10, and when they got to 10 would say "Ready or not, here I come." If we weren't ready, we were caught off guard in the middle of hiding and found right away. While it was enjoyable as kids, there isn't a lot of joy in being launched into a leadership role without feeling ready. "Ready or not, now you lead" is a lot riskier than our time as children because the stakes are so much higher for us and for everyone around us. It's not surprising that the idea of leaders becoming more developmentally ready has received increased attention over the last several years as we've learned so much about the importance of experience in shaping leaders, and the power of intention and mindsets in shifting our perspective toward learning and away from a singular focus on performance, effectiveness, or personality types. Like a sprinter stepping up to the starting blocks whose preparation for that moment included so much more than that moment, developmental readiness is the preparation for that next moment we'll lead. In the same way that a sprinter has months of training, mental preparation, coaching, and practice, every one of us who is going to step up to lead deserves to feel more ready when that starting gun goes off. Whether we are parents, marriage partners, CEOs, board members, or first-time managers, who among us wouldn't have benefited from more preparation from the start?

Imagine you had one year to prepare a person to sail around the world alone in a 25-foot sailboat, and they had never sailed before. Where would you begin? For starters we would probably want them to learn some basic skills like swimming, navigation, sailing, radio communications, and fundamental survival skills, along with many others. You would also likely want to make sure they had the right supplies and redundancies in certain materials like extra sails, life preservers, food, basic tools, and access to water. But, beyond the much longer list of supplies and skills, we would also want to prepare them for some less obvious things like dealing with long stretches of being alone, understanding their own natural skills and things that will be more difficult, and a bit of self-awareness so they understand how they are likely to deal with challenges and storms (literal and otherwise) that are sure to come. The list of things we would do is long and necessary.

Now imagine that the person you are preparing for this journey is one of your children. Imagine that the stakes were that high. How would you prepare your own child for a year-long journey alone around the world—a person who brings little to no experience of sailing or of a journey like that? I know what you would not do. Given that assignment, none of us would take our child down to the dock, put them in the boat, untie the line to the boat and say, "Well at least you know what your personality is like and your strengths. See you in a year!" We would not do that. Unfortunately, when it comes to leaders, that's mostly what we do. We give someone the responsibility for going first and being the leader, take them down to the "leadership dock," put them in the boat, untie the line, and push them off with the unspoken statement of, "Now go lead. See you on the other side." We do this over and over again, with people for whom the stakes will be so high—not only for them, but for everyone in their influence. We do this with presidents, CEOs, first-time managers, pastors, leaders in government and in not-for-profits, and even with parents.

What would it mean to do a better job of preparing a person to lead—to go first with a spirit of courage and sacrifice and for the sake of others in their sphere of influence? If we had a year to prepare a person to lead, and in most cases we do, where would we begin?

You Are Here!

If you've ever visited a shopping mall for the first time and you know the store you want to visit, where do you start? We look for that elusive directory that gives us the map of the mall. Once we find the legend that helps us find the location of our store, what's next? Most of us look for those three little words, "You Are Here." Even if we've established some understanding of where we would like to go, it's almost always necessary to identify where we are. In the same way that it's impossible to get to our destination without knowing where we're starting, we have to understand our developmental starting point to more intentionally achieve the learning and development goals we hope for.

There are so many things that brought us to the point of looking at that map. That oversimplified "You Are Here" has so much in it. You have the money to shop, and you may be shopping with somebody else. You may be loving or hating the moment at the mall, and you may be shopping out of necessity or out of joy. And, you may be shopping for yourself or someone else. So, as you think about your own "You Are Here" story regarding your development as a leader and as a person, where are you beginning? And where might you start? An incredible body of knowledge regarding leaders' preparation, readiness, and development offer us so much. If we had a year to prepare each of us for our next big moment to lead and in the full knowledge that it would include many different things, what would we do? We would start at the beginning. At the very least, we would welcome an understanding of our personality, developmental readiness, personal, organizational, and life context, character, performance, and current level of fulfillment. Imagine how powerful it would be to have an audit in every one of those areas as you start your whole leader development journey. It's just the beginning, but what a strong start. An invitation to get started begins with six questions that are invitations to begin:

- **Personality:** What are you like and what isn't changing about you?
- **Developmental Readiness:** Are you feeling prepared for what's next and ready to learn what's needed?
- **Organizational Context:** Who are you building with, and who is depending on you?
- **Character:** Who are you and how do others experience you?
- **Performance:** Are you effective at getting the right things done?
- **Integrated Fulfillment:** How's it going in different parts of your life and work and are you feeling fulfilled?

PERSONALITY: WHAT ARE YOU LIKE?

Are you in a season of accepting yourself or changing yourself? While there may be times that we emphasize one over the other, both are essential parts of our whole developmental story. Accepting ourselves is all about making peace with the parts of ourselves that are less likely to change over our lifetimes, and changing ourselves is all about the things we can work on and develop. The whole story is that typically we aren't doing one or the other, but some dynamic combination of the two. Here's another question I would love to invite you to consider: What would be different if you better understood the parts of yourself that are less likely to change and those parts of yourself that are very likely to change? Probably a lot, especially as we consider setting a foundation for our whole and intentional development going forward.

One of the questions I'm often asked is whether I believe leaders are born or made. When asked, it's usually a test someone is giving me. What they are asking is, "Rob, does what you believe align with what I believe?" While it is an important question, a mountain of research on personality is more important than my opinion or yours. Here's what we do know. When we ask whether leaders are born or made, we are questioning whether people either have what it takes to lead or not, and whether they could develop and become a leader. The honest answer is yes and yes. And, as I suggested earlier in the book, personality is an integral part of your developmental story.

As I will refer to it here, personality is the part of yourself that is less likely to change over your lifetime. While it's not the only thing that is important to understand, knowing something about your personality's traits is an important starting place. And it becomes potent as you begin to understand how your personality traits may be interacting with the parts of you that are changing—that's the learning and development part of yourself. While we are drawn to labels that stick on us, we also love messages that say we can be anything we want to be. The point is this. Personality is a vital part of what it means to get ready to lead well. So, how do we assess our personality?

There are five primary factors upon which most other personality "types" or "typologies" have been built that are shown to be relatively stable over our lifetime. While they are labeled a certain way, they each also have another side. In other words, if you are high on one personality trait, you are likely to be low on the flip side. They include extroversion (the flip side being introversion), openness to experience (the flip side being less open), conscientiousness (the flip side being less conscientious), agreeableness (the flip side being less agreeable), and neuroticism (the flip side being pretty well adjusted and stable). These traits are neither good nor bad, but each side of the five is necessary to understand not only for our awareness but to develop a deeper awareness of how we impact others, why we are perceived in specific ways, and how others can more effectively live and work with us. It's important to remind ourselves that personality is part of our developmental story, but it's only part. Even neuroticism is a funny thing. I rate halfway neurotic on most personality assessments and only halfway conscientious. What has been essential for me to understand is that my neuroticism is also a gift. It gives me the adaptive capacity and a creative edge that is necessary for me to lead. Again, while it's important, it's not the only thing.

More importantly, here is what I've learned about personality as it relates to leadership. It is a foundation upon which so much change happens. Like the foundation upon which a house is built that is often less visible, it impacts what can be built on top of it and how. If you've ever been under a house in the crawlspace, you know what I mean. The foundation of a home includes all the places where the wooden structures of a home sit. And, without spending a lot of money, the foundation doesn't change in most remodels. My wife and I once got really excited about buying a house that we planned to remodel, until the inspection indicated that the foundation underneath wouldn't support our dreams for the remodel. Understanding the foundation of your personality can help you structure your work, your relationships to your family members and your team, and may even help others see you more clearly—a key part of what it means to trust and become more trustworthy.

DEVELOPMENT READINESS: WHERE ARE YOU NOW?

If personality predicts only about half of what it means for us to be a leader and to lead well, what's going on in the other half (Judge et al. 2002)? The other half is everything about us that is likely to change, and with a little bit of intention, may vary on purpose—for our sake and the sake of everyone in our influence.

Being developmentally ready isn't just one thing. If it were, it would be as simple as answering the question, "Are you ready or not?" Why you are ready or not is what this is all about. Readiness is established through a lifetime of experiences that have brought us to this point. As I've already said, the process of assessing readiness is a vital part of becoming more developmentally ready. Like looking at your gas gauge before going on a road trip and deciding whether you need to fill up or not, assessing our developmental readiness gives us an indication of where we are and to what extent we are ready to learn and grow.

Developmental readiness is the extent to which you are prepared to enter into a season of learning and change that will not only be effective and impactful for you, but everyone around you. Developmental readiness is change readiness. Change readiness isn't something you have or don't have, but something you approach through questions. In other words, the best way to get ready to learn is to assess your readiness. Assessing developmental readiness across multiple interrelated factors in your life is a key part of increasing it. While answers sometimes bring clarity, questions are the gateway to learning and the guide through the unknown horizon of our development. When you assess your readiness, the goal is not only to see yourself as ready or not, but to accept the invitation to work through it as you learn.

If questions are the key to assessing our readiness and the gateway to learning, what questions should we be asking ourselves and others? Here are 14 different dimensions, each assessing one important aspect of your readiness. Each dimension of developmental readiness is followed by a question you can ask yourself. For each statement, on a scale from 1 to 10 (1 being to a lesser extent, 10 being to a great extent), assess the extent to which you are feeling each.

1. **Service:** To what extent are you serving others around you who require something that you are in a position to provide? Your rating _____.
2. **Conviction:** To what extent do you know what you want at this point in your life and career? Your rating _____.
3. **Network:** To what extent do you have the necessary support network in place to take a calculated risk? Your rating _____.

4. Purpose: To what extent are you doing what you are supposed to be doing at this point in your life, regardless of the expectations of others? Your rating _____.
5. Composure: To what extent are you composed under pressure? Your rating _____.
6. Experience: To what extent do you know what you would like to experience next in your life and career? Your rating _____.
7. Contribution: To what extent do you know what you are good at and what you cannot help but do well? Your rating _____.
8. Motivation: To what extent do you know what excites you and motivates you to learn? Your rating _____.
9. Investment: To what extent are you intentional about investing in the learning and growth of the people around you? Your rating _____.
10. Direction: To what extent are your goals and daily activities purposeful? Your rating _____.
11. Learning: To what extent are you applying lessons from your past in current and future opportunities and challenges? Your rating _____.
12. Calling: To what extent is there a transcendent reason you are doing what you are doing that is bigger than you? Your rating _____.
13. Character: To what extent are you becoming a better version of yourself for the sake of others around you? Your rating _____.
14. Context: To what extent are you able to walk into an unfamiliar environment and discern what people are thinking, what's happening, and what needs to happen next? Your rating _____.

After answering those questions, I bet you are thinking, "Wow, I have a lot to think about." That's true. The whole and intentional story of your learning and development includes a lot of things, and instead of looking at your answers alone, I would invite you to see those questions less like a test, and more like an invitation. There was nothing in those questions that was designed to evaluate you or to judge you, but because of the way we've experienced questions in the past and the lack of role models who actually cared about our answers, they often feel like tests. Take a look at your responses again. What would change if you believed those questions were invitations to understanding and awareness, and had nothing to do with proving you unworthy or underprepared? When you look at each question and your response through that lens, what do you see? You might see incredible openness for growth. You may notice that some of the questions relate to each other. You might see blind spots that need attention. And you may even see that you are more ready for change than you imagined. As you go through each of these chapters on building personal trust, I will repeat a process we describe as the A.I.M. Process—a process of thoughtful action. This process is a simple way to begin to dig into the learning and growth that questions offer us, and it is one of the most accessible ways to not only understand your whole self, but also for coaching and investing in others. It includes three simple steps.

1. **Awareness:** As you answer questions or look at their result, what did you become aware of that is worth paying attention to? Your answer likely includes those things that are consistent with your understanding of yourself, as well as what surprises you.
2. **Impact:** What are the implications of the awareness you gained? In other words, given what you are aware of, what is the impact of that on you and on others around you?
3. **Mission:** What are you motivated to change or do next based on your awareness and application you see? Getting specific and honest about what you feel inspired to do is a wonderful finish any time we can get there.

To that end, as you answered the 14 questions, what did you become aware of? What is the impact of that awareness? And what mission will you assign yourself? Given what you learned, what is one thing or area that would have the greatest impact if you were to spend intentional time focusing on it?

A whole person perspective on developmental readiness doesn't end with us as individuals, but broadens our understanding to include a team, organizational, historical, and environmental context that serve as the containers within which our readiness is occurring. We don't learn alone, and we don't lead alone in most cases.

ORGANIZATIONAL AND LIFE CONTEXT: WHAT'S HAPPENING?

Intersections are often more interesting than long straight roads because they offer choices, and an opportunity to see different things converging. What's happening at the intersection of your personality, developmental readiness, and the organizational, family, or community context within which you live and serve? In other words, what's important for you or others to understand about the things in you that are remaining the same, the things that are changing, and the larger system of people with whom you live and work? A growing awareness of that reality and that intersection is a great place to start getting ready.

If we did life in a vacuum, it might be really lonely, but it also might be a lot easier for some of us. The reality is that we don't, and our learning and growth are almost always connected to a larger group, system, or organization within which we have some responsibility and support. While focusing on our own personal development is really important, building trust with others is the ultimate goal. Our personality, character, learning, fulfillment, and our competence almost always happen in relationship to others. Whether that context is the organization you work within, the not-for-profit you serve, the family you lead or co-lead, or the community that surrounds you—your development and readiness is wonderfully interwoven within that larger story. In fact, based on the research out there, a huge portion of your development as a leader is dependent upon that larger story.

For that reason, one of the fundamental places to start in understanding where you are developmentally ready is about understanding that larger context. For simplicity's sake, when I use the term organization, I'm talking about whatever group you are a member of. Organizations are simply groups of people coming together for a common goal. In that way, your organization may be your family, your community, or the place where you work. The important thing to think about is that whole and intentional leader development is about you, and about you with others. That's what is often referred to as alignment. Are your direction, learning, and motivations in alignment with where your organization is going? That is probably not a simple yes or no, but a process of discernment. Discerning alignment is a critical part of building trust. And it's wrapped up in three easy questions.

1. **Organizational Mission:** What is your organization attempting to accomplish this year?
2. **Team Alignment:** What is your team or group attempting to accomplish within the context of your organization's mission?
3. **Individual Contribution:** What are you personally trying to accomplish in the context of your organization's mission?

Sometimes we hesitate to ask these questions because they call out the possibility that we don't know the answers. But beginning to answer them invites us to see the alignment between who we are and what others need from us as we begin to get intentional about our own development as whole and trusted leaders.

CHARACTER: WHO ARE YOU?

Why is it important to take a moment to assess our character? Our character impacts all kinds of things in our lives and work every day. Character is everywhere. We all have it, and yet understanding it is so elusive. By its very nature, our character is a unique combination of who we are and who we might become. In that way, it includes things that are related to our personality and development, but at a much deeper level. To prove it, imagine assessing your conviction, vulnerability, hopefulness, realism, courage, steadfastness, humility, and reluctance. These "characteristics" are not simply virtues, they are ways of being as we interact with others in our world. They are aspirations we hold for becoming better humans, and when we consider them at that deeper level within us, we realize they impact our interactions with others in our world every day.

A deepening of our character brings about a cadence in our presence that others feel and see. When we enter into conversations about our character and take an honest moment to assess where we are, we begin to see the possibilities in how others might perceive us and our impact on them. A deepening of who we are impacts the greatest outcomes we can imagine that are so far beyond success, effectiveness, and motivation. At that point others will begin to see faithfulness, joy, peace, kindness, gentleness, resilience, self-control, goodness, and even love. And, for a person aspiring to more wholeness and trust, can you imagine a greater impact than that?

Performance: What Are You Doing Well, or Not Doing Well?

How in the world can we trust ourselves and be trusted by others if we're not doing what needs to be done, and doing it well? It's not the only thing required for trust, but it is an important start for building readiness. Your ability to get the job done is a fundamental starting place for building personal trust, and an honest assessment is the start. It will require a conversation with others if we are to fully understand our performance and effectiveness, but beginning with your own assessment is the first step.

While performance in a job or in life always has specific things that are customized to the task we are being asked to do, there are some common areas of personal performance that serve as the starting place for all the specific things we need to get done to be effective each day. Some of the most important areas include:

- **Communication:** Being clear with others and also hearing others.
- **Engagement:** Being engaged and motivated.
- **Connection:** Being aware of others through empathy and connection.
- **Adaptability:** Being open, agile, and innovating.
- **Drive:** Being productive, effective, and intentional.
- **Direction:** Being strategic, purposeful, and reflective.
- **Presence:** Being confident, courageous, and steady.
- **Character:** Being generous, humble, and forgiving.
- **Belonging:** Feeling valued, secure, and heard by others.

While it might feel like a stretch to label these as performance, these are foundations within you that allow your greater expertise and competence to emerge. And the point isn't to simply evaluate your performance across these nine categories and judge yourself, but to do an honest assessment of what you are doing well, and where you could improve. Starting there is such an important and liberating step in getting ready and building whole and sustaining trust not only within yourself, but also with others.

FULFILLMENT: HOW'S IT GOING?

An honest assessment of how we are doing across the different areas of our life is so liberating. It can feel risky to rate your level of fulfillment across your work, career, finances, family, and even your friendships, but when you do it serves as an important barometer of your overall well-being.

While our satisfaction with this or that in our lives is an interesting start, it often leaves us with that feeling that it's all about us, and whether we are happy with things as they are. Fulfillment is more whole in that it calls out the idea of being fulfilled or not at different moments of our life and work. To what extent I am feeling fulfilled in my work, in my family, with my finances, or even in my career is so much more interesting and actionable than whether I feel satisfied. Like a meter on a tank or a level of charge on a battery, understanding our level of fulfillment opens up an awareness that things can and will change with a bit of intention. So, how are you doing? What is your level of fulfillment in your family, your friendships, your health, your finances, your work, in your faith, or even in your service to others? Your fulfillment in these areas will change in moments and different seasons of your life. That's natural. Readiness begins with where you are now.

Thoughtful Action: Developmentally Ready

How do we get more intentional about assessing our readiness and getting a sense of where we are? Readiness starts by simply taking a look at the map of our lives with a very simple scaffolding of questions. There is so much more to come after this first step, but it does start with that simple process of questions about who we are, where we serve, and where we are going next.

For a Conversation

1. What's happening at the intersection of your personality, developmental readiness, and current organization or life?
2. Are you in a season of accepting yourself or changing yourself?
3. As you read this chapter, what did you become aware of that may be important for you to pay attention to?

The WiLD Profile

If you are using the Wild Toolkit alongside *Whole Leaders, Wild Trust*, the WiLD Profile is designed to scaffold a more in-depth conversation regarding your personality, readiness, context, character, emotions, and fulfillment. The process is simple. Create an account at www.wildtoolkit.com to access the WiLD Profile or all of the robust whole leader assessments together.

CHAPTER 8

Purposeful

Start with a Why That Won't Let Go

A whole and trusted leader lives on purpose in the moment with an openness to be called deeper.

When a leader knows their purpose, trust follows. Not because they have all the answers, but because they're clear on what's driving them. Purpose is more than a motivational slogan—it's the north star that makes us more trustworthy to others. People trust leaders who know why they're here, because it gives context to their actions, consistency to their choices, and integrity to their decisions. When I'm grounded in a purpose, I'm not swayed by every wind of opinion or trend. I'm steady. That steadiness doesn't just feel good—it builds trust.

But the implications go beyond personal credibility. Purpose is deeply existential, yes—but it's also wildly strategic. When a leader is clear on their calling, others are more likely to align with them, or just as importantly, realize this isn't their path—and that clarity is a gift. A defined purpose increases retention, builds belonging, and strengthens alignment with mission. It invites people to make intentional choices about where they're headed and who they want to become. So, the question of "Why are you here?" isn't just personal—it's catalytic. For trust. For culture. For everything that matters.

Why Are You Here?

What would change if purpose was driving your next step forward instead of just checking boxes? What if your life and work were no longer defined by outcomes alone, but by a transcendent purpose and calling to be and do something that you are in a unique position to do? What would change if you could remain true to the deeper calling on your life instead of the sole purpose of upward mobility, success, and the number of followers you have? Who among us doesn't want that—for our lives to be a part of something that involves us, but is bigger than us? It all begins with this question:

Why are you here?

At some point in our lives, every human being asks that question. We want some understanding of the broader reason for us being on this earth and its relationship to our daily activities in work and life. Having a clear sense of purpose is one of the most powerful drivers in our lives. Your purpose is your reason for being here that is a combination of your unique design and what it is that you are determined to do. If you are clear about your purpose for being in the world, it impacts your well-being, your performance, and even your service to others. However, identifying your sense of purpose isn't as easy as just naming it. It involves a process of digging, discovering, and discerning why you are here and what you are uniquely designed to do. Your sense of purpose is critical because it provides an anchor in the challenging but important moments in your life as it helps you navigate forward in a way that is not only important for you, but for every person around you.

The calling on your life and work is what you are called to do, who you are called to be, and who you are called to serve. While purpose and calling are certainly related, there are times in your life where you are called to do things that you may or may not want to do or feel qualified to do, but nonetheless, are being called to do. Hearing and responding to that call on your life may be directly in line with your purpose, or it may even be a calling to make sacrifices for the sake of others.

It doesn't matter what you do for a living. Whether you work in the trades, are an accountant, or a nurse, you don't have to be a philosopher or work in a not-for-profit organization to feel a deep desire for answers to the questions "Why am I here?" and "Who am I called to serve?" There are few things more freeing for us as human beings than leaning into the reality that we are here for a purpose and that we are each being called to serve in some way. What's even more inspiring is to be able to discern that purpose and hear that calling more clearly.

Hearing the Call

A calling is a summons, a request, and invitation to serve, but too often we treat it as something we have and not something we listen for. We cannot be called if we aren't paying attention, and paying attention implies that there may be a cost—something to pay. Every day of our lives there are moments to pay attention. Calling is so often framed as a bigger-than-life concept we are supposed to figure out. What if calling isn't only about that bigger thing, but also about every detail of our day? Is it possible that every meeting on my calendar today is a moment to respond to a larger call on my life? Of course it is, if I were only willing to pay attention. Whether you're meeting with a customer, your spouse or child, a friend, or a new acquaintance, there is already a transcendent reason you are there whether you know it or not. Our temptation is to give in to the cultural assumption that I need to get something done. What if you are being called to something more profound than that? That call may be to say something tough with love, to simply be present and to see the other person more whole, or it may be to enter into each of those meetings with a clear agenda, and an openness to the conversation surprising you in some way. While I do believe and see evidence that there is likely a larger call on our lives that frames everything, some of the greatest power of calling is in our willingness to pay attention to the smallest moments.

It Involves Us, But It's Not All About Us

Hearing and discerning calling isn't always easy at first. While we wish that God or someone else would just send us an email or speak to us through a megaphone with clear instructions about what we're supposed to do and who we're supposed to be, it doesn't usually work that way. Like everything else about becoming whole, a purpose and calling is discerned over time, through the lives and influence of others who love us and will give it to us straight. To hear the call on our lives is to remain open to the possibility that the call may or may not be something I want to do, but will in the end serve some of the most unexpected people in my life.

The simple phrase "my calling" has flooded our generation and has become the statement of our time regarding how to bring purpose to work. It's the modern-day version of, "What kind of job would you like to have?" What's most troubling is that while it hints at the possibility of service to others, it's the same wolf dressed in clothes that make us slightly more comfortable with our fundamental assumption that it's all about us. The first four words in Rick Warren's book *The Purpose Driven Life* caught most of us by surprise. When he said, "It's not about you," he convicted us and enlightened us at that exact moment (Warren 2002, 17). And, when it comes to calling, we have the same problem. We've created a way to make ourselves comfortable with calling by diluting the idea of being called into whatever we may be called to, to something that is comfortable, suits us, and is only attractive if it serves others and pleases us at the same time.

When we ask college students in university career centers about their future and don't want to make it all about a job, we ask them, "What do you think your calling is?" At our worst, we follow that with a list of jobs that match a student's unique strengths and desires. I'm not slamming the power or importance of any young person discovering their strengths or desires, but to note that our current use of the word "calling" with them is incomplete at best, and reckless at worst.

The challenge in front of us is that our language regarding calling mimics our generational assumption about who or what matters most. We use the statement "my calling" to describe the transcendent answer to the question "why are you here?" which places us directly at the center of the question. When we ask someone what *their* calling is, we assume that the reason they're here and what they might be summoned to do next is fundamentally about them, making them the lead player in a story that includes them, but is not all about them. Even worse, using the words "my" or "your" turns calling from a request or communication to an implied ownership in an identity that defines us. When we assume that our calling is who we are, or some combination of our personality and strengths alone, we drive ourselves into the belief and the necessary outcome that it must go well—creating the possibility that when our purpose and calling aren't all that we hoped or something we despise, that we despise ourselves. I'm as guilty as anyone else when it comes to my words regarding calling. Changing our way of thinking about purpose and calling and rewinding our journey down a path that has made it all about us will first require us to reclaim the fundamentals of a call. The call we're receiving is for us, but it may or may not be about serving us—at least in the short term.

The Calling Curse

Mindsets matter. One of the most profound wake-up calls that the students and leaders in my care have received over the years is the moment they are confronted by the research of Carol Dweck. It's profound for them because they've never considered the possibility that the way they think about learning and performance may be just as important as their actual learning and performance. Her research opened up the reality that our beliefs about people being the way they are versus being able to change is a key driver in people's ability to change and even impacts the kinds of careers they will choose. Likewise, what if the way we think about calling as part of our identity is not only potentially damaging to us, but creating an obstruction to serving those in need around us in ways we could only begin to imagine? I'm always reminded of a good friend of mine who was told that *his* calling was to serve as a pastor in a church. That voice, planted in his mind in his mid-twenties, caused him to believe that this was not only his calling, but that *he* was his calling. The problem was that when he started to despise his job as a pastor, his only option was to despise himself. After years of witnessing his depression, from which he eventually emerged, I saw the impact of our language and assumptions about calling in the lives of some of the people I love most in this world. It's not their only challenge, but it certainly doesn't help. When we move calling from an identity to a rightful position as a summons on our lives, we realize that the burden of our response and of the outcomes is not something we bear alone, but bear with the caller.

DISCERNING YOUR PURPOSE AND CALLING

When it comes to understanding the greater "why" behind our lives, we may be the first generation (at least in the Western part of our culture) that walks into life with the fundamental assumption that most things start and end with us. Calling is no different. We too often see calling as a noun as opposed to a verb—something we have as opposed to something we hear. One of the simplest ways to understand the transcendent summons on our lives to serve those in need around us is to think about the ways we perceive calls in other parts of our lives—the simplest parts.

When we receive a phone call, it's *for* us, but it may or may not be *about* us. The basics of a phone call have more in common with earlier generations' thinking about calling than we might imagine. Throughout history and with few exceptions, a calling was seen as something received or heard and not something had—similar to a phone call. So, think about the fundamental aspects of a phone call. In most every case there is a caller, a receiver (you), a message, and a motivation to respond. Someone is calling you, and that someone may have a request, be responding to your need, or may just want to reconnect or stay connected. You, as the person being called, certainly have your motivations for answering the call, whether it's out of love for the caller, obligation, obedience to something greater than yourself, or because there is something in it for you—these are all reasons we decide to pick up the phone or not. Once we're listening, we're able to hear the message and make a decision about how to respond. The problem is that without an understanding of each piece (caller, receiver, message, and response), we can't fully understand the reason the person is calling us in the first place.

Understanding a phone call, in its simplest form, might help us understand calling in a way that would not only help *us*, but even more importantly, help us hear and respond to the most profound requests to be or do something for the sake of those around us in the greatest need. And, by definition, a call or a calling begins, continues, and ends in a relationship between the caller and the receiver. It also opens up the possibility that at certain moments of our lives, that transcendent voice calling us to be or do something in our world may be calling often, speaking sometimes, and silent at others.

WE ARE CALLED TOGETHER

We are rarely, if ever, called alone or in a vacuum of service to ourselves. The purpose and calling in our lives usually happens within a relationship to someone else. Whether it's someone you work with, work for, a spouse, our kids, or someone we feel called to serve, when we are called, it involves others. The greater "why" behind our lives is something we hear and understand in relationship to others.

Understanding that the purpose and call on our lives and work is inherently relational means there is always the potential to produce a controversy. The controversy of a purpose and call, from the will of another, is that the request might be to do or be something we don't fully comprehend, may feel underqualified to respond to, or even that we may currently disagree with. While we oftentimes simplify calling as something that fits for us or makes us happy, who among us hasn't had moments where we wrestle with the reality that someone else wants something from us that we don't want to do, but may need to do? Deepening trust with others is always a journey into increased knowing and understanding, and sometimes it takes several conversations. We rarely begin or even continue a relationship with a full awareness of everything others are thinking or asking of us. To be called is an ongoing process of knowing, understanding, and even wrestling with the will of another person or with God. To fully understand the interdependent relationship within a calling is to reveal the thinking process of both the caller and the called.

And, the purpose and call on our lives and work aren't just for us. If other people in your life matter, your response to the calls you receive also impacts them. In our personal and work relationships, being called is rarely something we receive or respond to alone. Those close to us have a stake in our response, and so we have to consider that in many cases, we receive and respond to calls together. Unless you live your life in a cloister apart from the will or feelings of others, you know what I mean.

> "No man (or woman) is an island, entire of itself, every man is a piece of the continent, a part of the main." (Donne 1624/1999, 108)

A call to be or do something in our world is rarely something we experience alone. The call on our lives most often gets discerned and worked out with the others we do life with. And trust is at the center of every one of those calling discernment conversations.

PURPOSE AND CALLING

If calling is a transcendent summons to be or do something in our world that is in response to the needs of others around us, then what does purpose have to do with it? Purpose is different but related. Whenever I describe purpose to groups of leaders, I often relate it to a common claw hammer. A hammer was specifically created for one of two purposes—to pound or to pull nails. Its design is clear. If a hammer had a brain, it would be important for it to know that it's designed for those two purposes. But, purpose goes beyond what we want and what we are good at. We're not only motivated by what we're good at doing, but also by intentions and deeper motivations and purposes. In other words, like the hammer, we have specific strengths and problems we're well designed to solve, but we also have things we want or that we were inspired to do that may or may not be in perfect alignment with our design. I'm really good at math, and more specifically, algebra. But, I don't love math.

Here is what I invite you to consider. Purpose includes our strengths, our unique contributions to teams and to the world around us, and it also includes our intentions, desires, and motivations. Our purpose is an extraordinary combination of our will and our design—both our agency and our unique skills and competencies. Like that common claw hammer with a unique and specific design and purpose, could we be called to respond to a need around us that's not a perfect fit with what we feel are our strengths or what we want? Of course we could. I'm not suggesting that we'll always be called to do or be something that's out of alignment with our purpose or strengths, but that we certainly might be. So, if calling is a transcendent summons from the will of another that is beyond or above us to serve in our world, and purpose includes both our motivations and our unique design, then how are they related?

What calling and purpose share is an issue of will—my will and the will of the another. Whatever your belief, the opportunity in front of us regarding purpose and calling is that understanding our unique and desired purpose is really important, but absent the willingness to edit our purpose in response to a call that may be different from what we want will make the difference between us being all about us, and about something bigger than us.

These are two of my favorite quotes about calling:

"The place God calls you to is the place where your deep gladness and the world's deep hunger meet." (Buechner 1973, 95)

"We have learned too late in the day that action springs not from thought but from a readiness for responsibility." (Bonhoeffer 1953, 98)

I love both of these quotes for different reasons. Buechner reminds us that there are huge needs in the world, and that deeper meaning is likely there for us if we respond to that need. But, taken alone, we might assume that a call is always going to make us feel fulfilled in the short term. That's not always true. Characters throughout history were called to do or be things that they didn't want to do or be. I think a deeper joy was waiting for them somewhere down the line, but to assume that Buechner's quote is a promise of short-term gladness is pretty short-sighted. The quote from Bonhoeffer is troubling and promising at the same time. Calling is recklessly understated when we assume it is fully captured in what makes us happy. As someone who died in service to others, Dietrich Bonhoeffer understood the stakes, but he also understood why he needed to respond. The statement reflects Bonhoeffer's deeply held conviction that calling is not abstract—it is lived through courageous responsibility in real time. Both quotes, when seen as short-term answers to our desired definitions of calling, are misplaced and misunderstood. In the longer perspective, they make better and more perfect sense.

I often get asked whether our jobs and our work should be our calling. First off, I think I've made it clear that we don't have a calling, we listen for it. So, of course, it would be amazing if our jobs reflected an active answer to a call on our lives and were aligned with our purpose. Regardless of whether you would consider your actual job or career as a call or not, my hope is that you are actively listening for how it may serve that greater call on your life, and how your unique purpose will play a role in it. Regardless of whether you feel called to your work, wouldn't it be amazing if each of us was not only clear about the call on our lives, and the purpose for which we are designed, but also feeling a sense of fulfillment in both? Who wouldn't want that? I know I do.

Thoughtful Action: Purpose and Calling

How do we get more intentional about hearing and discerning our purpose and the call on our lives and work? Calling starts with paying attention to our whole story, the people who have influenced or are influencing us, the things we may hold sacred and struggle to sacrifice, and the long-term potential that may open up for us or for others if we're just willing to listen. Purpose starts with understanding our unique contribution to our world, our specific design and the motivations and intentions that drive us forward. It's the awesome combination of the summons on our life and our unique purpose that takes our impact from something that is all about us, to something that is so much bigger than us.

For a Conversation

1. What is the transcendent summons on your life or work at this point? How are you differentiating between calls that you want to respond to versus calls that may be important, but you hesitate to answer?
2. When considering your purpose, what is something that you can't help but do well? What is your unique contribution to any group, team, or family system that you're a part of?
3. What's the relationship between your purpose and the call you are hearing?

The Purpose & Calling Inventory

If you are using the Wild Toolkit alongside Whole Leaders, Wild Trust, the Purpose & Calling Inventory is designed to clarify your purpose, discern the call on your life and work, and the people you are committed to serving. The process is simple. Create an account at www.wildtoolkit.com to access the Purpose & Calling Inventory or all of the robust whole leader assessments together.

CHAPTER 9

Productive

Crush the Important Things

A whole and trusted leader gets meaningful things done.

One of the most underrated sources of trust in our lives and leadership is progress—not just any progress, but *meaningful* progress. People trust leaders who get things done, yes—but even more so, they trust leaders whose actions are clearly anchored in something deeper. A purpose. A reason. A "why" that goes beyond checking boxes. When our goals are tethered to a compelling purpose, something shifts. We become more consistent. More human. And more trustworthy—because others can see the story behind the strategy. They can see we're not just in motion; we're moving with intention.

At its core, productivity without purpose is performative. It's exhausting. But when people experience us making progress toward something we believe in—something that includes them and benefits more than just ourselves—they don't just trust what we're doing. They trust *why* we're doing it. And trust accelerates alignment. It fosters commitment. It gives others permission to clarify their own purpose or make a decision to opt out—both of which are valuable. So, this isn't just a personal development exercise. It's a strategic act of leadership. Because people can't align with your purpose if you haven't named it. And if the people you serve don't see where your goals are taking you, it's hard for them to trust the journey.

While we aren't defined by what we do, we can never escape the reality that building trust with others and within ourselves is deeply connected to our capacity to get meaningful results. When we make progress on our goals, we build confidence to push forward and further again, and it tells others that we are paying attention to what they need to make their own progress. Meaningful progress shows others and ourselves that we can not only get the right things accomplished, but that what we get done will matter—a foundation of trust.

Next-Level Goal Setting

We know that goal setting is especially effective when goals are achievable, specific, and measurable. If that's the case, then why do so many of us still struggle with setting and achieving goals? Much of the answer may not be about our goals, but about being intentional about the overarching purposes in different areas of our lives. The purpose behind our actions is key to unlocking intentional goal-setting and achievement. While lots of people set goals, many fail to identify a guiding purpose and meaning that takes our goals from mundane tasks to meaningful progress.

But goals don't come in just one form or in the absence of others. Different goals in different areas of our life feed each other. As we make financial progress personally, it impacts how we feel about ourselves and our capacity to take risks. And, as we make progress in our families we enter into our work relationships with less anxiety and more composure. And the same is true of work. When our work is going well and moving forward on purpose, we show up better for our families and friends. Our progress in different areas of life impacts our progress in others.

Making Meaningful Progress

> What is important for you to get done, and why is your progress important for you and for others?

"Why" is a hard question and so many of us don't like hard questions. Our thoughts about what we want to achieve, the people we want around us, and what we did are so much easier to navigate and answer than why we did something. It's so much easier to deal with our actions on the surface or the actions of others and to lay down the consequences or express our feelings about them than it is to ask questions about why it's all happening. If you've ever watched a professional soccer game or any professional sporting event for that matter, it's funny how often we see one player provoke another without the referee seeing the provocation and then three minutes later the player who is provoked fouls the other player and gets kicked out of the game. If all we saw was the final foul we assume that the story ends there, and in so many cases that's all the referee sees. Sometimes as fans we see that initial provocation and giggle because we know there's more to the story than the final foul. Here's what's interesting. When we watch the game from our living rooms or from the nosebleed sections of some stadium, we assume that the physical altercation we saw three minutes earlier is the whole story. The whole story might be that the player committing the final foul whispered something nasty to the provocateur. When my sons were young, I can't tell you how many times one son came to me saying, "he hit me." Most parents' natural response is to go ask the hitter, "Why did you hit him?" which is so often followed by the response, "because he called me a name" or "I don't know." Like those brothers who naturally provoke each other, most everything in our life has a "why" behind it that is the core reason behind what we see on the surface.

Getting purposeful about what we are doing is the critical process of answering why before we begin to answer what we are going to do or what we did. Describing our purpose is the process of filling in all the words that follow the word "because" and when it's hard to find the words, doing the thinking that gets us beyond not knowing.

Taking Your First Step

It's nearly impossible to make a small or big step toward becoming more whole and trusted without some level of purpose behind that first step. For each of us, it's not a purpose that controls everything, but some level of a guiding direction that tells us, "This is why I'm in it." The reality is that we are probably guided by purpose whether we like it or not, the only difference being whether it was a purpose we chose, or a purpose that chose us. While maintaining some wide-open margin for some purposes to find us is certainly part of the formula for whole and intentional living, a lack of any articulated purpose can leave us at the mercy of our compulsions and emotions—reacting to our environment and the people around us as opposed to purposefully interacting with it and with them. Nevertheless, living a life with increased purpose requires a little bit of intentional investment.

I had a conversation with an executive several years ago that surprised me. Whatever she was describing to me caused me to ask her this question, "Why do you lead?" After a couple of moments, she went on to tell me about the 10-year strategic vision for her organization and for her business. To be honest, her statement of purpose was less than intriguing. So, in hopes that I would get a more interesting part of her story, I asked her the same question again, "Why do you lead?" It was slightly awkward because most people don't ask the same question twice. I knew that she may have thought I wasn't listening or that I didn't understand her business, but I avoided the pressure to explain to her why I was asking the question and just sat there in silence. After a couple of minutes of awkwardness, she told me in a somewhat sheepish voice that she got into her role because it was the next promotion available to her, and that she and her husband had become used to a new level of income that suited the lifestyle they were not accustomed to. I am not sure this is what she felt, but she sounded somewhat hesitant and somewhat ashamed that this was her explanation for why she leads. So, being the awkward provocateur that I am, I asked her again, "Why do you lead?" For a little bit of context this was a leader in the aerospace industry who was responsible for leading engineers who build airplanes. After a few more awkward minutes of silence, she said, "When I was nine years old, my sister and I made cardboard wings and got up on the roof of our house with me wearing them and she pushed me off and I fell and broke my arm. Ever since then, I have wanted to help people fly." As soon as those words came out of her mouth I thought to myself, I would follow this leader anywhere. In another conversation with a senior leader he admitted to me that it took him too long to realize that as he was climbing the corporate ladder over the years, it wasn't until much later that he realized he was climbing the wrong ladder leaning against the wrong building. With just a bit more intention, we could change that.

Purpose in Action

> What would change if there was purpose driving your next step forward instead of just checking boxes?

Most of us know something about the important power of goal setting. There is very little arguing that setting goals that are specific and measurable works, but is there more? Is it enough to just get goals accomplished without those goals being driven by a purpose, a reason, and a why? Purpose is the anchor that connects our daily actions and motivations to something that is about more than just getting it done. When we are purposeful and are fully aware of why we are in it in the first place, our daily actions are no longer at the mercy of our compulsion to just produce and execute, but rooted in something intentional and purposeful.

Our goals rarely should be driving our purpose. Unfortunately, too often, our purpose is in service of and defined by what we are doing. Our goals should almost always be in service to a greater purpose that connects them to the people we serve, the call on our lives, and the longer-term vision for why we are here. It's easier to get started than it is to chart the course or even describe why we are heading out on the journey in the first place, but that doesn't make it the right way to function.

Imagine what would change if every goal you set and the things you were doing every day were connected to an articulated purpose for why you are doing them. If you are still wondering what I'm talking about, take a moment to answer these questions.

- ◆ What is your purpose regarding your health at this point in your life?
- ◆ What is your purpose in your family?
- ◆ What is your purpose in your work?
- ◆ What is your purpose in your spiritual life?
- ◆ What is your purpose in finances at this point?
- ◆ What is your purpose regarding your personal development?

I know these are hard questions, but they are so centering. Like that executive I described earlier, it often takes a couple of iterations for us to get to the actual purpose, but it's important to start. It's also important to be as specific as possible and to consider your purpose as it relates to others around you. A purpose that says, "My purpose in my family is to be a good dad" is a lot less compelling than a purpose that says, "My purpose in my family is to be available to my teenage children at a time in life when my work is as busy as ever and life is so busy." A purpose that is as specific as possible is not only more compelling, but also more meaningful as I set goals to fulfill that purpose. Even some additional context regarding the age of my children causes me to set goals with increasing specificity regarding my purpose as a dad. The same is true of the purpose behind your finances. The purpose of finances changes throughout life, and that's where it gets interesting. For a college student, it's a lot more compelling and important to articulate that the purpose of their finances is educational debt, when later in life the purpose may be more about saving. That level of honesty regarding their purpose will likely impact the way they approach their finances for the rest of their lives and even reduce the shame they may feel about their debt in the present. Who knows, it might even cause that student to be less inclined to accumulate other debt on top of it.

Taking a moment to articulate and document your purpose across multiple areas of your life, and repeating that process annually, calls out many things. It calls out the relational aspect of purpose, highlights the reality that your purpose will change, and also the reality that the purpose in one area of your life is likely related to the others. Our finances impact our families, and our families impact our work, and so on. And my purpose is wonderfully linked to the purposes of others with whom I do life. Once again, a whole perspective on your life, work, and leadership invites us to see the interconnected parts of our development and learning.

Making Meaningful Progress

If I've motivated you to begin to excavate your purpose across the multiple areas of your life in any way and to make meaningful progress, where do you begin? First, ask yourself what's important to you and others in every area of your life where you know you must get things done. When we identify why it's important for us and others, our goals immediately get interesting. One of the litmus tests for making meaningful progress is whether you yourself find your goals compelling. If you don't find them compelling or aren't excited to share them with someone else, maybe take another shot at it. Second, be specific and connect your goals to a specific business or personal need. For example, if the purpose of my health is to remain healthy enough to play catch in the front yard with my kids while they still live in my home, the deeper and specific need is for me to have that real time with them doing something we both enjoy. And finally, our goal accomplishment gets motivating and meaningful when it's connected to a measurable outcome.

Purpose is the reason behind our being in any situation that is connected to the outcomes we aspire to achieve. We don't move with purpose so that something will occur, but we move with purpose toward the possibility that something meaningful and definable might occur. If my purpose this year is to be present and composed with each member of my team at work at a time when the pressure is really high, the connected outcome might be that I would hear them at a time when they need to be heard, and be an anchor for them in the storm as their leader. The purpose does not exist for the sake of the outcomes, but should be attached to them.

Thoughtful Action: Making Meaningful Progress

As I said at the beginning, people will trust us, and we will trust ourselves as we get the right things done. Be aware of the following things as you begin to take an audit of your purpose across many domains of your life and work.

- Your purpose and the meaning behind your goals will change—it's an iterative process and not a destination.
- Your brain needs permission to think below the surface.
- It feels risky to prioritize why you're doing something before taking action.
- It's countercultural to open up your purpose beyond yourself—defining your *why* for the sake of others and for you.

- Living your life on purpose requires remaining open while also leaving room for errors, mistakes, wrong turns—all part of the process of making meaningful progress.

For a Conversation

1. On a scale from 1 to 10, to what extent do you feel like you are making meaningful progress and getting the right things done personally, financially, at work, in your health, in your family, and in your personal development?
2. Identify one area of your life (finances, work, family, health, spiritual, personal) and take a moment to answer this question. What is important to you and to others in each area of your life and work?
3. What specific things can you do to make meaningful progress in each area?

The Meaningful Goals Assessment (MGA)

If you are using the Wild Toolkit alongside Whole Leaders, Wild Trust, the Meaningful Goals Assessment enables you to get intentional across the most important areas of your life including your finances, work, health, friends, family, and personal ambitions. The process is simple. Create an account at www.wildtoolkit.com to access the Meaningful Goals Assessment or all of the robust whole leader assessments together.

CHAPTER 10

Composed

Stay Anchored in the Storm

> *A whole and trusted leader is composed under pressure, anchored in the storm, and connected to the needs and convictions of others.*

There are at least two kinds of people who are nearly impossible to trust—those overly focused on themselves at the expense of understanding others, and those overly focused on others at the expense of themselves. The first group is difficult to trust because they don't see us; they make decisions and react solely based on their own convictions. The second group is hard to trust because they choose keeping others happy over being forthright and direct. To become the whole and trusted leaders the world needs, we must recognize our own tendencies and take intentional steps to be both clear about our positions and connected to others' wants and needs. *If your focus is on being liked, you will never get the results necessary for people to trust you. If your focus is on being right, you will never get the results necessary for people to trust you.* Different problems with the same result.

What would change for you—and for the people around you—if you could be a better version of yourself when conflict, pressure, and change come? If you spoke more clearly and listened more effectively? Whether it's a conversation with a loved one or a high-stakes moment at work, what difference would it make to be more composed, convicted, and clear?

One thing built into our wiring as human beings is the deep connection between who we are as individuals and who we are in relationship to others. As if life weren't hard enough, the real challenge begins when we have to navigate its hardest moments together. Emotional maturity means staying true to our convictions while remaining in touch with the convictions of others—leveraging our strengths and understanding our blind spots, especially during times of change, pressure, or conflict. Knowing your tendencies is the beginning. The next step is to become intentional about showing up as the most composed and present version of yourself—for your sake and for others.

Over the years, I've invested in the development of hundreds of leaders—emerging and seasoned alike. From those conversations, a few universal truths about pressure have emerged. First, high-pressure situations will happen often. Second, they will challenge you—emotionally, physically, strategically, and spiritually. And third, there are strategies that help you navigate these moments more effectively.

Whether it was students, first-time managers, doctors, parents, or CEOs, they had two things in common: they felt called to serve where they were leading, or they were seeking clarity on their calling—and they had no idea how much pressure leadership would bring. Many had top-tier technical training, but few were prepared for the emotional toll of being responsible for the work and development of others. And from our study of thousands of leaders, a single truth stood out: the rewards of leadership are great, but the pressure is coming. Be ready—for your team, your organization, and yourself.

Leading through personal and organizational pressure is hard work. These moments bring clarity about your strengths and limitations, and they shape your leadership and character. They also challenge you to take stands, listen continuously, and do both at the same time. Leadership is always uncertain. But when those around you feel unsure about their future or the direction of your organization, the pressure multiplies. These situations shake your sense of identity, your confidence, and your ability to stay connected to the people counting on you.

You may be tempted to lean on your competence—and in doing so, lose your capacity to empathize or connect. Or, you may feel a deep need to maintain relational harmony, even if it means compromising your convictions. That's what makes leading under pressure so difficult.

If there's one factor that differentiates leaders who sustain impact from those who burn out, it's their ability to manage themselves well when the pressure is highest. It's not just competence, training, or communication skills. It's what we call leadership differentiation.

The Composed Leader

Leaders are those who step out first, often alone, doing what others haven't yet done. But once they step forward, the real work begins. Everyone watching has opinions about their leadership and decisions. The leaders I've spent my life developing have the courage to go first—and the sacrificial awareness to pay attention. They pay attention to what's happening around them and what others need. They ask questions instead of filling every meeting with their voice. They edit their behavior while staying true to who they are.

They start each day knowing they must be clear about what matters and matters to them—and just as attentive to the needs, thoughts, feelings, and emotions of their followers. In high-pressure situations, what distinguishes these leaders is their ability to differentiate themselves from the anxiety of others. Differentiated leaders attend to what matters most—to themselves and those around them. Garry Ridge summed it up with remarkable clarity:

> "Leadership is a balance between being tough-minded and tender-hearted." (McKenna 2025)

That balance is at the very core of composure under pressure. Leaders who embody this duality can bring the full weight of their convictions to the table without crushing the voices of others in the process.

Why Pressure?

Pressure is an invisible force that signals change. Whether it's conflict with others, shifting relationships, systems, workflows, teams, or roles—change demands our best. And what we all want in these moments is more composure and more differentiation. Leadership differentiation is the ability to stay true to your convictions while remaining in touch with the convictions of others—and resisting the urge to simply appease or bulldoze (McKenna 2004).

While this skill is always vital, pressure and conflict tend to pull us in opposite directions: either doubling down on our own perspective or becoming consumed with everyone else's.

The Fundamental Tension of Leadership Differentiation

If you're asking yourself whether you're called to be a leader, you likely already understand this simple principle. It must be about you, but also about others. If you don't grasp that tension, you're probably defaulting to one or the other—either disconnecting from the needs of your team or losing yourself in the process.

Leadership differentiation means holding two competing truths at once and refusing to lead solely from habit. Instead, you lead from a position of truth *and* connection to others. If you've ever worked with a family systems therapist, this will sound familiar. Many therapists are trained to build both self-awareness and awareness of others. Leadership development borrowed this insight late in the game. In high-pressure moments, some leaders rely on convictions and gut instincts—at the expense of understanding the experience of others. Others rely on relationships—at the expense of direction. The shared challenge is navigating this tension with self-awareness and intentionality.

We all have habits under pressure—whether that's over-focusing on others' feelings or reacting with unchecked assertiveness. The place to start is by naming your default. Do you lead too strongly, or care too much about others' approval? The goal isn't to deny either instinct, but to manage the pressure of choosing one at the cost of the other. Leading well requires staying clear and staying connected.

THE PEACE KEEPER

Peace keepers are those who have a more natural tendency to connect with the emotions and the needs of others. We need these leaders in our world because they bring an ability to connect, to see others, and to even show compassion and empathy. The challenge for peace keepers is that they can in times of pressure and conflict focus too much attention on making sure everyone is feeling happy and satisfied, and as leaders, it is nearly impossible to do that without lying to someone. Peace keepers are not bad people, they just have a unique developmental challenge.

For many of us, the idea that it's okay to know what we want can feel self-serving. It may seem inappropriate to clearly state our desires, the direction for our family or organization, or the next steps we believe should be taken. For leaders who haven't given themselves permission to express their own convictions or lead with strength, doing so can feel heavy-handed—especially for those who care deeply about the thoughts and feelings of others. But when we fail to provide clarity about where we are going, we do a disservice to those we lead. In my work with leaders who struggle to attend to what matters most to them—those who spend most of their emotional energy trying to interpret others' reactions—I often ask this simple but revealing question:

What do you want, and when will they know?

THE TRUTH SPEAKER

For other leaders, the challenge looks different. Truth speakers tend to over-focus on themselves—so anchored in their own convictions that they lose sight of the people around them. These leaders are often described as Type A, nonemotional, and direct. They pride themselves on strength and decisiveness—and may even view emotional connection as weakness. If this sounds like you, you likely see yourself as a no-nonsense leader who gets straight to the point. You care deeply about how others perceive your leadership, but you may not think as often about how they perceive themselves in your presence. While you may acknowledge you have areas to grow, you might quietly believe others should toughen up or keep pace. We need these leaders just like we need the peace keepers because they bring a natural clarity and direction that is easy to follow. Their developmental challenge is maintaining that strength while working the muscles that allow them to more effectively connect with the experience of others.

Here's the most important advice I can offer: shut up.

Yes, really. That advice has been so vital to the leaders I coach that I wrote an entire chapter in another book titled "Shut Up." If you identify as a truth speaker, your next move isn't to explain yourself better—it's to stop talking. Create space for others to speak. Let their voices fill the room. Let their ideas emerge. You'll be tempted to jump in and fix, lead, or clarify. Resist. Let them own the answer. It will likely be better because they shared it.

Your Pressure Profile

To stop being at the mercy of external pressure, your first move is to increase your awareness—of yourself and those around you. There is a dynamic continuum between our capacity to be truth speakers and peace keepers. Figure 10.1 offers an opportunity to map where you land. Most of us lean toward one or the other—or fluctuate depending on the people or the moment.

What's the goal? Trending upward on both. As you read through the following four profiles, reflect on which one best describes you when pressure is high. If your profile shifts based on context, consider what drives the change.

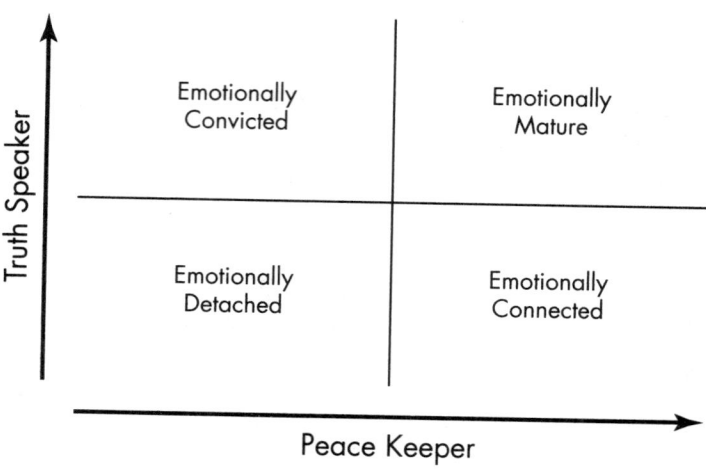

Figure 10.1   Your Pressure Profile

HIGH TRUTH SPEAKER—HIGH PEACE KEEPER
Strength—Emotional Maturity
Developmental Edge—Remaining Steadfast

You are attuned to both your convictions and the needs of others. Under pressure, you stay anchored and present, even when others are anxious or reactive. This is powerful—but be prepared. When you hold your ground calmly, those who are reactive may try to force your hand through aggression, flattery, withdrawal, or sabotage. Steadfastness will be your strength.

HIGH TRUTH SPEAKER—LOW PEACE KEEPER
Strength—Emotional Conviction
Developmental Edge—Emotional Connection

You're driven by what you believe is right, and you express it clearly—often regardless of what others may feel or need. While this clarity can be effective, under pressure it can lead to disconnection and mistrust. If this sounds like you, reflect on what you might be missing when others go unheard. Connection isn't soft—it's strategic.

LOW TRUTH SPEAKER—HIGH PEACE KEEPER
Strength—Emotional Connection
Developmental Edge—Emotional Conviction

You prioritize relationships, often putting harmony above your own convictions. You're likely well-liked, but you may find yourself avoiding difficult conversations or downplaying your perspective to keep the peace. If this resonates with you, consider what it would take to voice your convictions—even when they might disrupt the status quo.

LOW TRUTH SPEAKER—LOW PEACE KEEPER
Strength—Emotional Detachment
Developmental Edge—Emotional Presence

You tend to withdraw or go quiet under pressure or during conflict. This doesn't necessarily mean you aim to please or dominate—it may simply mean your confidence in either area is underdeveloped. Growth for you starts with showing up: developing the capacity to speak your mind and remain emotionally connected when it counts most.

A Strategic Response

Identifying your default tendencies under pressure is only the beginning of building composure. The next step is to act with intention—becoming a better version of yourself when it's most difficult to do so. After two decades of studying the developmental journeys of leaders, we've found that certain actions—what we call "differentiation strategies"—consistently help leaders regulate themselves and lead more effectively under pressure.

These strategies are not abstract. They are practical tools that can be practiced, developed, and refined. They help you connect your emotions, values, and leadership decisions in ways that build trust and confidence. Below is a self-assessment and questions that allow you to evaluate your strength in each area. Even more powerfully, invite a teammate, family member, or mentor to assess you as well. Use the insights to spark a conversation about who you are under pressure—and who you're becoming.

Differentiation Strategies Profile

Think of a high-pressure situation you are currently facing. Rate yourself on each of the dimensions in Table 10.1, noting the areas where you are strong and the ones being underutilized.

KNOW WHO YOU ARE AND WHAT YOU WANT

Chances are, you got into your current position because someone you knew had confidence that you were competent to do the job. That person probably also knew you had the courage necessary to make tough decisions, and the wisdom to get feedback from your key stakeholders before you act.

However, as the responsibilities of the job increase all around, many leaders become less and less effective and spend less time being deliberate about connecting why they lead with what they'll ultimately do. Without that reflection time, emotional pressure from others can cause you to act in the moment with emotional responses that may get you away from the things you know you want out of the situation and that might be best for those around you. Being reflective and deliberate as a leader provides direction and grounding in every situation, conversation and decision. Many leaders struggle with this.

Table 10.1 Differentiation Strategies Profile

Strategy	Low	Med	High	Coaching Questions
Purpose: The ability to think about the current situation in the context of a larger mission, purpose, and/or set of values.				What is your purpose for being in this situation? What would you do if you weren't afraid? How can you keep your eyes on your greater purpose?
Conviction: The ability to define what is important to you and express it with clarity and strength.				What do you feel is most important in this situation at your gut level? Who would benefit from hearing your convictions? When will you express what's important to you to others involved?
Control: Focusing more attention on what you can control versus what you can't.				What things are outside of your control? What are things that you have some control over in the situation? What do you need to let go?
Perspective: The ability to step back and see things from a broader perspective.				What will be the ripple effects of the actions you are considering in this situation? If you were to step onto the balcony above all the fray, what would you see? What in the organization's history might explain the way people are acting?
Potential: The ability to see positive potential outcomes when others may only see barriers.				For every obstacle that you have identified, what is the potential that might emerge? Who encourages you to see potential over problems? What unsolicited voices or unexpected opportunities are presenting themselves to you that you may have missed?
Listening: The ability to put yourself in the shoes of others and hear them, even those who may be the cause of pressure.				What valid motivation might be causing others to react the way they are? If you were in their shoes, how would you feel? How can you listen more effectively?

(Continued)

Table 10.1 (Continued)

Strategy	Low	Med	High	Coaching Questions
Empathy: The capacity to feel what others feel.				How would you feel if you were in their shoes? What possibilities would emerge if you asked others what is causing them to feel the way they do? What matters to others in the situation?
Objectivity: The ability to remain objective, even in situations that feel deeply personal.				What are you taking personally that likely has nothing to do with you? When you take things personally, how does it impact other people? If you remind yourself that most things aren't personal attacks, how would that change your perspective?
Awareness: The ability to know yourself and to know how others see you.				What do you know about yourself that might be causing you to react the way you do? What do others say are your strengths and areas for development? If you knew yourself better, what would change for you and others?
Composure: The ability to stand firmly under pressure, to make decisions, and to remain connected to others.				What is the smallest step you could take today that would have the greatest impact in moving you closer to your goals? Recognizing that there probably isn't a perfect solution, what are the advantages and disadvantages of the best actions you could take in this situation? What about you allows you to stay centered when you are the target of blame and sabotage?
Ownership: The ability to look at one's own actions before looking for other people to blame when things don't go well.				What is your contribution to the problems you are facing? How can you be honest about your contribution (good and bad) to the situation? What would change if you took responsibility for your contribution to the high pressure situation you are facing?

If you abandon any part of yourself for the sake of consensus, the outcome can be a lack of respect from your followers and even a lack of respect for yourself. The people in your organization may not always like the decisions you make, but they'll respect you more if they know you have the courage to follow through. One way to make sure you're following your gut in any high-pressure situation is to ask yourself some tough questions. While you may not need to communicate all the answers you come up with, they may give you permission to explore those things that are rarely negotiable for you.

- What do you want?
- What would you do in this situation if you weren't afraid?
- What do you need to do in this situation to look yourself in the mirror next week?
- What price are you willing to pay for the outcome you desire?

Leadership is rarely about getting everyone to agree, but more about getting as much input as possible, and being courageous enough to take a risk, sometimes risking relationships, consensus on satisfaction with the outcome, and being willing to have some resistance along the way.

Considering all the stakeholders involved, what are the tough decisions you'll need to make?

Paying Attention

Being true to yourself alone will not complete your leadership in high-pressure situations. For leaders who value high performance, celebrate and reward the tough-minded, and tap our ever-increasing reliance upon achievement as a means to feeling satisfied with our work, what does it take for you to stay connected to the key stakeholders around you?

As your successes add up, your influence grows, and you get more pressure to move forward, to produce, and to build a body of accomplishments, oftentimes your ability and willingness to hear others is decreased. Others know immediately when you no longer value their input. In fact, you might think and say you value the input of others, but the pressure to do more and do it better can completely mute your ability to stay in touch. So what's a leader to do?

Realize that your ability to stay connected, to slow down, and to hear the voices of others are key to your ability to truly lead well. And realize that pressure and adversity may hinder your ability to listen.

Here are some questions to ask yourself that can help you feel more confident that you're paying attention to the voices around you.

- *Who are the key stakeholders in the situation and what's at stake for each of them?* Take the time to make a list of those who'll be impacted or have a stake in the outcome. Hopefully you understand the adversity you're facing, but do you understand what others are feeling and why? For many of the leaders in our work, this means being deliberate about checking in with even the most challenging people, be they peers, bosses, subordinates, volunteers, family members, or the community.
- *Do you tend to fill the silence with your own voice?* Leaders often become uncomfortable with silence when they feel personal pressure. They feel they're expected to have answers, to be right and to produce results. Speaking into silence for the sake of filling the silence is an anxious response. Find a trusted other who can watch you under pressure in the presence of others and will tell you if you need to stop talking so much and begin listening.
- *How can you create an environment in this situation where people will come to you with good and bad feedback?* If you're a strong leader, even a good leader, those you lead may not communicate with you enough. Followers may dismiss the value of their contribution, think you're too busy for them, or may feel intimidated by you. Encourage feedback from others.
- *When you're confident you finally understand other people's perspective, how will you know you've got it right?* We often ask leaders if they know what others are thinking in the midst of organizational or personal adversity. Many leaders say, "Yeah, I know what they're thinking." How do you know? "I asked around the office and I brought up the issue at our last board meeting and no one had any objections, so they're on board." If you don't have much feedback, or haven't been deliberate about processing the different opinions of your stakeholders, chances are you don't really know their perspective yet.

The Power of Purpose—Why Are You in It?

Why have you chosen to be in a position of accountability for others? This is the reality of leadership. It's only a matter of time before that accountability will provide pressure, anxiety, opportunity, and challenge. One of the most powerful contributors to a leader's ability to handle the pressure is the extent to which they have clearly defined their purpose for being in the situation in the first place. The challenge to each of us is to be clear about why we are doing what we are doing. And the more specific the purpose the better. "Because I'm supposed to" is very different from "I'm supposed to be in this role because I have led through turnaround situations before, and that's why I'm here." Specificity of purpose keeps you and others clear when the pressure comes, and serves as an anchor in a harbor that will soon become stormy.

The power of adversity and times of high pressure are that they provide the crucibles upon which your leadership will mature, *and* the temptation to be reactive, to make decisions unilaterally, or to be frozen by the need for consensus will diminish. The advice of the leaders we have worked with is clear. Take the time necessary to step back and see the big picture. Regulate your emotions in real time so you can get the perspective necessary to manage the anxiety others are feeling. In other words, know your hot buttons and get perspective, so you can pay the necessary attention to what you know needs to be done and to the needs and wants of the other key stakeholders, even those bringing you the most heat. Maintain a focus on the possibilities in the midst of challenges, and differentiate yourself by refusing to react one way or the other when others push you. Regulating your reactivity will help others know you're a person who's in touch with their reality, and that you have the courage to follow your gut, even in the most challenging times.

Trust is built and reinforced when we are clear and direct while also connected to the needs and convictions of others. It's hard work, but it's necessary if we want to become the whole and trusted leaders others need us to be.

For a Conversation

1. Under pressure, do you tend to pay more attention to what others think is important or to what you think is important?
2. What would change for you and for others if you could be more attentive to what's important to you and what's important to others at the same time?
3. Which two or three strategies described in this chapter are most important for you to practice in the high pressure moments you are facing right now?

The Leading Under Pressure Inventory (LUPI)

If you are using the Wild Toolkit alongside this book, the Leading Under Pressure Inventory provides you with actionable insight into your default tendencies under pressure and specific strategies for becoming a more composed and differentiated leader in each high pressure moment. The process is simple. Create an account at www.wildtoolkit.com to access the Leading Under Pressure Inventory or all of the robust whole leader assessments together.

CHAPTER 11

Learning

Enter the Leadership Laboratory

> *A whole and trusted leader continues to edit themselves, learn, and grow over the long haul.*

We all have gaps. Gaps in our ability to get things done. Gaps in our character that cause us to double down even when we know we're in the wrong. And gaps in our competence that still need to be filled. But these gaps aren't our biggest barrier to becoming trustworthy. The greatest barrier is our incapacity to learn.

At the core of learning is editability—a willingness to change and to press the backspace key, even on parts of our character. Editing is hard. Whether it's someone asking us to change the way we think, adjust how we work, or revise something we've created, it confronts us with the possibility that we could do better. And that's uncomfortable. But here's the truth. It's nearly impossible to build a trusting relationship with someone who won't learn. If we were perfect all the time, learning would just be a nice bonus. But we're not. And because of that, learning—especially when it's difficult—is essential.

Real learning is messy. It's disruptive. It increases our capacity to change more quickly and intentionally while staying grounded in who we are. And it's powered by one essential source: experience.

Learning from Experience

A huge portion of your growth is happening in real time—right now—in experiences you've likely never had before and that sit outside your comfort zone. The more challenging the experience, the deeper the potential for transformation. Those moments when you feel underqualified, under pressure, or just exposed, often become the moments that change you forever. Whether you're managing people for the first time, launching something from scratch, or trying to turn a team or project around—these are the moments that matter.

What would shift if you treated those moments as incredibly powerful classrooms—and if you knew what kind of experience you needed next to grow?

Each of us has a story. Not just of what we've done, but of the moments that have changed us—experiences that shaped our skills, our confidence, and our direction. Some of them were positive. Some were painful. But all of them taught us something. And we're in the midst of more right now. Having intentional conversations about those experiences—past and present—can build trust and deepen connection. They help us understand each other's learning journeys and give us clues to how we can support one another moving forward.

One of my heroes in leader development is Morgan McCall. In his article "Recasting Leadership Development" (McCall 1999, 3–6), he outlines seven principles that have shaped my thinking for years:

1. To the extent leadership is learned, it's learned from experience.
2. Certain experiences matter more than others—managing people for the first time, launching a project, turning something around, or being shaped by a role model.
3. Challenge is what makes experiences powerful.
4. Different types of experiences teach different lessons.
5. Intentional design of experiences makes a difference.
6. People can access critical experiences if they know what to look for.
7. Learning is dynamic and takes time—it's full of twists and turns.

Changing the Paradigm

Most of us were trained to think learning means being taught—listening to someone talk, reading a book, watching a video. And while all of those have value, they're not enough. What really shifted my perspective was what I stumbled into in the classroom. In 1994, I was preparing to teach my first graduate course. I was young and didn't have much experience. My students, on the other hand, had real-world experience I didn't. The course covered the psychology of work—how people think and behave in organizations. I had a textbook, a foundation of theory, and some early consulting experience. But I realized I had something more valuable: the lived experience of my students.

So I made a choice. I'd only "teach" half the time. The rest would be space for students to process the material through their actual experiences. That commitment changed my teaching—and the way I build leader development experiences to this day. Effective learning happens when personal awareness, evidence-based insight, and real-world application all show up in the same space.

Personality Versus Learning

Are leaders born or made? Most research says it's both. Personality plays a role—certain traits remain fairly consistent over time. But our environments and experiences shape at least half of who we become.

Experience is a powerful mentor. Left unfiltered, it will still shape us. But with intention, we can guide that shaping process. Mentoring, coaching, therapy, reflection—these are ways we assert agency in our development. They're proof that we know our experiences can either expand or constrain us. With even a little attention and intention, those same experiences become the engine of our transformation.

THE LEADER LABORATORY

As kids, we intuitively understood experiential learning. That's why field trips were the best days. As adults, we need to bring field trips back—because the real leader laboratory is right in front of us.

Over the past few decades, a growing body of research has confirmed what many of us sensed. The most effective leadership development happens *in the doing*. Organizations that move beyond passive training and into active learning—assignments, stretch projects, turnarounds—unlock growth at scale. I call this the "leadership laboratory." Not a secretive place hidden behind closed doors, but the messy, daily environment we're all already in. And with just a little more intention, that lab becomes the perfect place to develop the next generation of leaders.

LEARNING FROM THE GOOD, THE BAD, AND THE UGLY

It's not just the positive experiences that shape us. Sometimes the most profound learning comes from the toughest moments—the crucibles we'd never choose but can't forget.

Research tells us that experiences with role models deeply shape leaders—and surprisingly, over a quarter of those role models were *bad* ones (Van Velsor et al. 2016). I often joke with leaders: if you're doing a terrible job, the good news is you're teaching someone a very important lesson. Moments like personal failure, turnaround situations, first-time management, or breaking out of a rut can reshape us permanently. They're not easy, but as my friend Megan Lawrence once said, "Hard is not the same as bad." Even when we'd never choose the experience again, there's something to learn.

As Robert Thomas writes in *The Crucibles of Leadership*, "It requires an awareness of one's vulnerability... and yet it demands a relentless sense of agency" (Thomas 2008, 10). Don't dismiss the hardships, but do mine for the learning.

EXPERIENCES OVER JOBS

Too often, when we think about what's next, we think in terms of jobs. But jobs are limited resources. Experiences are not. What if we thought about the experiences we want, just as much as the titles we hope to earn? Imagine showing up in an interview and naming the experiences you're looking for—not just for your sake, but in service of that organization's mission. Imagine reflecting on the experiences you need next to grow into your next season of impact. Learning doesn't have to pause for execution. We learn *as* we execute. That's the power of framing our growth in terms of experience.

Thoughtful Action: Learning from Experience

There's a myth that senior leaders have nothing left to learn. It's false. Even executives with decades of experience will tell you that one shift in context and they're learners all over again. A client of mine who had run a massive public sector agency once told me, "I knew how to run a department with thousands of employees. Running a four-person consultancy? That's where I got stretched." On the flip side, early-career leaders sometimes feel behind because they don't have the experience yet. But lack of experience isn't a weakness—it's an open runway. What matters is staying humble, open, and intentional. You get to shape who you're becoming. That's an incredible gift.

If we want to be trusted, we have to keep learning. It's not just about modeling growth for others—it's because learning is the raw material of trust. If I'm unwilling to change, how can I expect others to trust me? That's why building whole leaders and trust requires both confidence and editability. And the best lab we have? It's right in front of us—filled with challenges, moments of clarity, feedback, failure, and breakthrough.

We may wish it were easier. But if trust is the goal, learning is the path. Not just once, but over and over again. And it always starts with the courage to learn.

For a Conversation

1. What role have experiences had on the person or leader you are today?
2. What are you experiencing right now that's teaching you something about yourself?
3. What experiences are necessary for you to have next that will prepare you to be more effective in your current or a future role?
4. What should others in your life or work understand about the experience you are having or would like to have next that would help them trust you more?

The Transformational Experiences Audit

If you are using the Wild Toolkit alongside this book, the Transformational Experiences Audit will give you an inventory of the experiences you've had and the experience you want next to become the leader and person you aspire to be. The process is simple. Create an account at www.wildtoolkit.com to access the Transformational Experiences Audit or all of the robust whole leader assessments together.

CHAPTER 12

Competent

Build Trust Through Excellence

> *A whole and trusted leader is aware of their strengths and their limitations, and is continually turning their blind spots into deeper self-awareness.*

There are few places in the world where competence and our need for trust intersect more obviously than in a hospital. On a recent trip to the hospital with my dad, I was once again confronted with my need for trust and my need to believe in the competence of his caregivers. While I could assume that every nurse and doctor who entered his room brought the same high level of expertise, it would be naive to assume that is true. But, if that hospital we are entering is going to be a place we trust, the basic competence of every caregiver is one of the most critical drivers of trust.

Trust is defined as your belief in my integrity and that I will have your best interests at heart, my ability, my reliability, and my strength, and that I will tell you the truth if any of those things are missing. Your understanding of your competence is related to almost every part of trust. How can I do what you are asking me to do, do it well, and do it consistently if I don't understand what it is I am actually good at doing and where I am weak or untested?

When we understand our strengths and expertise and others know them as well, everything changes. The problem is that oftentimes we haven't been given the opportunity to do an honest audit of our skills and what we know and so we aren't even sure what we would tell others. And it's even worse when we not only lack the knowledge of what we do well, but the things we either don't do well or that remain as blind spots for us. When we become knowledgeable about the whole story of our skills as well as our weaknesses and we share that knowledge with others, we are able to put ourselves in a position to use those strengths or to have others help us where we are deficient. Trust begins there.

While we so often oversimplify leadership in many contexts as a calling or as a general principle, becoming aware of your specific competencies as a leader and the skills and knowledge you have or have not gained is one of the biggest favors you can do for people you lead. If we strip down our definition of skill, competence, and knowledge as the things we have mastered doing or knowing, that helps a lot. It's an understanding of our specific expertise. In some cases, our skill and competence at doing something is simply that—our ability to do something well. And yet our gained knowledge is equally important. So often we dismiss knowledge or even changes in our thinking as something less than a visible skill, but knowledge is a powerful thing too. The skills and knowledge we have gained over our lifetime are the basis of so many things happening within us psychologically. And that's just the beginning.

Think of the last time you learned to do something that you could not do prior to learning it. Cooking is that thing for me. Other than your typical pancake breakfast or grilling steaks or burgers, I just don't have that much experience cooking. More recently, I've started to cook a few times a week. In full transparency, the entire process produced a lot of anxiety for me. While I'm fully aware that some of you may have cooked all your life and are shaking your head that I'm just now realizing how stressful it can be, I get it. Cooking involves so much more than cooking; planning meals, checking the pantry to see if you have what you need, finding recipes, starting at the right time, shopping, calling home because you forgot to check for one ingredient, responding to three work emails in the middle, turning on the oven, and all the rest that comes after that—that's cooking. All you people who are good at this and laughing, I get that too. While I truly don't think I will ever love cooking,

I am getting better. I'm getting better at the little things. The more I practice each of those steps, the more confident I feel. The more feedback I get from my family, the better I'm able to adjust. The more I learn to search through the pantry, the more skilled I feel at walking the aisles in the grocery store. The more food I burn, the more knowledge I gain about appropriate temperatures. And finally, the more practice I get in real time, the more cooking feels like a skill I have and not a barrier or an unknown possibility. I may or may not ever consider myself a cook, but my hope is that the skill will last with me, and serve the needs of people who will eat my cooking. Just like the importance of the ingredients in a recipe and the process of cooking well, leadership has its own ingredients, things we know and things we do, that are required if we are to become better at leading and more trusted over the long haul. Whether it's listening, communicating better, confronting problem people, facing uncertainty, becoming resilient, learning to negotiate or to manage conflict, these skills and knowledge take practice to develop, and that practice involves lots of dynamic moving parts.

Expertise, Skill, and Knowledge

If skills and knowledge are the fundamental building blocks of our capacity to do specific things well, expertise includes the larger categories of skills and knowledge that tell the story of our increasing mastery in a certain area. Imagine a volume of books that sits on your bookshelf all published by the same publisher with a common theme. These are the books that we leave on our bookshelves because they look so impressive together. They're usually the same color, the same height, and they just seem like they're going to last. If you've ever staged a house, you know what I'm talking about. You don't put all the ratty paperback books on the shelf. You put the beautiful consistent volume of books that are even more impressive if they've aged a bit.

Expertise in different areas of leadership are like those volumes of books. Each book represents mastery relevant to a specific area—with the individual chapters of those books representing the more specific skills and knowledge that make up each area of expertise. In the same way that some chapters might be repeated in different books in the volume, some skills and knowledge relate to more than one area of expertise.

What trade or profession have you studied or experienced in which you have or are developing some level of expertise? Whether it's engineering, law, sales, medicine, education, music, a specific trade, or parenting, there are likely identifiable skills and knowledge necessary to function well within that area of expertise—and more specific skills and knowledge necessary to practice to become more of an expert. Even more interesting, while a standard and accepted list of competencies likely exists, you have your own unique and nuanced story of things that come more naturally to you—the things that have always felt like barriers to becoming skilled, and the things that are simply unknown because you haven't explored them yet.

Leadership Competence

One of the most common transitions people go through is the moment they shift from being a technical expert to a leader. Whether you become an engineer, an attorney, a salesperson, a doctor, a teacher, an accountant, a mechanic, a musician, an electrician, or a plumber, that moment comes when your technical expertise pulls you into a leadership role for which you may feel underprepared. The common saying is that "what got you here won't get you there," but the reality is that those technical skills will probably continue to play a key role in your development as a leader. It will likely be less about the practice of the skill, and more about the knowledge you gained that will be critical going forward. Knowing how to be an effective plumber will still be important because you know how plumbing works. However, if you make leading people all about being an expert plumber, you will fail to develop the new set of competencies necessary to become the leader of plumbers, software developers, or not-for-profit volunteers. Our deeply rooted expertise in a technical area often provides the springboard into the deep end of our leadership capacity.

When we become leaders—those with the responsibility for going first and responsible for others—our past skills and knowledge become the foundation for developing new and unexplored competence. The expertise required to lead is oftentimes informed by those skills while taking on new life in our learning and development. Leadership competencies are the fundamental building blocks of our ability to lead well, and to lead in our own unique way. Our skills, knowledge, and expertise tell the unique story of our areas of mastery, our areas needing attention, and areas where we may need help. It's necessary to see those competencies as a new volume of books in our learning and growth. The volumes making up our technical competence will still matter, but the new volume of books is going to include things that maybe we've never had to consider before. It's not just about identifying this new set of competencies, but also where they fit in the broader landscape of who we are and who we're becoming. Just like that new volume of books would require a new bookshelf, this newly discovered need to learn will require space in our minds and even deeper spaces in who we are.

From Technical Competence to Leadership Competence

When we move from technical expertise to leadership expertise, the fundamental shift is from it being about us to it being about us and others. While we sometimes practice technical skills and knowledge with others, leadership competencies share one common factor—an inherent and necessary connection to the needs and competence of our followers, peers, and even our own leaders. Thinking about followers may feel like an ego thing, but I'm suggesting something different. The relationship between leaders and followers is more one of responsibility than it is of a privilege. As leaders, we are now responsible for thinking about our own competence in direct relationship to the needs and competence of our followers and stakeholders.

As an example, three of the most common leadership competencies include strategy and vision, engaging and inspiring others, and process management. When we frame these three competencies as inherently connected to others, it changes everything. Why is it necessary for us to become skilled at strategy or inspiring others or at process management? To lead a group of people or an organization requires leaders who bring strength in these areas. Strategy exists for the sake of setting all of us up to take advantage of opportunities in the future. Strategy is necessary for us to get anywhere with intention.

And strategy is created by leaders who bring that competence, or a willingness to learn it or delegate it. Something magical occurs when we realize that the development of leadership competence is all done for our own sake and for the sake of others. I'll never forget the moment a leader in the aerospace industry with a deep background in engineering said to me, "You know what I learned in that experience, Rob? I learned that people matter." His statement wasn't a joke. There comes a time when we all realize that improving our own capacity no longer exists in a vacuum of self, but exists so we can all move forward together.

WE ARE MORE COMPETENT TOGETHER

As I already suggested, leadership competence is different in that it immediately includes other people. A whole leader approach to developing competence must include the reality that our ability to lead well does not occur in a vacuum. While we sometimes practice our competencies and do our skills alone, more often than not we are executing on things that require us to be effective together. Sometimes together means with one other person. Other times it means being effective as an individual while working as part of a team. And even further, sometimes our execution is done through others. Executing through others, often referred to as executive-level competence, occurs when we are no longer the ones doing the work, but are the ones creating the environment where other leaders can thrive.

BECOMING AWARE OF YOUR STRENGTHS AND YOUR GAPS

For most of us, watching a recording of ourselves doing just about anything is a painful process. For those of you for whom it's not painful, I would suggest you might want to pay even closer attention. Getting feedback on how we are doing at performing our skills and competencies is painful because it requires us to let our guards down to see things as they really are. Even if you don't "watch the tape" of yourself in action, the reality is that you probably are or are not performing at the level you desire anyway. It is so absolutely necessary that we become aware of our skills, knowledge, and expertise. When we become aware of our strengths, blind spots, weaknesses, and areas for development, we open actionable possibilities for us to become the leader we desire to be.

And that awareness and the courage necessary to muster it, is the foundation upon which great teams are built.

It's also important to step back and take in the bigger picture of our development as leaders by looking back, being aware now, and looking to the future. Looking back is about understanding the skills and knowledge you've learned in the past that provide the foundation from which this next stage of your learning begins. Being aware now is about understanding the competencies you are using and learning right now as a leader. And, looking forward is about the expertise I need to develop in the future that will not only allow me to be my best self, but be my best self for the sake of others around me. A whole perspective on the development of our expertise as leaders is about our past, our present, and our future.

When I begin to understand my own strengths, blind spots, weaknesses, and areas for development it impacts the makeup of my team, our functioning together, and my capacity to help you become more deeply aware of all these same things in yourself. Some skills I need to work on. Some skills I need to compensate for. Some skills I may need to delegate. And, in some cases, my awareness regarding your expertise may release you to develop skills that are still undiscovered. It can be hard to become more aware of my expertise or lack thereof, but it is absolutely necessary if we are to become the whole and trusted leaders we desire to be. Doing a job well and learning what we will need to learn to improve increases our confidence to do the next thing, and that confidence will help us be more honest with others about where we are strong and where we are weak—a necessity for building trust.

Thoughtful Action: Becoming Competent

How do we get more intentional about assessing our areas of expertise and the skills and knowledge we have now? Awareness starts through a simple annual audit of them and a conversation with others to ensure that what we understand is consistent with the experience of others. Leadership expertise is more than courage, conviction, compassion, and empathy. A whole perspective on developing our capacity as leaders includes a range of interconnected skills and knowledge that, when practiced, move us toward wholeness in our expertise as leaders. We become aware, we practice in real-life situations, we edit, and then we practice again.

For a Conversation

Rate yourself on the following areas of leadership competence on a scale from 1 (not competent) to 10 (highly competent).

Interpersonal Discernment/Relationships: You are skilled at managing relationships and interacting with others.
Your rating _____.

Organizational Adaptability/Agility: You are able to adapt and change your approach to work as necessary.
Your rating _____.

Creativity & Innovation: You take an innovative and creative approach to your work rather than relying on the way things have always been done.
Your rating _____.

Strategy & Vision: You are skilled at creating and communicating a vision or strategy.
Your rating _____.

Engaging and Inspiring Others: You empower and motivate others or your team.
Your rating _____.

Skills & Acumen: You have the necessary skills and acumen to perform your job optimally. Your rating _____.

Execution: You are known for getting things done.
Your rating _____.

Self-Development: You are intentional about developing yourself and your abilities.
Your rating _____.

Handling Conflict: You are effective at facing and dealing with conflict.
Your rating _____.

People Management: You are effective at managing those with whom you work.

Your rating _____.

Process Management: You are skilled at managing processes and directing work.

Your rating _____.

1. As you rated your high and low areas of competence, what are your greatest areas of strength? What are the conditions in which you are able to do those things at your best? What are your areas of weakness or areas that are untested?
2. What two or three skills are weaknesses, areas that have not yet been tested, or gaps in your competence? Are these things you should learn, compensate for, or delegate to someone else who may have strength in that area?
3. What is important for others to know about your competence that will help them trust you more?

The Skills & Knowledge Inventory

If you are using the Wild Toolkit alongside this book, the Skills & Knowledge Inventory is designed to scaffold a more in-depth conversation regarding your leadership expertise, skills, and knowledge. The process is simple. Create an account at www.wildtoolkit.com to access the Skills & Knowledge Inventory or all of the robust whole leader assessments together.

CHAPTER 13

Motivated

Inspire the Deeper Forces Behind Your Effort

> *A whole and trusted leader is motivated, and interested in the motivations of others.*

Have you ever found yourself waiting on someone—teammate, friend, partner—to do what they said they'd do, and they just don't? You know they're capable. You've seen it. But the follow-through never comes. It's frustrating, because when people repeatedly drop the ball, our trust in them starts to erode. But here's a harder question: What if there's more going on than just their failure? What if part of the story is us?

Yes, there are moments when people genuinely let us down. But our ability—and theirs—to perform, to follow through, and to learn something new isn't just about skill or good intentions. It's about motivation. Motivation is the spark, the fuel, the drive behind everything we do. It's not just whether we *can* do something, but whether we have the energy and fire to actually do it. And here's the trap: we tend to believe that what motivates us should motivate everyone else. It doesn't. When we start recognizing that people are driven by different things—purpose, achievement, connection, challenge—we stop managing behavior and start lighting fires.

If we want to become whole and trusted leaders, we need to get more honest about what moves us—and what moves the people around us. Because motivation fuels performance. And performance, repeated and consistent, builds trust. Not just trust in outcomes, but trust in each other.

Einstein famously said insanity is doing the same thing over and over again and expecting a different result. If that's true, then most of us are toeing the edge of madness. We all have areas in our lives where we want change, but we keep applying the same worn-out tactics, hoping they'll work this time. We relate to that kind of insanity because it's real. But let's be honest—avoiding insanity is a pretty low bar. We need something better than just staying sane. What we need is inspiration. We need something that lights us up, that reminds us why it matters, and that calls out the very best in us.

Learning and Motivation

If we aren't motivated, we don't learn. For 25 years I've been teaching students the fundamentals of two related topics—learning from experience and motivation. Back in the early 1990s, I became fascinated by the research on experiential learning. Study after study has shown that the place where most leaders learn is on the job and through experiences. While training, degrees, and the classroom were certainly important to some, experience was the primary teacher. In other words, the most powerful and impacting changes that occurred in leaders happened while they were leading. So many important discoveries were made regarding learning from experience. We learn on the job and through crucible-type moments that oftentimes push us to the edge of ourselves. We also learned that experiences teach us very specific knowledge and skills and lessons that we can apply for the rest of our lives. And we learned that for some crazy reason, sometimes we go through important experiences and we don't learn. We just repeat the same mistakes.

The reality that sometimes we experience incredible transformational moments and don't learn then inspired some of the smartest people in our world to study a huge question. What is the key to unlocking the door between the most profound experiences of our lives and the learning that is on the other side? The whole story is that there is a lot of amazing psychology regarding our learning and motivation that involves important moving parts. At a minimum, those parts include things like agency—my belief that I have choices

I can make, self-efficacy—the belief that I could actually learn something, and the reality that motivation to learn matters and that each person is motivated by different things. And, being motivated by different things isn't only about auditory or verbal learning, but also about something more deeply psychological.

The Power of Motivation

A few years ago I had the opportunity to drive a Ram TRX—a truck I've wanted to drive for a long time. I was being picked up by a client of mine and when I walked out of my hotel, there it was. A black TRX. The Raptor killer. If you don't know what it is, in 2021, the Ram TRX was the most powerful stock truck ever built…702 horsepower. A super truck. I almost started jumping around like a kid on Christmas morning. It may be a lost breed because it guzzles a lot of gas, but I can guarantee you that if you had a chance to drive one and push it to its limits, it would put a smile on your face. While some of you could not care less about what a TRX is, for me, it was a really fun moment that connected into my deep passion for trucks that is real and always has been.

The engineers who build cars and trucks build them with intention because they know that without something that connects the power of the engine to the tires on the road, nothing moves forward. What if we applied that same basic science of learning to our own experiences? We already know that motivation is the power that connects experience to learning and learning to doing. But what if we were more intentional about discovering our unique motivations to learn and to do anything that would propel us forward? Motivation, like the driveshaft in that truck I got to drive, is what connects the power between our experiences and our capacity to learn and to get things done.

Imagine what changes when you begin to understand your unique motivations, and the motivations of everyone around you.

- Learning is elevated.
- People are not only seen for what matters to them, but for what inspires them.
- Agility is accelerated, and our teams get engaged.
- And even the most taxing people on your team who are causing the most emotional labor for the rest of your team might begin to learn how to change, grow, and develop.

Motivation Fuels Performance and Learning

When I did my first TEDx, "Whole Leaders in a Broken World," I invited the audience to ask themselves eight questions. The questions were based on everything we know about leader development. But, instead of posturing them as the eight things to do, I postured them as questions. As invitations to develop at another level. Here are the questions.

- What would change if I knew why I'm here and what I should do next?
- What would change if there was purpose driving my next step forward?
- What would change if I was showing up better under pressure?
- What would change if I were applying the lessons from my past experiences?
- What would change if I knew my unique skills and competencies, and also my blind spots?
- What would change if I knew what motivates me?
- What would change if I were surrounded by cheerleaders, role models, and people who give it to me straight?
- What would change if I were intentionally investing in the team of people around me?

There was a question in the middle of all of those questions that was related to all the others. The question was this, "What would change if I knew what motivates me?" When I answered the question for myself on that stage, I immediately knew the answer. If I knew what motivates me, I would do those things. If I knew what motivates me, it would impact my response and my willingness to discover my answer to every one of those other questions. And, if I understood the unique motivations of everyone around me, what difference would it make in their learning and their own capacity to grow, and grow together?

Getting Real About Learning

Learning is a funny thing. While it's probably one of the most fundamental realities of the human experience, it is also one of the most elusive. If you don't believe me, just walk through any self-help section of any bookstore for the last several decades and its mystery and importance to us becomes immediately apparent. Whether it's for selfish or selfless motives, learning is the fundamental building block of our progress as individuals and as human beings together. If we don't learn, we don't progress. If learning is so common to the human experience, why is it so difficult for us to improve, to grow, and to learn?

If learning is such a critical aspect of becoming a whole and trusted leader, why is it so hard to master it and move on? Learning is hard because it requires editing—the possibility that we may have to be willing to hit the backspace key on things that may even feel like they are part of our character. To learn is to change, and to change is to edit. And learning also requires us to not only live in the future, but to live in a full awareness of our present and our past. We cannot learn without a whole perspective on our past, present, and future. If we dismiss our failures or misses as only distractions or obstacles to ignore, we miss out on that most fundamental thing for living and work and doing it well—learning.

However, while change is hard and we are drawn to forward progress over thinking about our past, incredible things open up when we start to learn from our present and past. When we start to get intentional about our learning and the learning of others, it's contagious. When we begin to provide invitations to change and provide intentional pathways to becoming more self-aware and aware of others, it impacts everything else.

Learning Motivators
Here's what we know.

- ◆ Motivation is one of the most powerful and studied concepts in leadership and organizational science. And whether you are thinking about your children, friends, or co-workers, understanding motivation is really important.
- ◆ Long-term motivation is about agency and an invitation to readiness. Even inviting the problem people and inviting them to change, or to find a place where they might be motivated to do so.

- Motivation to learn is different from a learning style. Learning styles are more about how we learn. Learning motivation is about the natural psychological and situational drivers that inspire each of us to learn.
- All motivational drivers fuel performance and learning, but some more than others in different people.
- Motivation plays a huge role in learning because it is what unlocks the gate between my experience and my growth.
- Motivation to learn is different for different people. While there are general principles that apply, the application of those principles looks different for different people.
- Motivations to learn may change over time. While some motivations may remain the same over different seasons of our life or work, motivation is not the same as personality. The context of our lives and work can impact our basic motivations to change.
- Trust is fueled by our ability to perform and get the job done, and performance is fueled by understanding our unique motivations and the motivations of others.

As you think about the people around you, I invite you to think about their unique motivators—their motivational drivers. Understanding our motivation to learn and the unique motivations of everyone around us is a game changer because it unlocks the gates and helps us understand each other and connects the powerful engine of our hearts and minds to action and change where the tires meet the pavement.

When I talk about "learning motivators," I'm talking about focusing on identifying each individual's personal inspirations to learn that likely increase the capacity to be more learning agile, to grow, to change, and even to be engaged. The fundamental shift caused by a focus on motivational drivers is that it moves our understanding of learning and motivation as an ability or willingness a person either does or does not possess, to include the reality that ability and willingness are developmental processes in and of themselves. Motivation is not only an end goal, but also a developmental process inside each of us that likely impacts everything.

Based on our research on thousands of leaders, we discovered that motivation to learn is not only something you can increase, but something you can inspire in others intentionally once you realize that different people are motivated in different ways. We discovered that learning and motivation weren't the same for everyone, but that each person's individualized motivational drivers and the contextual factors around them were playing a role (McKenna et al. 2007). Motivational drivers are the personal keys to unlocking your inspiration to learn and get things done. In that way, they are happening both while we are experiencing and when we are learning, as well as providing a connection between the two. In other words, a person's capacity to learn is not simply about looking for lessons and intentional reflection; rather, it is also about their unique motivations and inspirations to learn.

I will never forget the first time I realized that one of my learning motivators was influence or my capacity as an influencer. While the term "influencer" may sound a bit self-indulgent given our current feelings about "influencers" in our world, it went deeper than that for me. I realized that when I have the ability to impact others through speaking, writing, or sharing principles that I believe in deeply, something magical happens. My motivation to learn is elevated through the roof. While it's not my only motivation, it helps. That's why members of my team know that if they need me to execute something, remind me that without me getting my work done, they can't move forward. That awareness for me has changed everything for me, and I would suggest, for those who work with me.

Following are the 14 motivational drivers and a description of how to tap into the unique motivations of different people. As you read each of them, think first about yourself and consider the mix of motivational drivers that energize you and allow you to focus. Next, think about the people with whom you work or know, and consider the mix of motivational drivers that provide energy and focus for each person. Most of us are motivated by a unique combination of things and not just one thing, so you will likely come up with two or three for yourself and for others. What are their unique motivations to learn and to get things done that might give you insight into how to work with them, or even live with them? Once you have taken a shot at identifying the unique set of two or three motivators for each of the people around you, consider having a conversation with them about it to see if you are right.

- **Adaptability:** This person is driven by roles and tasks where there is flexibility in the way they get things done, manage change, and perform tasks with a high degree of variety. Be aware that flexibility and the chance to work on new projects may be more important to this person than money, stability, or influence, and identify opportunities for variety in their jobs.
- **Awareness:** This person is driven by self-understanding and direct feedback. Provide honest and constructive feedback to this person as they grow.
- **Care:** This person is driven by concern for others and seeing them accurately. Be transparent with this person about your life and work and provide opportunities in the job for them to connect on a deeper level with others.
- **Challenge:** This person is driven by risk-taking beyond what is comfortable. Give them the opportunity to do things that are difficult but achievable.
- **Collaboration:** This person is driven by working with others to accomplish things. Look for opportunities for them to get more done through working with others as opposed to alone.
- **Connection:** This person is motivated by networking and building support communities, building and maintaining relationships with others, and connecting with others. Ensure that this person has the opportunity to collaborate and work with others to get things done.
- **Expertise:** This person is motivated by applying their skills to solve a problem, doing things they are good at, and being an expert at something. Help them identify what they are really good at doing and give them opportunities to practice those skills on projects that matter.
- **Influence:** This person is driven by making a difference in the lives of others, seeing their impact on others through things that matter to them, and developing the skills and abilities of others. Clearly communicate the connections between what they are doing and the direct positive impact on others.
- **Integrity:** This person is driven by doing things that are consistent and aligned with what they say you are going to do, being honest about what they see happening—being direct and forthright with others.

- **Joy:** This person is driven by working with a team that laughs, people who see potential even when things are tough, and being around joyful people. Celebrate wins and be open to laughter with this person as an important part of work and life.
- **Learning:** This person is driven by learning for the sake of learning, actively reflecting, and applying lessons from their past to current situations. Provide opportunities for them to simply learn new things because they are motivated by the chance to reflect, grow, and simply learn something.
- **Purpose:** This person is driven by doing things that serve a higher purpose, feeling a sense of calling to what they are doing, and seeing a purposeful connection between what they are doing and something bigger. Communicate the purpose of tasks and the reason behind what they are doing.
- **Strategy:** This person is motivated by seeing the big picture, thinking strategically, and making strategic decisions based on the best knowledge available. Team members motivated by strategy get energy from thinking about how things will be done and not just getting things done, so provide space to step back and think about the structure and strategy behind tasks.
- **Success:** This person is motivated by work and tasks that require determination, measurable progress, and success. Give them permission to identify specific goals that will tell them that they are making progress.

A whole perspective on motivation and learning moves us from seeing it as our desired outcome (i.e., I just learned something) to our realization that our motivations change over our lifetime and in different seasons. And that great and lifelong drive to learn or even to get things done is an ongoing and repeating cycle. The greatest challenge is that many of us have been lured into a reality that we just need to get it done, fail fast, and then try again. Learning—deeper learning that eventually ferments into wisdom—takes time and intention. If just getting it done is the primary goal, the cycles of mindless repetitions and failures will likely continue. If an understanding of our deeper motivations in this season is the goal, then sustainable and repeatable learning is possible. Learning is hard, but also inspiring.

Repeatable learning is not only possible—it's powerful. Learning can be difficult, even uncomfortable at times, but it can also be deeply inspiring. What if the people around us understood what truly compels and motivates them to grow—not just to complete tasks, but to take the risk to stretch, change, and become better versions of themselves? What if each of us had greater clarity about our own personal motivators—what drives us to rise, to learn, and to improve—not only for our own benefit, but for the sake of those we lead and serve? The impact would be contagious. When people are clear on what fuels them, and we see them leaning into that growth, it ignites something in us. We catch the spark. And what once felt like a grind becomes a movement—of individuals and teams who are learning, growing, and showing up differently because they've found the drive behind their "why."

Thoughtful Action: Motivated and Driven

It's not enough to talk about building a "motivated team." Motivation isn't a one-size-fits-all driver—it's personal, differentiated, and deeply human. If we want to build teams and organizations that are truly alive with purpose and trust, we have to get better at seeing the unique and diverse motivations of every person we lead. That includes successors, high-performers, and everyone else in the system. Because the truth is this: every person is motivated to act, grow, contribute, and change—but for *very* different reasons. And if we assume that what drives us should drive them, we'll miss the mark and diminish trust in the process.

Motivation is the fuel behind performance, learning, resilience, creativity, and follow-through. When we begin to see those drivers clearly—not only in ourselves but in the people around us—we start leading in a way that is more personal, more effective, and more trusted. The work of becoming a whole and trusted leader requires this kind of curiosity: not just about what people do, but *why* they do it. And when we fail to understand those deeper motivations, we don't just risk disengagement—we risk becoming blind to the actual needs of those we are called to serve.

So ask yourself: Are you motivated by the chance to influence others, or by creating systems and strategies that hold things together?

Do you come alive in moments of deep reflection, or in real-time problem-solving? Are you driven by a desire to bring people together, or by your ability to provide clarity and stability in chaos? The answers matter—not just for your own development, but because your motivations shape the experience of those around you. And when you understand what drives you and what drives them, you're not just managing people—you're building trust.

This isn't just a strategy for learning. It's a blueprint for leadership. And it may be the very thing that takes us from being leaders who get things done to leaders who leave others better—because we paid attention to what truly moves them.

For a Conversation

1. What would change for you if you understood your unique motivations to learn?
2. Considering the motivational drivers described in this chapter, what is important for others to understand about your motivations that may help them energize you either in work or in life?
3. How does understanding your own learning motivators increase your capacity to inspire learning agility in others?

The Motivational Drivers Inventory

If you are using the Wild Toolkit alongside this book, the Motivational Drivers Inventory is designed to scaffold a more in-depth conversation regarding your unique motivational drivers and the ways you could intentionally ignite the linkage between your experiences and the learning on the other side. The process is simple. Create an account at www.wildtoolkit.com to access the Motivational Drivers Inventory or all of the robust whole leader assessments together.

CHAPTER 14

Invested

See Others Clearly

A whole and trusted leader makes an intentional investment in others.

One of the most overlooked truths about trust is this: when we invest in others, we don't just build their capacity—we also build our own. Every time we pause to consider someone else's growth, we develop greater clarity about who we are, what we value, and the kind of leader we want to be. That clarity builds self-trust. Investing in others stretches our courage, sharpens our emotional intelligence, and forces us to lead with both truth and compassion. It strengthens our sense of purpose and deepens our belief that we have something meaningful to offer.

But it doesn't stop there. When we take the time to see someone—really see them—and offer our insights with intention, it signals something powerful: You matter. I see you. I'm with you. That moment of recognition lays the foundation for deeper, more enduring trust. People trust those who make the effort to invest in them, especially when it's not required. And in return, they often rise to meet the faith you've placed in them. Over time, trust becomes mutual, and that mutual trust becomes the relational fuel that not only develops us as whole leaders, but builds sustaining trust.

Who is one person who made a meaningful investment in you? What made their investment so impactful? Maybe it was the time they gave, the questions they asked, or the simple fact that they truly saw you. Even if they didn't think their actions were significant, you know the difference they made.

Whether it was a mentor, a boss, a friend, a family member, or a colleague, most of us can name at least one person who changed our lives because they chose to see us and invest in us. The potential to have that same kind of impact is within all of us—but too often, we don't follow through. Not because we don't care, but because we haven't made investment a habit. The truth is: investing in others is a sacrificial act that starts with a small dose of intention.

Leaders Developing Leaders

It's no surprise that great leaders develop other leaders. But doing so with intention and consistency is less common than you'd think. Too often, our efforts are haphazard—or missing altogether. I don't say that to shame anyone, but to call it out plainly: we can do better. And the good news is, better is within reach.

Recently, I worked with senior leaders at a large corporation focused on building their capacity to invest in others. Halfway through the session, a VP pulled me aside and said, "If this is a tough crowd, it's because in Q1 alone, we had more turnover than in the entire previous year. In our exit interviews, the number one reason people are leaving is that their managers didn't see them—and neither did their coworkers."

That's devastating. You've heard it said that people don't leave organizations—they leave bad managers. But it's deeper than that. People leave when they're not seen. At our core, we long to be known for who we are, for the value we bring, and for the unique story we carry. Being seen doesn't just mean being praised. It means being respected. It means being acknowledged for strengths and being challenged on blind spots. Seeing someone whole includes character, competence, and the honest feedback they might need to grow. The tragedy isn't just that this kind of investment is rare. It's that it's completely doable. And yet, we've all experienced the barriers—awkwardness, fear, uncertainty. We've also experienced the cost of not doing it.

Investing in Others Isn't Easy—But We Must

"Every moment and every situation challenges us to action and to obedience. We have literally no time to sit down and ask ourselves whether so-and-so is our neighbour or not. We must get into action and obey" (Bonhoeffer 1959, 77). If investing in others is such a no-brainer, why don't more of us do it?

Because it takes courage. For the one investing, and the one being invested in. Intentional investment requires vulnerability. It means pausing to reflect deeply on another person—their character, their contributions, and where they could grow. Then it means sharing those insights in a conversation that could change everything. That's where many of us hesitate. We're not sure we know enough, or we're afraid it won't land. But courage means stepping in anyway. And here's the thing: the need for meaningful, growth-oriented feedback is huge. Most people aren't getting honest insight about what truly matters in their development. If we don't offer it, who will?

It's hard because it wasn't modeled for many of us. Culture tells us to look out for ourselves. And investing in others—especially in a work context—can feel strange or too personal. But real investment is always a bit countercultural. It's personal. It's sacrificial. And it requires us to push past the initial awkwardness. We don't have to be perfect. We don't have to know everything about a person. But we do have to start. Even a small conversation can make a massive difference.

The Power of Seeing People Whole

What if development conversations became normal? What if your team, your family, or your peers expected to be seen—fully and regularly?

It's amazing how many world-class organizations forget to invest in their own people. But no matter your context—whether you're leading a business, a not-for-profit, a church, or a global cause—your leaders need ongoing investment too. Intentional investment builds continuity and trust. It helps us see each other with greater accuracy, not just once, but over time. And when we see people through a developmental lens, we understand their motivations, purpose, competencies, and support systems. We also see the gaps, the strengths still hidden, and the untested potential waiting to emerge. I'm not talking about robotic systems, but a steady rhythm and common language that connect people's whole story with their current role. Imagine your team knowing that someone is regularly thinking about how to support their development—not just their performance.

Here's what research and practice show us:

- **These conversations are happening—just not at work.** Too often, we save them for close friends or late-night talks over coffee. But work is full of insights others don't see.
- **They don't have to take much time.** Five minutes of insight or affirmation can shift someone's life trajectory.
- **People want the truth.** They want to be affirmed, yes—but they also want to know what to work on.
- **You know more than you think.** You don't need to know everything. Just come with humility and a willingness to listen.
- **Development is not the same as performance.** But when development conversations are consistent, performance conversations become easier and more fruitful.
- **Diversify your investments.** Don't just invest in people who report to you. Up, down, sideways—everyone benefits when development flows in all directions.

Taking Action on Good Intentions

When I set out to build a system for whole leader development, I knew it had to be about more than self-awareness. As essential as it is to understand ourselves, that's only half the equation. Whole leadership doesn't happen in isolation. It's forged in the space between us—when we choose to invest in the growth of others with courage, intention, and a long view. That's why the foundation of our developmental philosophy had to go beyond self-reflection. Real change—in people, in teams, in culture—requires courageous *investment* in others. It means we pause in the middle of the rush, long enough to truly reflect on the people we're responsible for. It means asking better questions. And above all, it means preparing ourselves—not just them—for that investment.

Intentional investment isn't about creating a growth plan for someone else. It's about preparing yourself to show up differently—for their sake. It's an act of presence, not performance. That's where the **INVEST Model** was born. It's a framework designed to help leaders clarify what it actually means to invest in another person—not generically, but specifically and personally.

THE INVEST MODEL
Interest—What matters most to them?
Start with curiosity. What do they care about deeply? What gets their attention and pulls at their heart? You can't guide someone well if you don't know what they value.

Needs—What do they need from you?
Not everyone needs the same kind of leadership. Some need clarity. Others need encouragement. Some need a challenge. Ask yourself what they *actually* need—not just what you're comfortable giving.

Virtues—What do you admire in their character?
Point out what's good and true in them. Speak to the character you see—the grit, the kindness, the integrity. Naming virtues reinforces identity, not just performance.

Experiences—What would stretch or grow them?
Growth happens at the edge of challenge. What experience—big or small—could catalyze new insight or resilience in them? Leaders create environments where stretch is possible and safe.

Strengths—What are they uniquely good at?
Everyone brings something distinct to the table. Investing means recognizing those strengths and helping people use them with purpose.

Traps—What blind spots might limit them?
Every leader has them. Sometimes it's overconfidence, sometimes self-doubt, sometimes a repeated pattern that holds them back. Investment includes the courage to gently and honestly name those traps.

Now, imagine answering these questions—specifically—for each person on your short list. Imagine sitting down and actually sharing those reflections with them.

I created something called the People Investment Plan (PIP) to structure that very process. The first time I used it, I walked into a meeting with a team member, shared what I'd written, and said, "Here's what I see in you." They paused, then said something I'll never forget: *"I didn't realize you saw me this well."* The truth is, I wasn't even sure I had it right. But what I realized in that moment was that I knew more than I thought—and that I had the power to make a bigger difference than I imagined. Since then, I've seen that moment repeat hundreds of times. Leaders discover their own capacity to see others deeply. Team members saying, *"I didn't know you saw me."*

That's the power of intentional investment. It opens up potential like nothing else. It's not about fixing people. It's about seeing them. And when someone knows they're truly seen, something shifts—motivation is unlocked, trust deepens, and people begin to rise into the roles they were built for. If you want to be a whole and trusted leader, start by investing in the people around you—not someday, but today.

Every Conversation Is a Development Conversation

Investing in people is hard—until it's not. Every conversation is a chance to encourage, inspire, and challenge someone. Every moment has the potential to shape the future.

It's much harder when we've skipped the foundation. That's why—whether you're just starting out or have led for decades—the time to begin is now. True transformation rarely begins with "You should." It starts with a question, a relationship, and the belief that someone is worth investing in.

Thoughtful Action: Invested in Others

Some people credit their success to someone who invested in them. Others carry the ache of not having that person. Regardless of your title or role, you can be that person for someone else. Not everyone needs the same thing from you. But everyone needs something—time, questions, insights, presence. The people around you may be desperate for a real conversation about what matters most.

Becoming a whole and trusted leader isn't just about understanding yourself. It's about making a bold, intentional, and sacrificial investment in the lives of others.

If we don't, who will?

For a Conversation

1. Who made an intentional investment in you and what made it impactful?
2. Identify up to three people in whom you would like to make an intentional investment and ask yourself these two questions: (1) What is the unique contribution they bring to their team or the world, and (2) what, if it were further developed, would take them to the next level?
3. What would change if you shared these reflections with them? Not just thoughts—but responses. Thoughtful, intentional responses have weight. They build trust. They spark growth.

The People Investment Plan

If you're using the WiLD Toolkit alongside this book, the People Investment Plan will provide a simple structure for you to make an intentional investment in the learning and growth of the people around you—your team, your friends, and even your family members. The process is simple. Create an account at www.wildtoolkit.com to access the People Investment Plan or all of the robust whole leader assessments together.

CHAPTER 15

Supported

Move from Solo to Surrounded

The whole and trusted leader is never fully alone. They are actively seeking to be surrounded—by people who offer support, speak the truth in love, and care deeply in real time.

Becoming a whole and trusted leader is not a solo pursuit. We cannot do this alone. The presence—or absence—of strategic support directly shapes how much we trust ourselves and how much others trust us. When we're surrounded by people who will catch us when we fall, confront us when we drift, and celebrate us when we rise, we begin to operate with deeper clarity, confidence, and courage. That kind of foundation fosters real self-trust—not the kind rooted in ego or achievement, but in the deep knowing that we're not alone in this work.

And here's the opportunity: being surrounded not only builds our own trust in ourselves—it also builds others' trust in us. People are drawn to leaders who are willing to stay open, admit they don't have all the answers, and receive support from others. Why? Because those leaders aren't hiding. They aren't pretending to be invincible. When we live with that kind of vulnerability and connection, our trustworthiness becomes tangible. Whole leaders aren't just competent—they're connected.

So, let me ask you: what would change in your life if you were truly surrounded by cheerleaders, mentors, and people who give it to you straight? I've asked that question of leaders in every industry, and the answer is often the same: "Everything."

Now imagine having specific people in these distinct roles. Mentors who speak wisdom. Role models whose lives and careers you admire. A designated person you'd call if everything in your world came crashing down. Someone who tells you the unfiltered truth about how you're showing up. Advocates who cheer you on because they know your mission, not because they're just trying to be nice. Cross-organizational partners who share a vision with you, even if they come from different communities or industries. People you'd call during a job transition or life shift—not because you're networking, but because they know you.

That kind of strategic support structure changes everything. Now imagine all of it was taken away. What would that feel like? For many of us, the thought is sobering. Without these relationships, we're simply not at our best. These connections don't define us, but without them, it's hard to remain grounded, resilient, and fully trustworthy. When we lack strategic support, we don't just lose encouragement—we lose perspective, self-awareness, and in many cases, the courage to take meaningful risks.

But here's the challenge: many of us struggle to ask for that kind of help. Some of us don't want to burden others. Others of us were raised to believe that needing support is weakness. Some of us have asked for help in the past and been let down. And yes, there are those who lean too heavily on others—revealing another set of boundaries to navigate—but far more people live isolated, overextended, and unseen. The result? An undercurrent of self-doubt and a fragmented experience of leadership.

Here's the truth: it's not only okay to be surrounded and supported—it's reckless not to be.

If you had the right people walking with you right now, would you be more willing to take a calculated risk? More likely to pursue the growth you've been putting off? More confident in how you're showing up? For most of us, the answer is yes. Support doesn't make us less independent. It makes us more intentional. Strategic support provides something we can't generate alone: the courage to take the next step, the feedback we don't always want but desperately need, and the fuel to sustain us in seasons of both growth and strain.

We've all heard the phrase, "It's not what you know, it's who you know." But I'd push that further. It's not just *who* you know—it's *why* you know them. I once asked a leader how prepared he felt for a major transition in his life. He said, "When I think of all humans, I know I'm not the only one who feels this unready. But when I think about the people in my actual life—that's when the loneliness kicks in." The absence of meaningful connection was feeding his sense of inadequacy, even though the logic in his brain told him he wasn't alone. His heart hadn't gotten the message.

Have you ever found yourself in a season of struggle, whether in work, relationships, or life, and not known who to call? I've been there. That kind of silence—where you realize you're missing a sounding board, a truth-teller, or someone who just knows you—is a form of isolation that chips away at both your confidence and your capacity. Even if you know, intellectually, that you're not the only one feeling underprepared, unsupported, or overwhelmed, it's the lived experience of not having *specific* people to turn to that compounds the weight.

Here's the good news: you don't need to wait for a crisis to build a circle of trust. Strategic support isn't just for the emergency moments. It's for daily decisions. The tough conversations. The new ideas. The subtle but significant shifts in how you lead. The best time to build your circle is now.

To become a whole and trusted leader, you don't need to have it all together. But you do need people. You need to be surrounded. And you are worthy of that support.

We Become Our Best Together

We do not develop best on our own. At that intersection of our lives and work and our hearts and minds is the reality that our self-awareness and effectiveness as humans and as leaders will be stifled if we do not do this together. Most of our development occurs through and with others. Understanding your readiness and your personality, the call on your life, the experiences you need next or have had, the competencies you've learned, and how to become a leader who develops other leaders will all be reliant on the network of others who surround you at any given point in your life. Just like one part of our bodies can't survive without a healthy connection to all the other parts, we can't survive or thrive without a healthy connection to others.

A leader described the power of others in our aspiration to wholeness this way. She said, "The ultimate goal would be to build an organization where we realize we are completely reliant on others. Saying it is one thing. Doing it is another." She went on to say, "I have realized that I am completely reliant on others, and in a strange way, that is the goal…to work in an organization where you feel that level of trust. Building that can take time, and so often we don't want to wait."

Saying we want to build an organization where we support one another and rely completely on others is one thing. Doing it is another. We discern together, we often perform and are effective together, become convicted and clear together, are called together, edit ourselves together, become more mature together, and we move toward wholeness together. It's the way it is, and when we begin to move alone and fail to invite others into our learning and growth, we are stifled and stuck in the brokenness that does not need to define us.

The Power of People Around Us

As a Ph.D. student in the 90s I was always overwhelmed by the power and impact of social support. During that time, if you were doing research on anything about organizations and the psychology of the people within them, you had to think about social support as a variable. Research on social support made one thing clear. If people are surrounded by others who support them and feel an awareness of their presence, the impact is profound. If you had it, you were doing better. If you didn't, it wasn't a good thing. I even remember designing a few studies with professors of mine where we were considering different variables to include. We knew that if we included social support as a variable, it was likely to soak up all the variance in the study, leaving very little room for us to study the impact of other variables. When we studied social support, we asked questions like, "Do you feel supported at work?" or "Do you have social support at work?" Do you feel supported by others at work?"

That way of describing what it means to be supported sounds so generic and plain. But, in fairness to all the psychologists in the 80s and 90s studying it, we were just getting started.

Social support in life and work is about something deeply human…a need to feel a sense of being supported, surrounded, valued, and worth investing in. People who support us change our lives forever. They come alongside us in the toughest of times and remind us that these hard times will pass, that we've got this, that our ideas and dreams are worth pursuing, and that there are risks we must take. Being strategically supported is more than having friends. It's about having a sense that we belong, we are not alone, and that we can learn, grow, and develop. A supporting cast of people in our lives reminds us of our value and our part in something bigger than us, but that includes us.

Who to Call?

People who support you are like Volkswagens. If you buy one, you'll see them all over the road. Once you make an intentional move forward to identify the reason you need people in different roles, those people will emerge, or you will realize they were there all the time. Getting strategically surrounded by people who will support you and stretch you toward the purpose that is right in front of you in this moment of your life takes three things. First, some pre-work on the direction you are moving in and the purpose for you going in that direction. Second, courage to take an honest look at where you feel supported or don't. And finally, a moment to get intentional about identifying who you need around you and why. Every one of us needs strategic support. If we are going to respond to the riskiest calls on our lives with courage, it will be reckless not to be surrounded. As you work through beginning to build your strategic support, be open to surprises, look for new things, build with intention, and take a long-haul perspective.

The kind of support you need will surprise you. I cannot even begin to imagine where I would be without key people who have surrounded me at different points in my life and career. One key player is Dr. Bill Robinson. Bill and I got to know each other at a conference. We had mutual friends because Bill had been a college president, and we knew a lot of people in common. Each year during that conference we would sneak away to have a beverage together and just catch up. After about three years of this, I mustered the courage to ask Bill a question. I said, "Bill, would you be one of my mentors?" I'll never forget his response because it caught me so off guard. He said, "No, Rob, I won't." The second or two that followed his response felt like a lifetime because it wasn't what I was expecting. He went on to say, "But here is what I will do for you. I'll have your back, and that means that if anyone questions the character or competence of Rob McKenna, I will tell them they don't know Rob." Immediately I thought, I'll take it. I went into that conversation wanting one thing, but did not realize that through his awkward "No" I would receive support from him as a key advocate that I didn't fully understand how much I needed.

Looking for new kinds of relationships is also important. Over the last couple of years, one of the most powerful peer mentors and advocates has been Dr. Tiffany Powell. Tiffany probably doesn't fully understand her impact on me, but it's been profound. Tiffany is an expert in diversity, equity, and inclusion, and as a white male leader in our world, I have often wondered about my appropriate and most helpful place in the conversation regarding diversity. Meeting Tiffany was huge for me. Tiffany and I quickly became friends and advocates for each other, and we even had a chance to write together on the topic of diversity and whole leader development. I have learned so much about myself and my purpose—far beyond what Tiffany might imagine. And, she has been an encouragement to so many women in my own network in ways that I cannot fully be.

It is ok to build relationships and support with intention. While it can feel self-serving, if we don't, our support will feel flimsy and fragile at best, and downright missing at its worst. Recently I realized that if there was one place I needed additional support, it was my need for wisdom from leaders a few steps ahead of me who shared my worldview, who understood me and my vision for my life and organization, and who had significant leadership experience. The morning I identified that need I was on a call with Dr.

James McPherson, another new friend of mine, regarding a big challenge I was facing. A few minutes into that call James said, I would like us to meet on a regular basis, Rob. I almost fell out of my chair. To imagine being officially mentored by James McPherson, a guy who had spent decades in corporate leadership roles and in the highest level of government was overwhelming.

Support in the Moment and Beyond

Getting strategically surrounded is a long-term proposition. At one point in my journey, I set out to pursue a capital investment in the business I built. I knew I needed financing, but I wasn't sure where to begin because I had never done that before. During that time, I began to meet with Frank Haas. Frank was 84 years old and had been very successful in business. After six months of mentoring me, Frank did something I never imagined possible. He ended up being the one who made a significant investment in my business. I know that he did it because he believed in me and what we were trying to do, but that belief expressed through an actual financial investment changed everything. I will never forget how nervous I was the morning that I was heading to Frank's condo to negotiate the terms of the investment. I was so anxious. The crazy thing is that two months after Frank made that investment, he passed away. While it was tragic, I learned so many things after that. At the memorial service put on by his family, one of his sons came up to me and said, "My Dad debriefed with me every conversation he ever had with you." I had no idea that anyone outside of attorneys and accountants even knew. And then, the executor of Frank's estate came up to me and said, "Frank loved it when you were negotiating the terms!" Frank, as someone who surrounded me during his life, is still surrounding me after his death. He is someone who understood that his investment in me was going to outlive him, and he was teaching me even as he negotiated with me.

While I could go on and on about the people who have surrounded me over the years, including my parents and siblings who have been huge mentors and advocates, I played a role too. I only wish someone had told me about the power of building an intentional strategic network much earlier.

Strategic Support

During a conversation with my brother who had been coaching a very senior and famous leader, he said, "Did you know that every year this leader sits down and documents his strategic network of support...the specific names of people he needs around him to accomplish what he needs to accomplish this year?" I was immediately struck by the level of intention my brother Doug was describing in this leader he was coaching. Building strategic support is about identifying an intentional and documented network of people who will play a diverse set of specific roles in your life, and who exist in your support network for a specific purpose in this season of your learning and growth as a leader, or as a person. If you are an emerging or a seasoned leader, I invite you to the possibility that you could be strategically surrounded. Whether you have been a CEO for 20 years, transitioning back into the workforce after raising your kids, or just moving through college, the time to start is now.

> "The lives of all the men (and women) we meet and know are woven into our own destiny, together with the lives of many we shall never know on earth. But certain ones, very few, are our close friends. Because we have more in common with them, we are able to love them with a special selfless perfection, since we have more to share." (Merton 1955, 12)

It's impossible to deny the power of social support, but to actually be strategically supported is an entirely different thing. Imagine if you were not only surrounded, but you were intentional about identifying roles that different people would play in your life and work and the type of support they might provide. Getting to that level of intention invites us to think about more than just the kinds of roles they will play, but the purpose for which they will play those roles. Strategic networks of support are relationships and people who will set you up to take advantage of future opportunities.

Why is strategic support from others such a critical thing for us, and why do we struggle to get the support we need? There are many reasons. Some of us have baggage about things like networking because it feels selfish and everybody except the biggest narcissists hate that. And we don't want to be those people. It takes too much work. We feel like we are the only ones who don't have others around us. For too many of us, self-sufficiency is the lie we live. "You got this on your own" is the tale we tell, when deep down we know the only reason we can say "I got this" is because someone else told us we do. Some of us don't know who we can trust. And maybe the most powerful reason, at the deepest and most vulnerable level, we don't feel worthy of being supported. But what if I told you that there is a way, and that if we are going to be the people and leaders we aspire to be, we need to be intentional about it?

Here are the top 10 big ideas that could take your strategic support and turn it into a reality, where every year you have the support you need to make effective progress and move toward wholeness and trust.

1. Social support is one of the most powerful variables in a person's life. Whether it's healthy attachment, overall wellness, stress buffering and direct effects of stress, being surrounded is key. We are social people, even the most introverted among us.
2. There are typically more people around you than you realize who are just waiting to be asked to help you out. If they can't, the right support will tell you so.
3. A strategic network exists for a purpose. Knowing what you are wrestling with, the mission you are on, what you are trying to learn, what your needs are, and what kind of support you need is required to begin to think about who must be around you.
4. Networks are living and breathing and changing. The purpose different people will serve in your life will change. It will always involve many starts and stops. It's a process, not an outcome.
5. By its very nature, leading and going first is a lonely proposition. And yet, being surrounded is a critical component that takes intention, strategic focus and purpose.
6. Social support increases differentiation, agency, efficacy, and well-being.
7. Early-career people need leaders to invest back in them, but they often feel a sense of fear and resistance.

8. Building a strong network makes you more employable. A strong network builds nuance, interest, and awareness.
9. Specificity matters. Because your network of support is strategic and purposeful, the more you understand about what you are trying to accomplish this year, the more you will know about who needs to be in your network in this season of your life and work and the purpose they will serve.
10. It's not just about you. Oftentimes the real purpose behind getting you surrounded and supported will include the purpose that your network may serve in the lives of others within your influence.

The Roles People Play

As I said before, a strategic network of support includes people who will play a diverse and definable set of roles in your life and work. It's one thing to be surrounded, but a completely different thing to be surrounded on purpose (the reason and the role). We know that support matters but imagine how powerful it would be to know who is in your network, why they are there, and the specific type of support they will provide. Imagine what it would be like to identify specific names of people who would be willing to play these roles in your life.

- **Advocates:** People who have your back and would defend your competence and character.
- **Emotional Support:** People you would call if your life or career were falling apart.
- **Extended Team:** People who may not be a part of your immediate work team, but who will play a key role in achieving your goals or your team's goals.
- **Feedback:** Those who give you honest and challenging feedback about your development.
- **Mentors:** People you consider important voices in your life and career.
- **Organizations:** Organizations you resonate with that may provide important strategic connections in the future.
- **Role Models:** People who provide an example of who you would like to be, or not be.

- **Service to Others:** People who would likely include you as a part of their support network.
- **Your Team:** People who are a part of your immediate work team, or that you work with on a regular basis.
- **A Dream Team:** Individuals that are not in your network yet, but you would like to add.
- **Advisory Board:** A select set of individuals who will serve as your personal board of advisors.

It's important to note that when you begin to identify these different people who will support you, they don't get a message that says, "Rob just said you are his mentor!" The conversation about how they can support you will create a more complete picture of their role in your life. Be open to that.

Getting specific about your strategic network and supporting cast isn't hard to do. The real battle is with fear, our lack of intentionality, or our developmental laziness about getting strategic. Building a strategic network requires us to exercise a new and different muscle—the getting ready muscle. It's all about executing on purpose and getting supported on purpose, and that requires us to pause long enough to realize whether we have the people in place to support us in this coming season.

So many of us are challenged by specificity because it causes a dilemma. Specificity can highlight a lot of gaps. It's a lot easier to identify what's going well or where your network is stronger than it is to identify where you are missing something. When we get specific about what's missing, it creates an active over a passive dissonance (a realization that there is something to change) that is important, but hard to face. However, if we push through with the courage to see the whole story of our support or lack of it, new possibilities we never imagined begin to open up.

By its very nature, leadership can be very lonely. Stepping out to go first and lead can be a very isolating position. As a leader, you are now out in front, you are set apart, you are responsible for things that others are not, and you are different. People who used to trust you because you were a peer may criticize you, even when your intentions were as good as they come. Full transparency is something you are supposed to model, when in fact you know things about each of your followers that you cannot share with the others. That is a huge burden to bear alone.

Development is inherently a relational process, requiring us to think intentionally about those who will surround us in this present reality. Great leaders are intentional about surrounding themselves not only with support, but with those who will give them the tough feedback—the honest truth about who they are, where they are going, what needs to be affirmed, and what needs to change. It's not only a relational process, it's also a customized process. Just as you are a unique leader with a unique call and purpose, the nature of your strategic network must have that same uniqueness. For some that means diversifying or broadening your connections or increasing the quality of your connections over the quantity. Whatever your need is, the common factor is purposeful intent—building a network of documented support of people who will occupy unique roles in your life and work. Some of these people may be people you will know for the rest of your life, and others may support you in the short term and come back around later.

Your Dream Team and Advisory Board

It's hard to imagine something that you haven't given yourself permission to consider. That's why I always suggest that each of us start by identifying our dream team. These are people you would love to have in your network but may seem out of reach. The amazing thing is that dreaming up this "dream team" may or may not mean you will actually know those people but will help you realize what kind of people you could be supported by. Along those same lines, each one of us should have an identified advisory board. These aren't people who are on any kind of actual board, but people who are sitting in the virtual boardroom of your life. These are different people who are surrounding you for different reasons, but for a shared purpose of supporting you. And they are there because they each bring some unique combination of skills, resources, or wisdom, and that's why they are on your advisory board in this season.

At its core, building strategic support is about making trust visible. When you are surrounded by people who challenge you, advocate for you, and walk alongside you with purpose, your trust in yourself expands—and so does others' trust in your leadership. Support is not just about comfort in crisis; it's about formation. It grows us into the kind of whole leaders the world actually needs—leaders who aren't afraid to rely on others, because they know that trust is both given and grown in the space between us.

Thoughtful Action: Supported and Never Alone

If you want to become a whole and trusted leader, you won't get there alone. The most grounded and resilient leaders I know have one thing in common—they are deeply supported. But that support doesn't happen by accident. It begins with clarity.

Start by identifying your purpose and the calling on your life in this particular season. What's the work you've been given to do? Where are you being invited to grow? Whether you're a young leader stepping into the unknown or a seasoned leader navigating complexity, knowing what you're after makes all the difference. Because once you have clarity on your purpose, you can start to build the support around you that aligns with it.

And remember: this isn't about collecting contacts—it's about creating relationships that sustain, stretch, and sharpen you.

- Begin by identifying your purpose and the calling on your life this year or in this season. Whether you are young or older, an emerging or existing leader, knowing what you are looking for is key.
- Understand the different roles people will play. Your network will look unique compared to those of others.
- Change your mindset from what you will get to looking for mutually beneficial relationships while remaining open to the possibility that some people just want to help you.
- Take a risk to live in a healthy relationship with others. Maintaining your sense of yourself with an openness to edit is important. Be bold about what you're looking for and give people an out if they feel like they can't help you right now.
- Remember that building a strategic network is a process and system of relationships, not a destination. Get started building your strategic network and then keep maintaining it. Like most things in life that are important, it's about finding rhythms in relationships and purpose.

The truth is, we were never meant to do this on our own. Building a strategic network—one grounded in purpose and trust—isn't about proving your worth or climbing a ladder. It's about surrounding yourself with people who will challenge you when you need it, hold you up when you're tired, and remind you of who you are when you forget.

This isn't a weakness. It's wisdom.

You don't need to have it all figured out to start. Just take the next right step—reach out, ask a question, offer value, receive wisdom. And as you do, you'll find that you're not just building a network. You're building a foundation for whole leadership—one relationship at a time.

For a Conversation

1. What is the purpose of you being surrounded in this season? Consider what you are trying to do this year or how you are trying to develop as a person or a leader.
2. Given your understanding of a strategic network as an "intentional and documented network of people who will play a diverse set of specific roles in your life, and who exist in your support network for a specific purpose in this season of your learning and growth as a leader, or as a person," how would you rate your strategic network on a scale from 1 to 10 (1 = my network needs a lot of work, 10 = I could not feel more strategically surrounded right now).
3. Take a moment to identify one mentor, one role model, one person who gives you honest feedback, and another who provides you with emotional support or is your greatest advocate.
4. What would it be like to have a conversation with each of these people letting them know that you consider them a part of your strategic network, and that you are grateful for them?

The Strategic Support Assessment

If you are using the Wild Toolkit alongside this book, the Strategic Support Assessment is designed to help you build an intentional network of support that exists around you for a purpose—a network of specific relationships in definable categories of your life and work. The process is simple. Create an account at www.wildtoolkit.com to access the Strategic Support Assessment or all of the robust whole leader assessments together.

CHAPTER 16

Intentional

Lead a Whole and Intentional Life

A whole and trusted leader never stops learning.

One of the most powerful ways we build trust—in ourselves and in the eyes of others—is by committing to our own development. People trust leaders who are actively learning, not just because they're gaining new skills, but because they're showing up with curiosity, humility, and a willingness to grow. When others see that we are taking our development seriously, it signals integrity and responsibility. And when we see that in ourselves, it deepens our confidence that we can rise to meet the moments ahead. A whole and trusted leader isn't just reacting to life—they're choosing to live and lead with intention. That kind of trust doesn't just happen. It's cultivated over time, and it starts with a plan.

What would change if you had an actionable plan for what you will do and how you will do it—one based on what you've already learned and what you're learning now—and that plan genuinely excited you? It's one thing to get things done. It's another to get them done well and on purpose. Imagine what it would be like if everyone around you had a development plan for the year—not a to-do list, but a living blueprint for how they'll learn and grow while doing the work. Unfortunately, many people move through their days without a plan for their learning, even though their development plays an immeasurable role in how they show up for the challenges ahead.

The truth is, many of us have never imagined having a documented plan for our development. We often move through our experiences without extracting the insights that could help us be more intentional in the future. A development plan that matters is a reflection on who you are, where you're headed, who you hope to become, and the key variables that will determine whether you move forward with awareness or stay stuck in old patterns. A good plan is informed by others but ultimately shaped by you—because it belongs to you. Whether you're part of a company, a school, or a church, the best systems provide a framework for asking deeper questions, while leaving room for your story to shape the answers.

It's been a powerful process for me personally and professionally. I'll never forget the year I chose "conviction" as my developmental theme. I was passionate about developing leaders and knew that my conviction often helped others move forward. But a few months in, I received some tough feedback. Several clients found my presence intimidating and were unsure if they wanted to bring me back. I was stunned—until I realized they were feeling the intensity of my conviction without enough care to balance it. The next year, I added "care" to my theme. I still wanted to speak the truth boldly, but I also wanted people to feel supported. That next year was a game changer.

There's too much at stake for us to move through life without intention—especially when it comes to our growth and the growth of others. An intentional learning plan isn't just about personal goals; it's about impact. It's about how we show up for others and how we help others show up for themselves. Even in my own journey, I've seen the power of planning as I've worked through my calling and purpose, explored my personality and readiness, and considered the people I'm investing in. I'm not naturally drawn to structure when it comes to my own development, but I've seen what happens when I use a system that breathes—one that creates space for growth without locking it into a rigid mold. That structure has impacted my relationships, my leadership, and my movement toward wholeness.

I had a conversation with my nephew that reminded me of how intention drives curiosity and trust. Every year, he would take a solo trip somewhere new. That year, it was the Shakespeare Festival in Ashland,

Oregon. When he mentioned the trip, it sparked dozens of questions from our family—not because we doubted him, but because his plan clearly had purpose. Why Shakespeare? Why go alone? What does this trip represent for him? He's introverted, works in tech by day, and acts in theater by night—his dream role is Macbeth. He explained that these trips are about stretching his introverted tendencies, connecting with strangers, and embracing the aliveness he feels in theater.

What struck me most was how open his plan was. He had clear intentions but also held space for what the trip might become. He was pushing himself, but not forcing a fixed outcome. That's what a whole and intentional plan looks like—clarity with room to grow. It includes both what we aim to do and the openness to what we might discover. A plan like that matters. It goes deeper than where we'll sleep or when we'll leave. It considers who we are, what motivates us, the kind of experience we want to have, who we'll serve, and how we'll grow. And ideally, it's not just about us. It's about how our intentional growth will help us lead, love, and serve better.

Knowing, Practicing, and Identity

Our journey of learning and leadership is filled with paradoxes. Growth requires both structure and spontaneity. It demands that we take action while remaining open to correction and change. When we begin to live with more intention—while still allowing space for surprises—transformation happens, not just for us but for everyone within our influence. It starts with knowing—gaining insight into who we are and what we're called to. Then we practice—trying new behaviors, learning from mistakes, and applying what we've learned in real relationships. And over time, what we know and practice becomes a part of who we are. It gets woven into our identity and becomes how others experience us. The shift isn't just behavioral—it's relational. You begin to see that your development is not just about you. It's about becoming someone others can trust.

Making a Plan

Making a plan is about getting ready. Readiness starts with awareness—of where you are now, the lessons you've learned, and what you haven't yet been intentional about. It involves reflection, experimentation, and new beliefs about yourself and others. If you're just beginning this journey, whether as a student, manager, parent, or CEO, you've likely already noticed areas that need intention. The second time through, things begin to shift. You try new behaviors and see the difference intention makes. And eventually, what began as awareness becomes a more rooted identity. You're never done. New challenges will arise. But you'll have a foundation to stand on—a mission that affirms and stretches you, both for your sake and for the sake of others.

As you begin to build your plan, the goal isn't to tie everything up neatly. It's to pause, reflect, and take action that feels both purposeful and energizing. The questions listed in Table 16.1 are designed to spark that action. Take a moment to quickly answer each of the questions and tell your whole story. Don't overthink your answers. Respond with honesty and courage. And notice which questions matter most right now—they'll change over time.

Table 16.1 Your Whole and Intentional Plan

Question	Your Whole Story
Where are you leading right now?	
In what ways are you feeling ready for what's next in your life or work?	
What do you feel like you are being called to do next?	
Where in your life and work are you making meaningful progress?	
In what ways are you becoming more composed under pressure?	
What experiences are important for you to have next?	
What is the unique contribution and competencies you bring to any team or group?	
What motivates you to get things done or to learn new things that others should know about you?	
What kind of support do you need in this season of your life and work?	
In what ways are you going to invest in the team or people who surround you in the coming year?	
Based on your responses, what is your developmental theme for this coming year?	
What are three things you'd like to commit to doing based on that theme?	

The key to a meaningful development plan is paying attention. A plan doesn't need to be complicated, but it does need to be intentional—anchored in your past, grounded in your present, and aimed at your future. Here are five litmus tests to ensure your plan matters:

- Did it come from you, and does it energize you?
- Does it include both your strengths and areas for development?
- Will you talk about it with someone you trust?
- Does it reflect changes in how you think and how you act?
- Will it help both you and others at the same time?

Thoughtful Action: Your Plan for the Future

Your whole story is just that—whole. Not perfect, but integrated. And being a whole and trusted leader means intentionally learning from all that has shaped you. The brokenness we carry doesn't disappear, but when we face it with intention, it becomes the raw material for transformation. That's what allows us to lead with wisdom and build trust in others. The tensions we experience become gifts—pathways to growth and deeper connection. I've seen systems that breathe—rooted in trust and intention—change lives. That's why I believe so deeply in this. And why I believe in you.

For a Conversation

1. What are three things you are aware of today that you weren't aware of about yourself a year ago?
2. What is your developmental theme for the coming year, and how will you act on it?
3. What would change for others if they had the opportunity to develop their own whole and intentional plan?

The WiLD Plan

If you're using the WiLD Toolkit alongside this book, the WiLD Plan will provide you with a moment to pause to get intentional as you move into the next year of your development. The process is simple. Create an account at www.wildtoolkit.com to access the WiLD Plan or all of the robust whole leader assessments together.

PART III

Creating a Whole and Trusted Team

Trust begins within us at the personal level as we more deeply understand ourselves. When we start to work with others and our understanding of ourselves and our ability to get things done bumps into that same reality in others, that is where trust impacts our experience every day. Whether on a team or in other relationships in our lives, when our reality comes face-to-face with the reality of others and we start to do life and work together, trust moves from something we are preparing for to something that we must experience together if anything positive is going to occur. In *The Five Dysfunctions of a Team*, Patrick Lencioni wrote, "Trust is the foundation of real teamwork. And so the first dysfunction that must be addressed is the absence of it" (Lencioni 2002, 43). That foundation is not built by accident. It requires clarity, humility, and the courage to work through what's hard instead of avoiding it.

If people were perfect and never let one another down, we wouldn't understand our need for trust. But, we are not perfect. None of us are. Facing that reality is the foundation upon which trust must begin to be built because it is the whole story. Trust is necessary for us to not only accomplish things together, but for us to feel healthy and whole. This is where the rubber meets the road when it comes to trust. At the level of relationships and teams is where trust is enacted. As Lencioni continues, "Teamwork begins by building trust. And the only way to do that is to overcome our need for invulnerability"

(Lencioni 2002, 58). Within teams, those we are in the foxholes of life and leadership with every day, trust creates the capacity, to perform together in service of a larger purpose, and it creates the healthy connective threads between us that cause us to experience deep gratitude, progress, and even the deepest joy in our work. In the words of Harvard researcher Amy Edmondson, "Team psychological safety is defined as a shared belief that the team is safe for interpersonal risk taking (Edmondson 2019, 45)," and this is precisely the soil in which team trust grows. The drivers of team trust are more than aspirations of hope. At the team level, trust has teeth because the drivers and foundations upon which trust is built include both perceptions about each other, and behaviors that make it possible.

In Part III, Chapters 17 through 19 explore the foundations of team trust—truthfulness and transparency, consistent and courageous execution, and the clarity that enables us to move forward together without confusion.

CHAPTER 17

Truthfulness and Transparency

The Courage to be Candid

Team trust lives and dies by truth.

If you've ever been part of a team where trust was high, you probably knew it because you could say things others might avoid. You could be honest about your challenges. You knew the person you reported to had your back. You could be open with teammates about your limitations, and they could be open with you. You weren't guessing at who people really were—you *knew* them, and they knew you. That kind of clarity and confidence doesn't happen by accident. It happens in environments where truth and transparency are expected, practiced, and safe. If you're not sure you could say the same about your current team—or if you're even slightly hesitant—it's worth taking a closer look because working on a whole and trusted team changes everything.

- Whole and trusted teams have team members who trust their manager.
- Whole and trusted teams have team members who are open with each other about their strengths, their limitations, and their weaknesses.
- Whole and trusted teams have team members who know each other.

Trust at the team level is built on the willingness to say what's necessary—and to hear what's necessary. When team members tell the truth and show who they really are, even the hard parts, trust increases. When they don't, it erodes. It's as simple and as difficult as that.

When you think about the relationships in your life that you trust the most, how would you describe them? For most of us, those relationships are defined by truthfulness and transparency. They are the relationships where we feel seen and where we see others. These are not shallow, surface-level dynamics. They're courageous, real, sometimes messy, and always marked by people who are willing to speak honestly even when it's hard. That's not just emotional—it's emotional maturity. Building that kind of trust takes guts. It requires the courage to speak what we believe is true while being open to being corrected if we're wrong. It's about being honest, but also humble. And on teams, that blend of candor and care is essential.

Telling the Truth

Truthfulness is the backbone of team trust. But there's a catch. Telling the truth in teams is a risk. Sometimes we hold back because we're afraid of how the truth will land. We're afraid it might hurt someone, or hurt us. We fear rejection, retaliation, or just the awkwardness of conflict. So, we avoid it. We also avoid truth-telling in subtle ways. We triangulate—talking to others about a team member instead of to them. We soften our words or remain silent when clarity is needed. We avoid naming the thing that everyone is feeling but no one wants to say out loud. These aren't just communication breakdowns. They are trust breakdowns. "We are not at peace with others because we are not at peace with ourselves. . . And we will never be at peace with ourselves if we are not truthful about ourselves" (Merton 1961, 181).

Teams that thrive in trust aren't fearless—they're just practiced. They've built a muscle for saying hard things in healthy ways. They don't make assumptions without checking them. They ask honest questions. They tell the truth, and they make space for others to do the same.

So why don't more teams tell the truth?

- **Truth can be rejected.** It's painful when we offer feedback and it's dismissed or shut down. Over time, that discourages us from speaking up again.
- **Truth requires vulnerability.** It means risking the relationship, even temporarily. Not everyone is ready for that.
- **Truth exposes imperfection.** Some teams live under the illusion that strong equals flawless. But teams with the highest trust have learned to say, "Here's where I need help," and "Here's where we need to grow."

Here's a truth worth telling: High-performing, trusted teams don't just succeed because they're smart. They succeed because they're honest. In fact, as Ron Carucci reminds us in *To Be Honest*, reinforceable honesty is a learned skill—not just a trait: "Honesty is not a character trait. It is a muscle, a capability. It's something you have to be good at, and if you want to be good at it, you have to work at it every day" (Carucci 2021, 68).

Being truthful isn't limited to offering feedback or naming team dynamics. It's also about being honest regarding our own competence and skill gaps, the clarity (or lack thereof) we have about our purpose, our need for support, and how we're actually showing up under pressure. Some of the most transformational team moments happen when someone has the courage to say, "I don't know how to do this yet," or "I'm overwhelmed and could use some help," or "I'm not sure if I'm living out the purpose that drives me." Telling the truth in these moments isn't weakness, it's wisdom. It invites collaboration, clarity, and deeper connection. As Adam Grant reminds us, "If knowledge is power, knowing what we don't know is wisdom" (Grant 2021a, 25). Naming our gaps, asking for help, and acknowledging uncertainty are acts of leadership, not liabilities. And on trusted teams, those moments of humility often unlock our greatest strength.

A Manager I See and Who Sees Me

Think about the best manager you've ever had. Chances are, they didn't just tell you what to do—they saw you. They gave you feedback that mattered. They called out your strengths. They helped you grow. They weren't perfect, but they were present—and they were honest. Now think about a manager who never quite invested in you. Maybe they were too busy, distracted, or unsure how to help. Maybe they avoided hard conversations or only checked in when something went wrong. At first, that might feel tolerable. But over time, it creates distance. And that distance becomes distrust.

We trust managers who take the time to know us and give us insight into how we're showing up. Especially when that insight is both caring and challenging. A manager who only praises without correction may seem kind, but ultimately isn't helping us grow. And a manager who only critiques without encouragement may be telling a version of the truth but won't be trusted. We need both.

And when we experience that kind of investment from a leader—someone who knows us, speaks the truth, and sticks with us—trust doesn't just grow. It spreads.

Transparency: The Courage to Be Seen

If truth is what we say, transparency is what we show. It's not just about being honest—it's about being known.

A transparent team is one where people don't hide. They're not performing or posturing. They're not spinning the truth to look good. They're real. That doesn't mean they say everything that comes to mind. It means they're willing to be seen as they are—including their strengths and their stretch points. Transparency doesn't mean oversharing. It doesn't mean leaking emotion or saying, "Well, that's just how I am." It means showing up with the kind of openness that invites others to do the same. It means bringing your full self to the table, not just your curated self.

Being transparent includes letting others know what drives you—your deeper purpose—and where you're unsure about that purpose. It means being open about your blind spots and triggers, your motivations and insecurities, and what kind of support you actually need in this season. That level of transparency unlocks something powerful in teams. When we show up whole, we give others permission to do the same.

A team with real transparency:

- Talks about what's working and what isn't.
- Names tensions instead of pretending they're not there.
- Gives permission to say, "I don't know," or "I need help."
- Invites challenge, even from newer or quieter voices.

Transparency builds safety, but not the false kind where no one is allowed to disagree. It's the kind of safety where disagreement is welcomed because people trust each other enough to say what's real.

Strategies for Building Truth and Transparency in Teams

If you want to build truth and transparency on your team, start with these practical moves:

- **Go first.** Leaders and team members alike need to model what openness looks like. Be the first to admit a mistake. The first to name an issue. The first to ask a hard question with kindness.
- **Establish rules of engagement for honesty.** Create a shared understanding that truth-telling is expected and valued. This includes truth about performance, about culture, and about relationships.
- **Avoid triangles.** When you're tempted to vent or avoid, pause and ask, "Have I taken this directly to the person first?" If not, don't skip that step.
- **Use structured feedback tools.** Tools like the WiLD Toolkit or a regular team check-in process can create predictable, safe rhythms for surfacing truth and inviting transparency.
- **Give permission to challenge and receive it well.** Team trust grows when challenges aren't punished but appreciated. Receiving feedback without defensiveness sets the tone for everyone else.
- **Celebrate moments of truth.** When someone says something courageous, acknowledge it. "That took guts—thank you for saying it." That simple affirmation can reinforce a culture of trust.

If we want to build trust at the team level, we have to stop hiding. We have to say what's true and show who we are. Telling the truth, especially in love, is never easy—but it's always worth it. And transparency, when done with wisdom, invites others to meet us in the middle. Trust is the reward of that risk, and the beginning of something stronger.

For a Conversation

Use these questions to spark a deeper conversation about truth and transparency on your team:

1. What's one truth that's hard to tell in our team, and why?
2. When do you feel most seen and known by your teammates? When do you feel least seen?
3. What could we do as a team to increase both our truthfulness and our transparency in the next 30 days?

CHAPTER 18

Productivity, Consistency, and Conflict

Forward Progress, Faithful Practice, and Fighting Well

Teams with high levels of trust do what is necessary, even when it's hard.

If you've ever been part of a team that gets things done on time, with integrity, and under pressure, you know how powerful that experience can be. You also know it's rare. We feel it when our teammates consistently follow through. We notice when they have the skills to contribute meaningfully. We lean in when the people around us show up again and again, ready to do their part. That kind of team culture doesn't happen by accident. It grows from three powerful ingredients: competence, consistency, and a commitment to fighting well.

- ◆ Whole and trusted teams do the things that need to be done so that others can be effective in their jobs.
- ◆ Whole and trusted teams have team members who have the skills and knowledge to be effective in their jobs.
- ◆ Whole and trusted teams have team members who are timely and consistent at getting things done.

- ◆ Whole and trusted teams have team members who are effective at doing the job they are assigned to do.
- ◆ Whole and trusted teams are effective at handling conflict.

We trust people who do what they say they'll do. We trust teammates who know what they're doing and know when to ask for help. And we especially trust the ones who show up the same way on Monday morning as they do Thursday afternoon—steady, composed, and present. But trust isn't just about capability. It's also about courage, especially the courage to lean into hard conversations and healthy conflict. Because without conflict, trust stalls. Teams that avoid conflict may feel peaceful, but that false peace comes at a cost. When we fail to disagree well, we fail to innovate, to learn, and to grow.

Consistency

Consistency is the quiet force behind trust. It's not flashy. It doesn't seek recognition. But it builds a track record that people come to rely on. Consistency means following through on commitments. It means showing up with your full self—not once, not sometimes, but over time.

On high-trust teams, consistency shows up in the small things: starting meetings on time, delivering on deadlines, communicating when something changes. These are the behaviors that build the foundation of reliability. When consistency is missing, trust begins to erode. A team member who says the right things but fails to follow through sends a mixed message. We start to wonder, *Can I count on them when it matters most?* Trust breaks not because people are bad, but because their behavior becomes unpredictable.

> "Faithless is he that says farewell when the road darkens." (Tolkien 1954)

High-trust teams know that consistency doesn't mean perfection. It means presence. It means being aware of how your actions affect the people around you and committing to reliability as a form of respect.

Competence

Competence is more than technical skill. It's the ability to contribute in a way that makes others better. Competent team members bring their knowledge, but also their willingness to learn. They stay sharp. They adapt. And they take ownership when something is outside their expertise.

> "The fundamental task of management is to make people capable of joint performance, to make their strengths effective and their weaknesses irrelevant." (Drucker 1954)

On trustworthy teams, competence is acknowledged and encouraged—but it's never weaponized. When we compete instead of collaborate, we build silos. But when we share our knowledge, coach others, and admit where we still need to grow, trust grows with us. Being truthful about our competence is one of the greatest trust-builders available to us. It's saying, "I've got this part," and "I could use help here." It's refusing to fake it, and instead committing to learning it. High-trust teams are full of people who take responsibility for sharpening their skills and recognize when another team member may be more equipped for a particular challenge.

Conflict

High-trust teams don't avoid conflict. They fight well. Too often, we assume conflict is the problem. But on the highest performing teams, conflict is necessary. It's how ideas evolve. It's how clarity emerges. It's how trust is tested and strengthened. The issue isn't conflict, it's how we do it. On unhealthy teams, conflict is hidden or hostile. On healthy teams, it's honest and human. Conflict becomes a place where people show up with care *and* conviction.

> "For good ideas and true innovation, you need human interaction, conflict, argument, debate." (Heffernan 2011)

When we avoid conflict, trust breaks down. We peacemonger instead of progressing. We protect feelings at the expense of learning. We talk around issues rather than through them. And eventually, the avoidance creates more harm than any single disagreement ever could. On high-trust teams, conflict is embraced as part of the culture. It's not personal, it's purposeful. Team members disagree when it's important to do so, and they do it with respect. They bring their convictions to the table while holding space to be challenged and changed.

FIGHTING WELL

What does it mean to fight well?

- It means disagreeing respectfully, but not too cautiously.
- It means putting real issues on the table with care.
- It means not talking behind each other's backs, unless it's to better understand someone's perspective.
- It means being led by a differentiated leader who values truth over harmony.

Fighting well is not a sign of dysfunction; it's a marker of maturity. When a team fights well, trust deepens, and communication sharpens. The culture becomes one of learning, not avoiding. One executive we worked with told us, "We don't fight well—and we don't fight at all. And that's very dangerous. Trust is low, and progress has slowed to a halt." Fighting well is not about aggression, it's about alignment. When we stop fighting altogether or when we fight poorly, we stop growing, we stagnate, and the cracks in our trust begin to show.

HOW TO BUILD A TEAM THAT FIGHTS WELL

Here are a few ways teams can develop the capacity to handle conflict with trust and truth:

- **Allow Collisions:** Honesty sometimes means friction. Don't fear it—facilitate it. The best answers emerge when everyone's perspective gets airtime.
- **Model for Error:** Like statisticians build margin for error, leaders should leave space for the possibility that they might be wrong. Come with evidence-based convictions, but hold 25% of your mind open to another angle.

- **Hire Editable Individuals:** Look for people who are sharp but also willing to learn. People who know that others matter as much or more than they do. Curiosity and humility beat raw brilliance over time.
- **Deal with the Problem People:** Avoidance kills trust. Leaders who don't address consistent behavior problems, especially when those behaviors hurt the team, create doubt and confusion. Kindness without clarity is not kindness.
- **Put Systems in Place for Seeing Each Other:** As Henry Cloud says, "Trust begins not with convincing someone to trust you; it starts with someone feeling that you know them" (Cloud 2023). Use tools, practices, and check-ins that foster real connection.
- **Turn the Lights On:** Don't let your team operate in the dark. Shine light on what's happening. Make it normal to name the tension. Culture drifts toward secrecy unless we intentionally choose clarity.
- **Look for Third Options:** Healthy conflict isn't binary. When a team is locked into one of two sides, creativity dies. Step to the left or right. Look again, and often there's a better way just out of sight.

Disagreement is a necessary part of progress. If we don't disagree face-to-face, we'll disagree in silence through gossip, blame, or passive resistance. High-trust teams know that conflict isn't a detour. It's part of the path. Show me a team that trusts deeply, and I'll show you a team that fights well.

For a Conversation

Use these questions to spark a deeper conversation about competence, consistency, and conflict on your team:

1. Where do we need to be more consistent, and how would that impact our trust?
2. What would it look like for each of us to be more truthful about what we do well and where we need help?
3. How do we currently handle conflict as a team? What would it look like to "fight well" instead?

CHAPTER 19

Clarity and Planning

Plans Don't Kill Trust, Confusion Does

> *Trust doesn't grow in confusion. It grows when people know what they're doing, why it matters, and how they're getting better at it.*

High-trust teams don't just happen; they're built on purpose. If you've ever been part of a team where trust was strong, where roles were clear, and where growth was expected, you've likely experienced the impact of clarity and intentionality. You knew what was expected of you. You knew where you were going. And, just as importantly, you knew how you were going to grow along the way.

Two powerful signals of trust at the team level are present when every team member has (1) a clear and current job description, and (2) a development plan that strengthens both performance and personal well-being. When these systems are missing, teams drift. When they're present, trust takes root.

The Power of Job Clarity

Think about anything in your life that works well—a relationship, a process, a routine. Behind almost all of it is a system and a layer of clarity. While there's always space for beautiful surprises and the unexpected gifts of collaboration, most things that function well don't do so by accident. Teams are no different. Too often we treat team trust as a hopeful outcome, or we invest in one-off activities like an inspiring offsite or a book club on leadership trends. While those can be valuable, they rarely change the day-to-day dynamics of trust. Real transformation requires structure.

That structure starts with clarity—specifically, clarity about what each person is expected to do. A clear job description isn't the one from your onboarding packet that hasn't been touched in years. It's a current, dynamic articulation of what success looks like in your role today. It helps define responsibilities, identify gaps, and set priorities. It offers a shared understanding of who's doing what and why. And in a team environment, that clarity is essential. Without it, team members are forced to guess, and guessing erodes trust. Why is this so critical? Because it's difficult to trust what you don't understand. If your job or your colleague's job is unclear, how can either of you truly know how to contribute? How can you hold each other accountable? How can you collaborate with confidence? Clarity isn't just a leadership best practice; it's a trust builder.

Job clarity also invites alignment. When roles are well defined and up to date, it becomes easier to see where responsibilities overlap, where they don't, and where collaboration should happen. It creates more room for others to understand the value of your contributions. When everyone has a clear job, the work becomes visible, and so does the person doing the work.

Building Development Systems That Matter

The same is true for development plans. Not the kind that gets filled out and filed away, but a real, living plan that reflects where someone is trying to grow personally and professionally—a plan that's as much about purpose and motivation as it is about skills and outcomes. When done right, development plans become conversation starters. They help teammates see each other more clearly. They create room for feedback, curiosity, and connection. They help leaders coach with intention. And they create a cadence of growth that supports not just performance, but wholeness.

Real development plans energize. They remind us that we're becoming. They give us permission to not be fully there yet because we've named where we're going. And when these plans are shared with teammates, they become catalysts for deeper understanding. We stop assuming and start asking. We begin to know not just what someone does, but why they do it, where they're headed, and how we can help. High-trust teams normalize development. They don't treat it like a side project, and they integrate it into the rhythm of work. That might mean regular one-on-one check-ins, quarterly reviews, or team conversations about growth areas. Whatever the format, the goal is to make learning and feedback a consistent part of the culture.

Development systems also give leaders a practical tool for building trust through care. When a leader asks, "How can I support your growth this quarter?" or "What would help you stretch into your next level of leadership?" that's more than a performance question—it's a trust question. It signals, "I see you," and "You matter."

From Confusion to Clarity

Teams that consistently use clear job descriptions and personal development plans experience a ripple effect. Expectations are aligned, communication improves, and motivation rises. And, perhaps most importantly, trust begins to take root in real and measurable ways.

One of the biggest obstacles to trust in teams isn't conflict, it's confusion. And confusion is a systems problem. When we build systems that clarify what matters and how we grow, we move from reacting to our environment to shaping it. That's what whole leaders do. They don't just work hard; they build ecosystems of trust. And here's the key: these systems don't need to be complex. A job description should be simple and specific. A development plan can fit on one page. What matters is that they're real, current, and used. When they are, they become the scaffolding for team trust.

Practical Steps for Teams

So how do we bring this into our daily work?

- ◆ Start by reviewing every team member's job description. Is it current? Does it accurately reflect the role today?
- ◆ Encourage each person to draft or update a development plan that includes goals for both their performance and well-being.

- Build review rhythms into your calendar—quarterly or biannually—to keep both job roles and development plans alive and aligned.
- Make these systems visible and relational. Share job descriptions within the team. Use development plans to guide coaching conversations.
- Model transparency. Leaders should share their own development plans too. Trust grows when vulnerability is modeled from the top.

Let's stop guessing. Let's stop treating trust in our team members as something we hope for and start treating it as something we build—with intention, with clarity, and with systems that support people as they are and as they're becoming. I'm not talking about systems that treat people like robots, but systems that breathe. Let's build systems that are energizing for all of us and create the necessary scaffolding and structure for great conversations that build whole and sustaining trust between us.

For a Conversation

Use these questions to spark a deeper conversation about clarity and systems on your team:

1. How clear is each person's job on our team, and where do we need more alignment?
2. What would it look like if everyone had a living, meaningful development plan?
3. How can we build clarity and learning into the rhythms of our team—not just once, but regularly?

PART IV

Building a Whole and Trusted Organization

Imagine working in an organization where your job is clear and you have a direct line of sight between what you are doing in your small piece of that organization and the final product or service you provide. You see that connection. You see where your results are meaningful because even if you don't have daily interaction with your frontline customers or the people you serve, you can see the linkage between what you produce, and the increased level of flourishing experienced by those customers.

Imagine that you have a respect for your manager, and you work with a manager or senior leader who sees you while working at maintaining appropriate boundaries. Imagine an organization where toxicity and blame are not tolerated, and performance and care for people are rewarded. Imagine an organization that is intentional about connecting the systems, the performance, the production, the operations—everything—to the heart of the people who walk its halls or fill its virtual offices every day.

This is the heart and soul of a whole and trusted organization.

In Part IV, Chapters 20 through 23 explore what it means to build and sustain that kind of organization—from the maturity of its leaders, to the culture that holds its people, to the integration of engagement, performance, and trust at every level.

CHAPTER 20

Leadership Maturity
Convicted and Caring

We don't trust leaders because they're perfect—we trust them because they're learning, they're real, and they've done their own work.

We often associate leadership trust with decisiveness, charisma, or even vision—but at the core, trust in leadership is about something deeper. It's about emotional maturity. When leaders lead from a place of wholeness, not only does their competence become clearer, but so does their character. They become people we trust—not just because they get things done, but because they're grounded, self-aware, and invested in our growth too.

Trusting leadership is felt across an entire organization. You feel it when the leaders are honest and caring, when they make hard decisions with transparency, when they lead with conviction and character, and when they invite others to grow by modeling their own growth.

- The leaders we trust are invested in the learning and growth of the people they lead.
- The leaders we trust are both honest and caring.
- The leaders we trust practice an appropriate level of vulnerability.

Emotional Maturity: Honest and Caring Leadership

We've all experienced leaders who lacked emotional maturity. Leaders who were reactive, who claimed to be open to change but gave little evidence of it. Some were overly direct, blind to the needs of their people. Others were so afraid of discomfort they tiptoed around issues that desperately needed addressing. Emotional immaturity comes in many forms—control masked as decisiveness, avoidance disguised as empathy, or ego cloaked in expertise. But we've also experienced the opposite. The leaders who changed us. The ones who had the guts to tell the truth—even when it was hard—and the heart to deliver that truth with compassion. These leaders didn't always get everything right, but we trusted them. Not because they were perfect, but because they were present. They were anchored. And they led with a blend of courage and care that made others want to follow.

Emotionally mature leaders embody honesty and empathy. They don't weaponize the truth, but they don't avoid it either. They don't pander to emotions, but they understand them. They are discerning and self-aware. They have developed the internal capacity to both name reality and stay connected. And that combination—truth with relationship—is what makes people trust them. In emotionally mature leadership, consistency and character matter as much as capability. Leaders who demonstrate emotional maturity don't just act out of impulse or comfort. They lead from conviction, while making space for others to be human. That doesn't mean they overshare or dissolve into emotion at every turn, but it does mean they're willing to be seen, and it means that they've developed a deep understanding of the impact they have on others.

Leaders Who Develop Leaders

One of the strongest indicators of leadership maturity is a leader's investment in others. Not just managing performance, but developing people. And not just saying that development matters, but actively making it happen.

Unfortunately, in many organizations, leadership development becomes something delegated—an initiative sponsored but not embodied by those at the top. We hear talk of "senior leader buy-in" as if agreement is enough. But buy-in is a starting point, not a finish line. What teams need is not just permission, but participation. We need leaders who are visibly and actively involved in the development of their people.

Trust grows when people believe their leaders are genuinely invested in them. That investment shows up in practical ways—through coaching, feedback, sponsorship, and intentional development planning. But it also shows up in how leaders talk to their teams, how they hold space for growth, and how they create a culture where learning is seen as strength, not weakness. Developing others doesn't require a formal mentorship program or a perfect curriculum. It requires attention. It requires presence. It requires the willingness to say, "I see who you are, and I want to help you become who you're meant to be."

And when leaders build systems to support that kind of growth—platforms, check-ins, development plans—they not only show commitment to learning, but they also make it scalable. They create frameworks where growth is normalized, supported, and expected.

Leaders Who Develop Themselves

The most compelling leaders are not just those who develop others. They are those who are still developing themselves. And nothing undercuts trust faster than a leader who acts like they've arrived. Leaders who are uneditable, who resist feedback, or who see themselves as exempt from learning create cultures of fear and stagnation. But leaders who model growth—who openly share what they're learning, where they're stretching, and what's still unclear—build trust through humility.

When a leader stands in front of their organization and says, "Here's what I'm learning about my own competence and purpose," it does more than inspire. It invites others to do the same. It creates space for others to be honest about their own growth edges. It models that learning doesn't stop with a title or a corner office. It sends a signal. Growth is not just for emerging leaders—it's for all of us.

Vulnerability That Builds Trust

Of course, modeling growth requires vulnerability. But not all vulnerability is created equal. Healthy, trust-building vulnerability is discerning.

It doesn't mean spilling everything. It doesn't mean blurring boundaries or seeking validation from your team. It means telling the truth about what matters, in a way that serves others.

Discerning vulnerability shows up in moments like these:

- A leader owning a misstep and sharing what they've learned.
- A leader acknowledging fear or uncertainty in the face of a big decision.
- A leader sharing a personal story that connects to a bigger lesson.
- A leader inviting feedback—and responding with grace, not defensiveness.

This kind of vulnerability communicates both strength and humanity. It says, "I'm leading, but I'm still learning." And that posture is magnetic because people don't need perfect leaders, they need present, grounded, and real ones. Discerning vulnerability is also what separates emotional maturity from emotional exhibition. The former builds trust, the latter erodes it. Great leaders know the difference, and they develop the wisdom to show up in a way that's transparent and responsible.

A Culture of Trustworthy Leadership

Leadership maturity doesn't just impact individual relationships, it shapes culture. When leaders lead with integrity, consistency, vulnerability, and a commitment to development—both for themselves and others—they model what it means to be a whole leader.

And when those leaders populate the top levels of an organization, trust becomes a defining characteristic of the culture. It doesn't mean everyone always agrees. It doesn't mean the organization is free from conflict. But it does mean people feel safe to speak, to stretch, and to show up as themselves. This is what the best organizations are building—not just skillful leaders, but mature ones. Leaders who develop leaders. Leaders who develop themselves. Leaders who are honest and caring. Leaders who lead in a way that builds real trust.

For a Conversation

Use these questions to spark a deeper conversation about leadership maturity in your organization:

1. What qualities make a leader feel trustworthy to you?
2. Where do you see evidence of emotional maturity in your organization's leadership—and where is there room for growth?
3. How could your leaders more actively participate in their own development and the development of others?

CHAPTER 21

People and Culture

Where People Belong, They Build

> *You don't build a trustworthy culture by trying to make everyone belong—you build it by getting clear about who you are, what you stand for, and who's in for the ride.*

When people say they trust an organization, they're rarely talking about policies or benefits. They're talking about people. They're talking about culture. They're talking about what it feels like to be part of something that matters—and to belong there.

At the organizational level, trust is grounded in the belief that this is the kind of place where people grow, where the culture is strong, and where the right people stay. That trust is reflected in four essential realities:

- The people in the organization belong there.
- The organizational culture attracts great people.
- The right people stay in the organization.
- The culture is aligned through a trusted mission.

Not everyone belongs everywhere, but everyone belongs somewhere. A whole and trusted organization is one where people don't just work—they belong. And not because the organization tries to be all things to all people, or because it claims to be a place where everyone belongs, but because people *actually* belong. There's alignment—between strengths and roles, between mission and motivation, between identity and action. Trusted organizations help people find that place.

A Culture of Belonging

Belonging isn't entitlement—it's alignment. And it's not just the responsibility of the organization. Yes, it's on leaders to clarify the mission, to make the culture real, and to create systems that support growth. But it's also on each of us to see the connection between our role and the larger mission. That's what makes trust mutual. It's not something we're given—it's something we build. Think about a nurse in a hospital or a plumber working in your home. Their job is deeply connected to something essential. The hospital doesn't function without that nurse. Your house doesn't run without that plumber. And when that connection is clear—when purpose is visible—trust is natural. It's earned. It's shared.

The same applies in any organization. When we can clearly see how our role connects to the mission, when that mission is consistent and real, and when others around us are just as invested, trust becomes a cultural current. We feel it. We're drawn to it. We stay because we believe in it. But if the mission is vague—or constantly shifting—it's hard to align. And without alignment, belonging fades. That's why mission clarity isn't a PR statement, it's a trust driver.

To trust a mission, it needs three things: consistency, courage, and character.

CONSISTENCY

Peter Drucker once said, "To trust a leader, it is not necessary to like her. Nor is it necessary to agree with her. Trust is the conviction that a leader means what she says. It is a belief in integrity. A leader's actions and a leader's professed beliefs must be congruent" (Drucker 2008, 290). The same is true of organizations. We trust a mission not because it's trendy or clever, but because it endures. Consistency isn't the enemy of innovation. It's the foundation of it. Without consistent patterns and shared values, culture becomes noise.

Edgar Schein defined culture as "a pattern of shared basic assumptions that the group learned as it solved its problems of external adaptation and internal integration" (Schein 2010, 12). Those patterns, when validated, become the behaviors and beliefs we teach to new people. And when those patterns are aligned with the mission, we get a culture that works. Culture isn't just what's written on the wall—it's what's reinforced every day. It's the stories we tell, the behaviors we reward, the language we use. It's the iceberg beneath the surface. If the visible artifacts of the culture don't align with what's actually happening, trust erodes.

Consistency builds identity. It helps people know who we are and how we do things here. And in a fast-changing world, it's one of the few things people can hold onto. That's why trust in the mission is also trust in the memory of the organization. Our past matters, and great leaders don't dismiss history, they build on it.

COURAGE

A trustworthy mission also takes courage. It takes courage to say, "This is who we are," and to align systems, strategies, and staffing around that truth. It takes courage to edit outdated practices and to name when we've drifted from our core. And it takes courage to ask hard questions about what we're building, and who it's really for. Too often, culture becomes either a marketing slogan or a sacred cow—something we perform or protect, but never refine. Trustworthy organizations don't fall into either trap. They're brave enough to challenge what's not working, and wise enough to protect what still matters.

CHARACTER

At the end of the day, a mission worth trusting must reflect something real. That's where character comes in. Organizational character is the lived integrity of the institution—how its decisions align with its values, how its leaders embody its mission, and how its systems support its people. This character shows up in the hard moments—layoffs, crises, pivots. It's easy to claim a culture when things are going well, but real character is revealed in how an organization navigates what's difficult. Trusted organizations don't just talk about values; they act on them. And that alignment builds the kind of culture that people want to be part of.

Culture That Attracts

Great cultures attract great people. Not because of ping-pong tables or perks, but because of purpose. When a culture is clear, aligned, and lived, it becomes magnetic. People want to work there—not just because it's a job, but because it's a place where they can contribute, grow, and belong.

Imagine an organization where:

- The mission is clear and lived out daily.
- People are seen, supported, and developed from day one.
- Leaders don't just endorse development—they participate in it.
- The story of the organization is shared, not siloed.
- The values are more than words—they're behaviors.

That's the kind of culture that doesn't just attract great people—it keeps them.

Aligned Retention

Retention isn't just about keeping people; it's about keeping the right people. Trusted organizations don't aim to retain everyone. They aim to invest in, develop, and retain people who are aligned with the mission, the culture, and the team. We call this aligned retention. It's the belief that when culture and purpose are clear, the people who are meant to be here will stay, and they'll thrive. Others may move on, and that's okay. Alignment isn't about exclusion, it's about honesty.

When an organization prioritizes aligned retention, it doesn't chase engagement with gimmicks. It builds it through clarity, consistency, and care. People stay not because they're stuck, but because they're seen. Because they matter. Because they believe in what's being built, and in who they're building it with.

A Culture Worth Trusting

A culture worth trusting doesn't happen by accident. It's designed. It's lived. It's edited over time with honesty and courage.

When people in an organization

- know they belong,
- see that the right people are staying,
- are surrounded by consistent patterns and stories, and
- are invested in,

. . .trust becomes more than a feeling. It becomes a feature of the culture itself.

For a Conversation

Use these questions to spark a deeper conversation about people, culture, and trust in your organization:

1. Where do you see alignment—or misalignment—between your organization's mission and daily culture?
2. What consistent stories, patterns, or practices define your team's culture?
3. What would it look like to invest more intentionally in aligned retention—and how would that impact trust?

CHAPTER 22

Engagement and Performance
Visible Progress Builds Invisible Trust

> *When people know the score—and believe they can change it—engagement becomes fuel, and trust becomes unstoppable.*

What drives performance in a trusted organization? It's not just incentives or pressure. It's clarity, alignment, and a deep sense of shared belief in the mission. When people are engaged, they show up differently. And when engagement is connected to real performance—and measured in meaningful ways—trust deepens at every level.

We trust what we see. Imagine going to the ER with a severe headache. A scan is ordered, and you wait anxiously for results. But the doctors never follow up. They say, "We're not sure we can show you what we found, and we might never be able to." Would you return to that hospital? Would you trust their process? Or would your mind immediately begin to make up a story to fill in the gap?

It's the same in organizations. When we put in effort—when we try something hard—and never see a result, trust erodes. But when results are made visible, when effort leads to forward motion, even small steps build belief. And belief builds trust.

Trust, Measurement, and Results

Results are more than metrics—they are evidence. They tell us what's working and invite us to keep going. Even creating a clear plan can be a kind of result. It's progress. It says, "We're moving."

There's a dynamic relationship between results, belief, and trust. When we see a result, our confidence grows. And as our belief in ourselves or our team increases, so does our performance. It's a cycle worth feeding. At every level—individual, team, and organizational—measurable progress creates momentum. Personal wins become team wins. Team wins become business results. And business results, especially when aligned with mission, build lasting trust. But when we skip measurement—or hide it—we create space for doubt, speculation, and breakdown. Performance and engagement suffer, and trust unravels.

A Story About One Million Cards

Let me tell you about John. He worked for a company that sold high-end greeting cards—specifically, the "blank inside" variety. No pre-written messages, just quality paper, beautiful design, and room for a personal note. The cards were elegant, simple, and more expensive than most. But they sold, because they were excellent.

John ran quality control. His work directly impacted trust—among his team, among retailers, and with customers. For years, John delivered. He grew production without sacrificing quality. His confidence, and the trust in his leadership, was rooted in results.

Then a new manager arrived.

The new executive was focused on scale. His mandate? To quadruple the company's revenue in 12 months. The goal was aggressive, and the pressure was immediate. When John voiced concern about feasibility—"I can double production without compromising quality, but quadrupling it isn't realistic"—his manager's response was cold: "Get it done, John." That phrase echoed. And it wasn't just the goal that rattled John. His new manager was unavailable, disinterested in personal context (including John's wife's declining health), and offered no support.

Six months later, one million Valentine's Day cards were delivered to a major retailer. When the buyer opened the first box, every single card had these words printed on the inside:

"Blank Inside."

Not a blank space. Those exact words. A literal printing of the category label. The buyer resealed the box and sent it back. That mistake didn't start at the printer. It started the moment trust began to unravel—when communication broke down, when pressure replaced partnership, and when performance was demanded without alignment.

John had always trusted his team. They trusted him. But when his own sense of belief was shaken, everything shifted. He missed a detail he never would have missed. Because his trust in the system—and in himself—had been compromised.

What's the takeaway? Trust and results are not separate. They're symbiotic. And when trust is fractured, performance suffers.

Engagement Feeds Performance

Performance isn't just about effort. It's about alignment, support, and meaning. And that's where engagement comes in. If you've ever driven a stick shift, you know the moment when the clutch engages, and the engine's power finally hits the wheels. That's engagement. It's the moment when effort meets direction. And it's what drives everything forward.

But engagement doesn't happen by accident. It happens when:

- People are seen.
- Leaders care about more than output.
- Learning and development are embedded in the work.
- Performance is measured in ways that make sense.
- The mission is clear, and people believe in it.

When those things are in place, people engage. And when people are engaged, they perform. Not because they're forced to, but because they want to. They feel connected—to the work, to the team, and to the purpose. And when that happens, it shows up everywhere: in customer experience, in operational excellence, in innovation, and in margin. The integration of the visible (systems, strategies) and invisible (trust, belief) creates a flywheel that moves the entire organization forward.

Performance That Builds Trust

Trusted organizations:

- Align performance expectations with purpose.
- Create systems that show people where they're going—and how they're doing.
- Make results visible and meaningful.
- Celebrate progress.
- Invite feedback and adjust.

They also understand that accountability isn't the enemy of trust—it's the fuel. When people know what's expected, how they'll be measured, and why it matters, performance becomes shared. And shared performance builds shared trust.

Accountability is not pressure, it's clarity. Clarity of outcomes, clarity of roles, and clarity of feedback—all of it builds trust.

Six Strategies for Engagement and Aligned Performance

If trust is the foundation and performance is the outcome, then alignment is the bridge between them. The most effective organizations don't separate engagement from execution—they connect them through clarity, consistency, and care. Here are six practical strategies we've seen leaders use to create environments where people are not only showing up, but growing—and where results aren't just expected, they're energized by trust.

- **Connect Every Role to the Mission:** Make sure every team member understands how their work drives the broader purpose.
- **Make Results Visible:** Don't assume people know how they're doing. Show them. Celebrate wins, track progress, and course-correct in real time.
- **Establish Clear Performance Expectations:** Every role should have metrics or milestones that are understood, actionable, and aligned with success.
- **Invest in Development:** Learning drives performance. Equip people with what they need to grow and contribute meaningfully.

- **Practice Whole-Person Check-Ins:** Regularly talk with your team not just about output, but about experience, motivation, and well-being.
- **Measure and Revisit Often:** Build systems that allow for regular review of progress. Adapt when needed, and communicate changes clearly.

Moral of the Story

At the intersection of trust and performance is a deeper truth about how people and organizations grow. These aren't just lessons from leadership theory—they're patterns we've seen again and again in real teams doing real work. If you want to build something that lasts, these are the truths to remember and return to:

- Performance breeds belief. Belief fuels performance. It goes both ways.
- Every business result is the product of individual and team results. Trust grows when we see the link.
- When we deliver what we promise, we earn trust. Consistency and clarity create organizational traction.
- People need autonomy and clarity. They need to know the score—and how to influence it.
- Engagement and performance are not perks. They're strategic imperatives. They are the ground on which trust stands.

For a Conversation

1. Are you and your team members clear on the results you're expected to deliver every day?
2. Are those results aligned with your systems, processes, and strategy?
3. Do you have regular whole-person conversations about both performance and development?
4. Are you addressing the necessary, honest conversations to ensure you're not just producing results, but producing the right results?

CHAPTER 23

Whole Leaders Building Wild Trust
The Fight for What Matters Most

> *Building bold, wild trust in the middle of our real and human brokenness demands self-awareness within us, life-giving patterns between us, and courageous systems around us—systems strong enough to carry trust through generations. This is the story of whole leaders. This is what it means to build wild, life-changing trust.*

We trust a courageous mission when it comes from a leader with the courage to lift the veil—to be both visible and vulnerable. Not performative vulnerability, but sacrificial courage. The kind that costs something. We will trust a mission that refuses to sacrifice service and love for the sake of a buck. A mission that confronts self-interest with other-interest. That asks not, "What can we gain?" but "For whose sake are we doing this?"

Adam Grant asked the question:

"How do you know when it's safe to be vulnerable?" (Grant 2021a)

The answer? You don't. But if we only offer vulnerability when it's safe, we've missed the point. Vulnerability requires courage because it is inherently unsafe. And trust? Trust grows in that tension—where leaders are courageous enough to let others see them, not because it's strategic, but because it's necessary. Contrary to popular belief, vulnerability is not the foundation of trust. Sacrificial courage is. The courage to change for someone else's sake. The guts to edit who you are for the benefit of those you lead. No qualifiers. No expected return. Just editing. That's the raw foundation of trust.

Character That Carries the Mission

A mission we can trust doesn't just come from thin air. It comes from a leader whose character has weight—someone deeply grounded in self-awareness and fully committed to seeing others. Not seeing others as objects to be managed or problems to be solved, but as whole people with purpose and potential.

Trust isn't built by leaders who are consistent only. Consistency matters, but so does permeability. Are you open? Are you willing to change? Are you strong enough to edit when your actions no longer align with the mission you've claimed? People who consistently treat others poorly may be consistent—but they're not trustworthy. The leader we will follow is one we trust enough to leap with, even if we don't always like them. Because they are *clear, connected, courageous*, and *constantly growing*. These leaders are not unicorns. They exist, but they are rare. Rare because it's hard to be strong and humble. Rare because listening is harder than speaking. Rare because changing for someone else's sake requires maturity many haven't seen modeled.

But I believe we can fill the world with them.

The Courage to Invite and Confront the Challenging Few

One of the greatest inhibitors of trust in any organization is the *challenging few*. Not the whole team. Just a small number of people whose toxicity, reactivity, or repeated resistance to feedback goes unaddressed. These are not just difficult personalities—they are people whose unchecked behaviors begin to dominate the team dynamic.

And here's the truth, they are not the core problem. Avoiding them is. When leaders fail to step in, trust doesn't just erode in that one relationship. It begins to break down across every level of our organization. People stop believing that problems will be dealt with. They stop believing they matter. And that creates a ripple effect far more damaging than the challenging person alone. Addressing them isn't just about confrontation. It's about an invitation. The invitation to be seen. The invitation to grow. The invitation to change.

Here's what courageous leaders do:

They separate identity from behavior.

They stop tiptoeing and start naming what's true.

They make expectations painfully clear.

They provide tools and support for change.

And when change doesn't come, they protect the team.

Every leader will face the moment where one person's attitude, actions, or unwillingness to grow has a cost to the many. The easy road is avoidance. The brave road is a boundary. And trust grows when a team sees their leader choose what is hard for the sake of what is good.

Gratitude and grace can also play a role. Gratitude says, "I see what I didn't earn but received anyway." Grace says, "You can get it wrong and still be welcome to grow." But neither of these are permission to tolerate destruction. Grace and gratitude are part of the path, but not a substitute for truth. The courageous leader doesn't fix every problem, but they do face them. They do name them. And they never let the challenging few derail the growth of the many.

The Shared Foundation: Trust

After working with leaders across every imaginable industry and stage of growth, what I've seen is this over and over again. When the veil is lifted, what people want most is wholeness and a plan for getting there. They want to feel like they are making progress—not just professionally, but personally. They want to know they matter. They want to feel seen. They want to become more of who they were meant to be. And the two things we can't live without? Love and truth. That might sound soft to some, but it's not. It's hard. Love requires sacrifice. Truth requires courage. They are compassion and candor, grace and grit, all rolled into one. Love says: I see you. I want the best for you. I'll take a risk on your behalf. Truth says: I will be straight with you, even regarding the things that are fragmented in me. Truth and love, in action, become trust. And trust becomes the systemic oxygen in the air we breathe that makes everything else work. When it's gone, everything slows. When it's present, we move.

And here's the pattern we've seen again and again in our work with leaders and organizations around the world. Trust must be built at three essential levels—the Personal, the Team, and the Organizational. These are the Circles of Trust, and each one requires its own attention and action. At the personal level, trust begins with knowing yourself and being known. At the team level, trust expands through truth-telling, consistency, conflict, and clarity. At the organizational level, trust takes the form of culture, systems, and a mission people can believe in.

When these circles are fractured, we find ourselves in the Jungle of Trust—a place where assumptions grow out of control, communication gets lost in the underbrush, and people feel unseen and unheard. But when we build trust intentionally across all three levels, we emerge into the Stronghold of Trust—a place where people are aligned, known, and supported. A place where the ground beneath us holds.

Systems That Align the Invisible and Visible

Building trust isn't just about conversations. It's about systems. We know that the invisible matters as much as the visible. That's why I committed my life and my organization to providing a system where whole leaders could emerge and grow, and trust could be built—to integrate development with performance. To give people a way to know their skills, their motivations, their blind spots, their calling—and to measure it all. Because if you can't see it, it's hard to trust it.

Trust is not a sentiment. It's a measurable, buildable, and *restorable* reality.

And here's what's wild: the basics matter. Do your people know what's expected of them? Do they know how to grow? Do they feel seen? Are they invited to invest in others, and are others investing in them? If not, don't wait. Build that system. Break the silence. Because when we stop talking, trust shrinks. Silence multiplies assumptions, and assumptions fracture relationships. The fastest path to wholeness is not strategy. It's truth, transparency, and intentional development.

The One Thing We Want, the One Thing We Need, the One Thing We Must Build

Every person wants wholeness and intentionality. Every person needs love and truth. And every organization needs wild trust.

Trust is the bridge between our belief and our action. It's what allows us to take risks for each other. It's the expression of belief in our systems. It's the foundation of a team, the fuel of performance, and the path to wholeness. It's not perfect. It never will be. But it is worth the fight.

We started with a dream: to see whole leaders leading whole teams, building trust that is deep, measurable, and long-lasting. Trust that changes everything. Not as a slogan, but as a reality. And here's where it gets personal. It starts with you. It starts with me.

Not with a program. Not with a consultant. But with a leader who says:

> I will know myself.
>
> I will see others.
>
> I will edit.
>
> I will measure what matters.
>
> I will risk being known.

Let that be your manifesto. Let that be ours.

Let's fill the world with whole leaders who build wild and life-changing trust.

Let's do this.

Bibliography

References

Bonhoeffer, Dietrich. *Letters and Papers from Prison.* Edited by Eberhard Bethge. Translated by Reginald H. Fuller et al. London: SCM Press, 1953.

Bonhoeffer, Dietrich. *The Cost of Discipleship.* New York: Simon & Schuster, 1959.

Brown, Brené. *Daring Greatly.* New York: Gotham Books, 2012.

Buechner, Frederick. *Wishful Thinking: A Theological ABC.* New York: Harper & Row, 1973.

Carucci, Ron. *To Be Honest: Lead with the Power of Truth, Justice and Purpose.* New York: Wiley, 2021. P. 68

Cloud, Henry. *Trust: Knowing When to Give It, When to Withhold It, How to Earn It, and How to Fix It When It Gets Broken.* Worthy Publishing, 2023.

Covey, Stephen M. R. *The Speed of Trust: The One Thing That Changes Everything.* New York: Free Press, 2006.

Covey, Stephen M. R. *Trust & Inspire: How Truly Great Leaders Unleash Greatness in Others.* New York: Simon & Schuster, 2022.

Donne, John. *Devotions upon Emergent Occasions and Several Steps in My Sickness.* Meditation XVII. 1624. Reprint, Ann Arbor: University of Michigan Press, 1999.

Drucker, Peter F. *The Practice of Management.* New York: Harper & Row, 1954.

Drucker, Peter F. *The Effective Executive.* New York: Harper & Row, 1966.

Drucker, Peter F. Revised and updated by Joseph A. Maciariello. 2008. *Management: Revised Edition.* New York: HarperCollins. Originally published as *The Essential Drucker.*

Edmondson, Amy C. *The Fearless Organization: Creating Psychological Safety in the Workplace for Learning, Innovation, and Growth.* Hoboken, NJ: Wiley, 2019.

Fukuyama, Francis. *Trust: The Social Virtues and the Creation of Prosperity*. New York: Free Press, 1995.

Grant, Adam, host. "How to Be Vulnerable at Work Without Spilling Everything (with Brené Brown)." *WorkLife with Adam Grant*. Podcast audio, April 19, 2021a. TED.

Grant, Adam. *Think Again: The Power of Knowing What You Don't Know*. New York: Viking, 2021b. P. 25.

Heffernan, Margaret. *Willful Blindness: Why We Ignore the Obvious at Our Peril*. Walker & Company, 2011.

Heschel, Abraham Joshua. *Who Is Man?* Stanford, CA: Stanford University Press, 1965.

Judge, Timothy A., Joyce E. Bono, Remus Ilies, and Megan W. Gerhardt. "Personality and Leadership: A Qualitative and Quantitative Review." *Journal of Applied Psychology* 87, no. 4 (2002): 765–780. https://doi.org/10.1037/0021-9010.87.4.765.

Lencioni, Patrick. *The Five Dysfunctions of a Team: A Leadership Fable*. San Francisco: Jossey-Bass, 2002.

Lewis, C. S. *The Four Loves*. New York: Harcourt Brace, 1960.

McCall, Morgan W., Jr. "Recasting Leadership Development." In *Executive Development and Organizational Learning for Global Business*, edited by William Pasmore and Richard W. Woodman, 1–24. Oxford: Elsevier Science, 1999.

McKenna, Rob B., and Paul R. Yost. "The Differentiated Leader: Specific Strategies for Handling Today's Adverse Situations." *Organizational Dynamics* 33, no. 3 (2004): 292–306.

Ridge, Garry. Interview by Rob McKenna. "Garry Ridge on The "Dumb-Ass" Way to Build Trust: Leadership Lessons from WD-40's Former CEO." *The WiLD Conversation* (podcast), June 17, 2025. https://wildleaders.org/the-wild-conversation-podcast/.

McKenna, Rob B., Paul R. Yost, and Tanya Boyd. "Leadership Development and Clergy: Understanding the Events That Shape Leadership Development." *Journal of Psychology and Theology* 35, no. 3 (2007): 179–189.

Merton, Thomas. *No Man Is an Island*. New York: Image Books, 1955.

Merton, Thomas. *New Seeds of Contemplation*. New York: New Directions, 1961.

Palmer, Parker J. *Let Your Life Speak: Listening for the Voice of Vocation*. San Francisco: Jossey-Bass, 2000.

Reagan, Ronald. "Remarks at the Signing of the Intermediate-Range Nuclear Forces Treaty." *Ronald Reagan Presidential Library*. December 8, 1987.

Schein, Edgar H. *Organizational Culture and Leadership*. 4th ed. San Francisco: Jossey-Bass, 2010.

Thomas, Robert J. *Crucibles of Leadership: How to Learn from Experience to Become a Great Leader*. Boston: Harvard Business Press, 2008.

Tolkien, J. R. R. *The Fellowship of the Ring*. London: George Allen & Unwin, 1954.

Tutu, Desmond. *No Future Without Forgiveness*. New York: Doubleday, 1999.

Ulrich, Dave. "The Leader as Human Capital Developer." In *The Leader of the Future 2: Visions, Strategies, and Practices for the New Era*, edited by Frances Hesselbein and Marshall Goldsmith, 219–226. San Francisco: Jossey-Bass, 2006.

Warren, Rick. *The Purpose Driven Life: What on Earth Am I Here For?* Grand Rapids, MI: Zondervan, 2002.

Van Velsor, Ellen, Corey Criswell, Katie Puryear, and Neil Hollenbeck. *Learning Leadership in the Military: Key Developmental Events & Lessons from Senior Officers*. Greensboro, NC: Center for Creative Leadership, 2016).

Further Reading

Allport, Gordon W. *Personality: A Psychological Interpretation*. New York: Holt, 1937.

Dweck, Carol S. "Motivational Processes Affecting Learning." *American Psychologist* 41, no. 10 (1986): 1040–1048.

Fiedler, Fred E. *A Theory of Leadership Effectiveness*. New York: McGraw-Hill, 1967.

Hemphill, John K., and Alvin E. Coons. "Development of the Leader Behavior Description Questionnaire." In *Leader Behavior: Its Description and Measurement*, edited by Ralph M. Stogdill and Alvin E. Coons, 6–38. Columbus: Bureau of Business Research, Ohio State University, 1957.

Hersey, Paul, and Kenneth H. Blanchard. "Life Cycle Theory of Leadership." *Training and Development Journal* 23, no. 5 (1969): 26–34.

Katz, Robert L. "Skills of an Effective Administrator." *Harvard Business Review* 33, no. 1 (1955): 33–42.

Likert, Rensis. *New Patterns of Management*. New York: McGraw-Hill, 1961.

Locke, Edwin A., and Gary P. Latham. "Building a Practically Useful Theory of Goal Setting and Task Motivation: A 35-Year Odyssey." *American Psychologist* 57, no. 9 (2002): 705–717.

McKenna, Rob. *Dying to Lead: Sacrificial Leadership in a Self-Centered World*. Maitland, FL: Xulon Press, 2008.

McKenna, D. Douglas. Personal conversation with the author, March 14, 2016.

McKenna, Rob. *Composed: The Heart and Science of Leading Under Pressure*. Oklahoma City, OK: DustJacket Media, 2017.

Stogdill, Ralph M. "Personal Factors Associated with Leadership: A Survey of the Literature." *Journal of Psychology* 25, no. 1 (1948): 35–71.

Acknowledgments

I am profoundly grateful to everyone who helped turn decades of research, experience, and hard-won lessons into this mountaintop manifesto on trust and whole leader development. This book took a village—and what a remarkable village it has been.

Daniel Hallak, for leading with me and taking the risk at different points in your journey to go to battle together for whole leaders and wild trust.

Megan Lawrence, for holding up our brand and leading strong and being an anchor for me in the normal storms of leadership.

Claire Jenkins, for working behind the scenes with me to ensure that the engines are running smoothly so our team can move boldly—and for every bit of editing.

Sabeth Kapahu, for protecting and projecting our mission, brand, and understanding my unique voice, and being a real-time editor for this book.

Chris Shaffer, for seeing that we would serve courageously together and bringing your expertise to elevate our missional platform on trust and whole leader development.

Ron Worman, for seeing me, and for joining the WiLD Leaders mission and showing me that we must dive deep into trust for the sake of changing lives.

Frank Haas, your belief in me and your willingness to invest in the vision of WiLD Leaders. And Mike MacDonald, for stewarding Frank's legacy with me.

The Board of Directors at the WiLD Foundation, Amanda Holland, Ann Klein, Greg Hunter, James McPherson, John Brekke, for your unwavering support.

My brother Doug McKenna, one of the most powerful mentors in my life for decades—teaching me the power of research, critical thinking, and leadership.

My sisters Suzanne Kinzer and Debra Blews, for your unwavering support and for being benevolent she-wolves—modeling strong leadership with great discernment.

Jeff Smiley, one of my closest friends who is a constant sounding board and my most important muse for how this book would land for senior leaders and executives.

Greg Leith and Sheryl Clutter at Convene, Tami Heim at CLA, Al Lopus at BCW, and Mark Vincent at Maestro Level Leaders, I sure love you all.

My research team over the years and to those who served at WiLD Leaders in the early days, your wisdom and willingness to edit and learn changed everything.

WiLD Affiliates and Coaches who became experts on our methodology for the sake of investing in whole leaders and building wild trust.

Every leader and organization with the courage to measure and build trust and invest in their people, I could not be more grateful to you.

The team at Wiley, your expertise in producing and marketing this book was a game changer. That kind of partnership is what I always have wanted with a publisher.

My sons Aidan and Ryan McKenna, you have kept me fresh and relevant and gave me living examples of trust as you entered into your "big boy jobs."

My wife Jackie McKenna, you are the rock behind all of this. Your encouragement and listening to my moments of writing struggle made all of this possible.

To the countless friends, family, former teammates, and mentors not named here—thank you. And above all, I thank God for being the ultimate source of any wisdom found in these pages, and for being the source of trust, wholeness, and grace in every chapter of my life.

About the Author

Dr. Rob McKenna is the Founder of WiLD Leaders Inc. and creator of the WiLD Toolkit and the WiLD Trust Index, used globally to develop whole and trusted leaders. Named one of the top 30 most influential Industrial-Organizational Psychologists and a leading voice in organizational culture, Rob has spent more than 25 years working with Fortune 100 companies, government agencies, universities, and nonprofits to transform how leaders are developed. He is known for combining cutting-edge research with personal transparency, humor, and heart. Rob lives outside Seattle with his wife Jackie.

You can follow Dr. Rob McKenna on LinkedIn, Instagram, X, and Facebook at @drrobmckenna. For more information on the WiLD Trust Index or the whole leader assessments in the WiLD Trust Platform, go to www.wildleaders.org.

Index

A

Accountability, 64, 127, 222
Achievement, 25, 108, 145, 165
Adaptability (motivational driver), 91, 142, 152
Adversity, power, 127
Advisory board, role, 175, 176–177
Advocates, role, 174
Agency, increase, 173
Aligned performance, strategies, 222–223
Aligned retention, 216
Alignment, belonging (equivalence), 214
Allport, Gordon, 18–19, 22
Argument, need, 197
Aspiration, 14–15, 45–46
Assertiveness, 118
Autonomy, people (need), 223
Awareness, 117
    A.I.M. component, 88
    motivational driver, 152
Awareness, Impact, Mission (A.I.M.) Process, 88

B

Becoming, awareness (moving toward), 1, 13, 33–34, 53, 55, 73, 90, 122
Behaviors
    identity, separation, 227
    values, equivalence, 216
Belief
    performance, impact, 223
    results/trust, relationship, 220
Belonging
    alignment, equivalence, 214
    culture, 214–215
Blanchard, Ken, 20

Bonhoeffer, Dietrich, 103, 159
Brokenness, 28, 34–35, 37–38, 45, 168, 185, 225
Brown, Brené, 41
Builder, 3–6
    role, 24
Business
    imperative, 12–13
    result, product, 223
    success, 13

C

Calling (transcendence)
    attention, 97
    curse, 99–104
    discernment, 97–99, 100
    extent, defining, 87
    language, 98–99
    phrase, usage, 98
    purpose, relationship, 102–104
    relationship, 101–102
    thoughtful action, 104
    understanding, 101
Candidness, courage, 189
Care (motivational driver), 152
Carucci, Ron, 191
Challenge (motivational driver), 152
Challenging few, confrontation, 226–227
Change, 5
    development, equivalence, 43, 49
    identification, 50
    practice, method, 49–55
    signal, pressure (impact), 117–118
    tools/support, providing, 227
Character
    defining, 90
    importance, 215
    improvement, extent (defining), 87
    mission, 226
    understanding, 83, 129

Circles of Trust™, 61–64, 62f
Clarity, accountability
   (equivalence), 222
Cloud, Henry, 199
Coaching, 88
Collaboration
   enhancement, 12
   motivational driver, 152
   team trust, impact, 63–64
Collisions, allowance, 198
Communication
   channels (poisoning), distrust
      (impact), 11
   clarity, 11, 64, 67, 91, 117, 190,
      198, 203
Compassion/empathy, display,
   118–119
Competence, 135, 140, 195, 197
Composed leader, impact, 117
Composure, 87, 115
Compulsions, impact, 110
Confidence, loss, 9
Conflict, 59, 195, 197–199
Connection (motivational
   driver), 152
Consistency, 195, 196, 214–215
Contingency theory, 22
Contribution, extent
   (defining), 87
Conversation, 162
Conviction, 23, 86
Cooperative behavior (discouragement),
   distrust (impact), 11
Core truths, inclusion, 48
Courage, 23, 37, 215, 225
Covey, Stephen M.R., xiii, xv, 12,
   44, 63, 231
Crisis response, strengthening, 13
Crucibles of Leadership, The
   (Thomas), 132
Culture, 14
   attraction, ability, 216
   people, relationship, 213
   shaping, 54
   trust, 216–217
   trusted mission, alignment, 213
Customer loyalty, improvement, 13

D
Daily activities (direction), extent
   (defining), 87
Daily work experience, 68
Daring Greatly (Brown), 41
Debate, need, 197
Desperation, 9, 73, 79
Destiny, lives (relationship), 172
Development
   change, equivalence, 43, 49
   conversation, 162
   investment, 222
   leader participation, 216
   performance, contrast, 160
   perspective, 52
   plan, 201, 203
   scaffolding, 79
   systems, building, 202–203
Developmental readiness, 83, 85–88,
   92, 141
Differentiation, increase, 173
Differentiation strategies profile,
   122–125, 123t–124t
Direction, extent (defining), 87
Discernment, process, 89
Distrust, 14–15, 59
Doubt, presence, 9
Dream team, role, 175, 176–177
Drucker, Peter, 21, 22, 31
Dweck, Carol, 99

E
Economic transactions, tax
   (imposition), 11
Edelman Trust Barometer, 13
Editability, 43, 78, 133
   importance, 129
Editable individuals, hiring, 199
Edmondson, Amy, 188, 231
Effectiveness, team trust (impact),
   63–64
Efficacy, increase, 173
Efforts, invisible parts
   (consideration), 18
Emotional maturity, 42, 60, 208
Emotional support, role, 174

Emotions
  impact, 110
  regulation, 127
Empathy, 91, 118, 124, 141, 208
Employees
  data, 68
  engagement, improvement, 12
Engagement, 42, 58, 219, 221–223
Error, modeling, 198
Executive effectiveness, 31
Existence, reasons, 96–97
Expectations, clarity, 227
Experience, 130, 133
  extent, defining, 87
  intentional design, 130
  INVEST model component, 161
Expertise, 137–138
  motivational driver, 152
Extended team, role, 174

F
Faithful practice, 195
Family, purpose, 111
Fear/uncertainty, leader acknowledgement, 210
Feedback, 126
  clarity, 222
  invitation, 222
  leader invitation, 210
  role, 174
  structured feedback tools, usage, 193
Fiedler, Fred, 22
Fighting well, 195, 198
Finances, purpose, 111
Five Dysfunctions of a Team (Lencioni), 187
Flexibility, 152
Flourishing, 62–63
Forgiveness, 45
Forward progress, 195
Foundation, building, 62–63
Fragmentation, shift, 45–46
Fulfillment, 92
  level, understanding, 83
Future, plan, 185

G
Gallup (*State of the Global Workplace 2023 Report*), 12
Gaps, awareness, 140–141
Generational investment, 9, 39, 46, 73, 98, 100, 132
Gift, stewardship, 24
Goals
  direction, extent (defining), 87
  service, 111
  setting, 108, 111
God, silence, 37
Grant, Adam, 191, 225
Growth mindset, 42
Gut intuition, shift, 57

H
Haas, Frank, 171
Harvard Business Review, 12
Health, purpose, 111
Hersey, Paul, 20
High peace keeper, characteristics, 121
High truth speaker, characteristics, 121
Hiring, reason, 49
Honesty, 40, 193
Hope, 1, xi, xvi, 9, 14, 34, 45, 71
Human being
  human doing, tension, 18, 27
  part of life, 23
  question, 96
Human doing
  human being, tension, 18, 27
  part of life, 23
Human experience, dilemma, 27
Human interaction, need, 197
Humanity, connection, 33
Humility, 52, 90, 160, 181, 191, 199, 209

I
Identity
  behavior, separation, 227
  importance, 183
Impact (A.I.M. component), 88
Imperfection (exposure), truth (impact), 191

Individuals
  contribution, impact, 90
  focus, 53–54
Influence (motivational driver), 152
Information revolution, 9
Inner darkness, exposure, 27
Innovation
  increase, 12
  needs, 197
  team trust, impact, 63–64
Inspiration, 6, 35, 79–80, 146, 151
Integrated fulfillment, 83
Integrity (motivational driver), 152
Intentional change, 47
Intentional development, 42–43
Intentionality, 79–82, 118, 181, 229
Intentional leader development, 55–56
Intentional life, leading, 181
Intentions, 42–43, 160–162
Interest (INVEST model
    component), 161
Interest, Needs, Virtues, Experiences,
    Strengths, Traps (INVEST)
    Model, 161
Interpersonal challenges, 4–5
Investment, 157
  difficulty, 159
  diversification, 160
  extent, defining, 87
Invisible, 22–24
  visible, systems alignment, 228–229
Invisible dynamics, 60
Invisible trust (building), visible
    progress (impact), 219
Invitational questions, 50
Islands of Trust, 65
Isolation/aloneness, feeling, 49

J

Job descriptions, 2–3
  clarity, importance, 201
  sharing, 204
Jobs
  clarity, power, 201–202
  experience, 132
  responsibilities, increase, 122
Joint performance, capability, 197

Journal of Applied Psychology, 12
Joy (motivational driver), 153
Jungle, 67–71
Jungle of Trust, 59, 60, 66
  daily work experience, 68

K

Katz, Robert, 19–20, 22
Kindness, 90, 161, 193, 199
Knowing, importance, 183
Knowledge, 137–138
  usage, 4

L

Leaders
  becoming, possibility, 79
  composed leader, impact, 117
  courage, 227
  development, 52–53, 158,
    208–209, 216
  fear/uncertainty
    acknowledgement, 210
  growth, modeling, 207
  laboratory, 131–132
  missteps, ownership, 210
  personal story, sharing, 210
  self-development, 209
  term, neutrality, 43
  tone, setting, 14
  trust, 207
Leadership
  balance, 117
  brokenness, impact, 34
  competence, 138–141
  contingency theories, 20–21
  development, 11, 42
  differentiation, 117–120, 122
    tension, 118–120
  dock, 82
  honesty/care, 208
  knowledge, 17
  laboratory, 129
  loneliness, 89, 165, 173, 175
  maturity, 207
  navigation, 37–38
  perception, 119

Leadership (*continued*)
  principles, oversimplification, 44
  reason, 110
  strategic act, 107
  timewarp, 18–21
  transition, 29
  trust, 13–14, 210
  uncertainty, 116
  understanding, 14
  whole leaders, 33, 38–42
Leading, meaning, 40
Leading Under Pressure Inventory (LUPI), 74, 128
Learning, 129
  continuation, 181
  crucibles, 132
  dynamism, 130
  experience, impact, 130, 133
  fueling, motivation (impact), 148
  goal, 50
  lessons (application), extent (defining), 87
  messiness, 129
  motivation, 146–147, 150
  motivational driver, 153
  motivators, 149–154
  occurrence, 29
  personality, contrast, 131–132
  reality, 148–149
  scaffolding, 79
Lencioni, Patrick, 187–188, 232
Life-changing trust, building, 225
Life context
  occurrence, 89–90
  understanding, 83
Life-giving patterns, demand, 225
Likeability, focus, 115
Listening, 97, 103, 116, 123, 126
Litmus tests, 10
Lives
  destiny, relationship, 172
  story, knowledge, 34
Long-term motivation, meaning, 149
Love, vulnerability (equivalence), 28
Low peace keeper, characteristics, 121
Low truth speaker, characteristics, 121

M
Management by objectives, 22
Management, task, 197
Managers
  quality, 191–192
  unrealistic goals, example, 220–221
Master builder, 6–7
McCall, Morgan, 130
McKenna, Rob, 38, 117–118, 151, 170, 232, 234
Meaning, 42–43, 51
Meaningful Goals Assessment (MGA), 74, 114
Measurement, 55–56
Measures, 47, 51
Mechanics, integration, 51
Mental health, 23
Mentors, 122, 158
  role, 174–175
Merton, Thomas, 172, 190, 232
Methods, 47
Mindset, 47, 48
  integration, 51
  shift, 54
Mission
  A.I.M. component, 88
  clarity, 216
  contribution, 23
  integration, 51
Mission, role (connection), 222
Mistakes, making, 49
Moment, experiencing, 30
Motivated team, building, 154
Motivation
  extent, defining, 87
  forces, 145
  impact, 148
  importance, 154–155
  learning, relationship, 146–147
  long-term motivation, meaning, 149
  power, 147, 149
  questions, 148
Motivational drivers, 151
  impact, 150
Motivational Drivers Inventory, 74, 155

Index

N
Needs (INVEST model component), 161
Network
　building, 174
　extent, defining, 86
　validity, 173
Next-level goal setting, 108

O
One-off solution, 80
One-on-ones, 54
Operational systems, 19
Organizational context
　events, 89–90
　understanding, 83
Organizational culture, impact, 213
Organizational effectiveness, 22
Organizational mission, defining, 90
Organizational trust, 64
Organizations
　focus, 53–54
　improvement, 21
　knowledge, 17
　people, presence (reality), 213
　role, 174
　shared story, 216
　term, usage, 89
　whole/trusted organization,
　　building, 205
Organizing, process, 7
Orientation, 55
Outcomes, connection, 113

P
Palmer, Parker, 27
Paradigm, change, 131
Party metaphor, 22
Peace keepers
　characteristics, 121
　impact, 118–119
People
　autonomy/clarity need, 223
　care, 41
　contact, identification, 169, 171
　courageous investment, 160
　culture, relationship, 213
　development, 30, 54–55, 216

investment, 162–163
observation, power, 159–160
perspectives, understanding
　(confidence), 126
power, 168–169
problem people, handing, 199
roles, 174–176
support, 216
visibility, 216, 221
People Investment Plan, 75, 162, 163
Performance, 219
　aligned performance,
　　strategies, 222–223
　belief, impact, 223
　defining/rating, 91–92
　development, contrast, 160
　engagement, impact, 221
　expectations, 222
　focus, 81
　fueling, motivation (impact), 148
　impact, 60, 222
　joint performance, capability, 197
　measurement, 221
　reviews, 54
　strengthening, development plan
　　(impact), 201
　understanding, 83
Personal context, understanding, 83
Personal development
　focus, 89
　plans, usage, 203
　purpose, 111
Personality
　learning, contrast, 131–132
　types/typologies, 84–85
　understanding, 83
Personal performance areas, 91
Personal trust
　foundation, building, 62–63
　organizational trust, relationship, 60
Personal well-being (strengthening),
　development plan (impact),
　201
Plan, creation, 183–185
Practicing, importance, 183
Preparation, 77
Pressure
　profile, 120–121, 120f

Pressure, impact, 117–118
Problem people, handing, 199
Productivity, 107, 195
Progress
  celebration, 222
  making, 108–109, 112–114
Progress mapping, usage, 56
Purpose, 23, 95
  action, 111–112
  calling, relationship, 102–104
  defining, 87
  description, 109
  discernment, 100
  motivational driver, 153
  performance expectations, alignment, 222
  power, 127
  questions, 111
  relationship, 101–102
  sense, 96
  specificity, 112
  strengths, 102
  thoughtful action, 104
  understanding, 101
Purpose & Calling Inventory, 74, 105
Purpose Driven Life, The (Warren), 98

Q
Quality control, example, 220–221
Questions, asking, 49–51

R
Readiness, 77, 85
Reagan, Ronald (Gorbachev conversation), 57
Real-time development, involvement, 51
Real trust, 10
"Recasting Leadership Development" (McCall), 130
Reflection, action (absence), 48
Relationship-motivated styles, 20–21
Relationships, 12, 177
  struggle, reason, 49
Relativism, fundamentalism (tension), 43–44
Responsibility, readiness, 103

Results
  belief/trust, relationship, 220
  visibility, 222
Review rhythms, building, 204
Revolution, 44–45
Ridge, Garry, 13, 117, 232
Risk, taking, 51
Robinson, Bill, 169–170
Role models, 174

S
Scaffolding, 79, 92
Scale (process), 53
Schein, Edgar, 14, 215
Self-attention, 125–126
Self-awareness, 28, 55, 63, 118, 225
Self-development, 42
Selfless perfection, 172
Self-trust, question, 91
Service
  defining, 86
  role, 175
Shadows, facing (refusal), 27
Shared foundation, 227–228
Shared language, impact, 55
Shell of Trust, 65–68
Short-term gladness, promise, 103
Silence
  importance, 52–53
  voice, usage, 126
Situational Leadership, 20, 22
Skill
  importance, 137–138
  usage, 4
Skillset, impact, 6
Skills & Knowledge Inventory, 74, 143
Skills theory, 22, 135
Social support, 173
Social transactions, tax (imposition), 11
Society, distrust, 11
Soviet Union, arms control agreement, 57
Speaking, space (creation), 120
Specificity, importance, 174
Spiritual life, purpose, 111
Stagnation, 48
Stakeholders, identification, 126

Index

Story
  moral, 223
  understanding, 55–56
Strategic alignment, 56
Strategic moment, seizing, 28–31
Strategic network, existence, 173
Strategic response, 122
Strategic support, 172–174
Strategic Support Assessment, 75, 179
Strategy (motivational driver), 153
Strengths
  awareness, 140–141
  INVEST model component, 161
Stronghold of Trust, 60, 65
  Jungle, 70–71
Structured feedback tools, usage, 193
"Styles Approach," 19
Success
  conditions, 64
  defining, 52
  motivational driver, 153
Support, 165, 171, 177–178
  emotional support, role, 174
  purpose, 174
  social support, 173
  strategic support, 172–174
Systems/resources, connection, 25

T
Team members
  contact, identification, 169–171
  job description, review, 203
  promotion, 39–40
  trust/openness/knowledge, 189
Teams
  alignment, defining, 90
  building, 198–199
  dynamics, improvement, 71
  extended team, role, 174
  job descriptions, usage, 203
  meetings, 54
  personal development plans,
      usage, 203
  protection, 227
  role, 175
  steps, 203–204
  transparency, 193–194

trust, 63–64, 189, 195
truth, building (strategies),
    193–194
Teamwork, 167
Technical competence, 139–141
Technical training, usage, 116
Thomas, Robert, 132
To Be Honest (Carucci), 191
Tolkien, J.R.R., 196, 233
Training/development efforts, 26
Trait theory, 22
Transcendent summons, 100, 102
Transformational Experiences
    Audit, 74, 134
Transparency, 35–36, 189
  building, strategies, 193–194
  modeling, 64, 204
  requirement, 36
  visibility, courage, 192–193
Traps (INVEST model component), 161
Triangles, avoidance, 193
Trust
  appearance, 60
  belief/promise, 61
  birthplace, 53
  breakdowns, 71
  bridge, 25
  challenges, 60
  chemistry, 57, 60–61
  confusion, impact, 201
  creation, 73–74
  crisis, 44
  defining, 26
  earning, 223
  fostering, 63
  foundation, 15
  fueling, 150
  growth, 201
  impact, 219
  importance, 57
  invisible trust (building), visible
      progress (impact), 219
  leadership, equivalence, 13–14
  leader trust, 207
  meaning, 11, 26–27
  misplacement, 10–11
  need, 10–11
  path, 1–2

Trust (*continued*)
  personal trust, organizational trust (relationship), 60
  prioritization, 64
  problem, 58
  questioning, 71–72
  realities, 213
  real trust, 10
  results/beliefs, relationship, 220
  rethinking, 69–70
  risk, 33
  shared foundation, 227–228
  signals, 201
  story, understanding, 67–68
  vision, 3
  vulnerability/transparency, relationship, 35–36
  wild trust, 33, 43–46
Trust, building, 61, 225
  efforts, 39
  excellence, impact, 135
  performance, impact, 222
  vulnerability, impact, 209–210
Trusted leader, 1, 77–78
  becoming, 73–75, 78–82, 109–111
  intentional investments, 157
  learning, continuation, 181
  motivation, 145
  people, impact, 165
  self-editing, 129
  strengths/limitations awareness, 135
Trusted mission, culture (alignment), 213
Trusted team. *See* Whole/trusted teams
Trustworthiness, 10, 13
Trustworthy culture, building, 213
Truth
  building, strategies, 193–194
  desire, 160
  facing, 3
  impact, 60
  moments, celebration, 193
  rejection, 191
  telling, 190–191
  vulnerability, requirement, 191
Truthfulness, 189
Truth speakers
  characteristics, 121
  impact, 119–120

Turnover, reduction, 12
Tutu, Desmond, 33

U
United States, arms control agreements, 57
Unseen, observation, 25f

V
Values, behaviors (equivalence), 216
Veil, lifting, 225, 227
Verification, importance, 57
Virtual work, 205
Virtues (INVEST model component), 161
Visibility, 17
  courage, 192–193
Visible
  focus, 24
  invisible, systems alignment, 228–229
  paradox, 22–24
Visible progress, impact, 219
Vision
  method, 48
  sharing, 4–5
Voice, usage, 126
Vulnerability, 35–36, 42, 51
  discernment, 210
  impact, 209–210
  levels, 64
  moment, 49
  requirement, 35–36, 191
  safety, 225

W
Warren, Rick, 98
Well-being
  barometer, 92
  increase, 173
Whole/intentional plan, 184t
Whole leaders, 1, 33, 38–42, 77–78
  becoming, 73–75, 78–82, 109–111
  development, 49
  impact, 22
  intentional investments, 157
  learning, continuation, 181
  mindset, core truths (inclusion), 48

motivation, 145
people, impact, 165
self-editing, 129
self-perception, 41
strengths/limitations awareness, 135
Whole life, leading, 181
Wholeness, 34–35
  desire, 229
Whole-person check-ins, practice, 223
Whole self, understanding, 88
Whole/trusted organization,
    building, 205
Whole/trusted teams
  actions, 195–196
  creation, 187–188
Wild aspiration, 45–46
WiLD Leaders, 38–39
WiLD Line of Sight, 49
WiLD Plan, 75, 186
WiLD Profile, 74, 93
Wild story, 36–38
WiLD Toolkit, 74, 163

Wild trust, 33, 43–46
  aspiration, equivalence, 45–46
  building, whole leaders
      (impact), 22, 225
  faith/belief, 45
  miracle, 45
WiLD Trust Index™ (WTI), 59–60, 63
WiLD Trust Platform, 47, 55
WiLD Trust Quadrant™, 64–72, 65f
  age group categorization, 70f
  individuals, categorization, 68, 69f
  organizational categorization, 66f
  organizational location, 65–66
  story, 66–67
  team location, 65–66
  trust story, understanding, 67–68
Work
  learning/development,
      embeddedness, 221
  purpose, 111
  relationship, 108
Workplace, trust (appearance), 60

WiLD LEADERS™

Leadership = Trust

WiLD Leaders is the first company to measure trust and provide data-informed tools to build it—connecting the purpose of the individual with the vision and performance of their organization.

Through our WiLD Trust Platform, we help leaders and teams meet the moment they're experiencing and build an intentional pathway to the organization they are becoming.

- Measure trust for yourself or your team with the WiLD Trust Index and download insights from Dr. McKenna's latest research.
- Develop your leadership capacity.
- Invite Dr. McKenna to speak at your next event.

Scan the QR code or go to **www.wildleaders.org** to take the next step toward building trust: